THE AFFORDABLE BABY

THE
AFFORDABLE
BABY
❖

*A Complete Consumer
Guide to Costs and Comparisons
for Parents-to-Be*

DARCIE BUNDY

1817

HARPER & ROW, PUBLISHERS, New York
*Cambridge, Philadelphia, San Francisco, London
Mexico City, São Paulo, Singapore, Sydney*

FIRST EDITION

Designer: Helene Berinsky

Library of Congress Cataloging in Publication Data

Bundy, Darcie.
   The affordable baby.

   Includes index.
   1. Child rearing—Economic aspects—United States. 2. Maternal health services—United States—Costs. 3. Childbirth—Economic aspects—United States. 4. Infants—Care and hygiene—Economic aspects—United States. I. Title.
HQ769.B7755   1985   338.4'76491   84-48581
ISBN 0-06-015446-2   85 86 87 88 89 10 9 8 7 6 5 4 3 2 1
ISBN 0-06-091263-4 (pbk.) 85 86 87 88 89 10 9 8 7 6 5 4 3 2 1

To my husband, Stuart Day. Not only because the original idea was his, but for being a sounding board, a supporter—and frequent dinner cook. Thanks to him for perspective.

Contents

ACKNOWLEDGMENTS

There are always many people who help, in large ways and small, to bring a project like *The Affordable Baby* to fruition. During my research, I worked with consumer advocates, a tax expert, analysts at health associations, a life insurance executive, doctors, a maternity clothing manufacturer, a layette buyer, a toy safety expert, directors of birth centers and HMOs, childcare researchers, even the owner of a diaper service, as well as many new parents across the country. I'm grateful to all of these people, although I can single out only a few here.

First, my special thanks to Ivan Jacobsen, M.D., for taking the time from his busy Manhattan obstetrical practice to review the medical chapters in the book. It was a source of reassurance to know that a physician of his stature would scrutinize those sections.

Thanks, too, to relatives, friends and college alumnae groups across the country who helped distribute my research questionnaire. And of course I'm particularly grateful to all the new parents who took the time to fill in that long questionnaire, providing facts and figures, insight and advice—even poems!—making me the beneficiary of their pregnancy and parenthood experiences.

And where would I have been without the man on the

word processor? Jack Mayer, with good humor and amazing speed, transformed my scrawl into clean copy—version after version. He certainly knows more than he wants to now about diapers and daycare.

Jeanne Drewsen, my agent, gets warm thanks for responding so immediately and positively to the book, and for her constant expressions of confidence. The same to Sallie Coolidge, my editor.

And finally, I thank family and friends—especially my parents, brother and sister-in-law, Betty and Mark, Kathy, Carla, Nicole, Joan, Louise, Antonia and others—who not only helped in practical ways, but more important, always asked how it was going and cared about the answer.

INTRODUCTION

The Affordable Baby is about financial planning and preparation for parenthood. More than that, it's a comprehensive, practical and specific consumer guide to all the goods and services that parents-to-be and new parents need and want.

The Affordable Baby explains these goods and services—why and when you need them, how to select the best versions of them, what they usually cost and, if possible, how to mitigate that cost. The point is to help you identify the many choices you'll face in the next few months and years, and the many options from which you can choose.

This book, then, is all about preparation—about well-informed choices, about avoiding unpleasant surprises, and planning those things that can be planned for. Most first-time parents-to-be can use this kind of help. How often during my research did I hear such things as "I had what I thought was a good health insurance policy—until I got pregnant and found it provided no coverage for obstetrical fees at all!" Or "The cost of prenatal vitamins really surprised me. I took them all during pregnancy and for six months of breastfeeding. Altogether, they cost more than $85—just one more in a string of unexpected expenses." Or "We had no idea the hospital would make us pay in advance for my maternity stay!" "I bought a complete, prepriced layette in the newborn size—what a waste." "We bought a car seat from a store without a return policy, and it turned out to be a kind we couldn't install in our car." "We didn't know enough to claim the childcare tax credit the first year." "We were persuaded to buy a whole-life policy on my husband. It's so expensive we realize we should have bought term." Or "Why do we need wills? If I die won't my wife automatically get everything and vice versa?"

And what about you? Do you understand the extent of maternity coverage in your particular health insurance policy? Do you know that health insurance will not pay for "well-baby" visits? Do you know it's not uncommon for obstetricians to ask that their fee be paid in full several weeks before delivery? Or that it can make a significant difference in your hospital bill if you choose a nonprofit rather than for-profit hospital? That women frequently get billed by the hospital for the services of an anesthesiologist even if they're not used during delivery—because the doctor is there on standby? Would you know how to comparison-shop for a pediatrician? Do you know what an alternative birth center is? An HMO? Why HMOs are often especially good value for a young couple starting a family?

Do you know how to recognize good value in maternity and baby clothing? Have you considered the diaper service alternative to disposables and cloth diapers? Are you aware that commercial baby food is at least two to three times more expensive than homemade? Do you know what items you don't want to see on the label of a commercial baby-food product? Could you select a good, safe highchair? Crib and mattress? Car seat, stroller, changing table, walker, toys?

For parents who both work outside the home, how will you choose good childcare? If you're looking for a group care situation, what's the desired ratio between caregivers and children? If you have someone come into your home, are you aware of your legal obligation to pay social security and unemployment insurance? What these add to the going rates for such care? What the risks are of paying your caregiver off-the-books? How much the federal childcare tax credit amounts to?

Do you know why it's vital for both parents to write wills? Do you need a lawyer? What information will the lawyer need from you? How do you calculate the amount of life insurance you need? Should you buy term or whole life? How do you comparison-shop for policies? Should a full-time homemaker have life insurance? Should you buy a policy on the baby? Disability income insurance—do you know what it is, why it's important? Saving for your child's education—do you know why it should involve some tax planning? That an appropriate tax-advantaged educational savings plan can save even moderate-income people thousands of dollars over the years?

Chances are, you don't yet know the answers to many of these questions. And they're just a few of the hundreds of consumer and financial choices you'll soon be facing. But don't be discouraged. After all, until now, you haven't had a need to know. Now you do. *The Affordable Baby* can help.

❖ I ❖❖❖❖❖❖❖❖❖❖❖❖❖❖❖❖❖❖❖❖❖❖❖❖

Medical Care and Costs

❖ 1

HEALTH INSURANCE

The majority of Americans have some form of health insurance. Few of us, however, understand exactly what we have. Often, healthy young adults have had little cause to use their insurance, and so no specific incentive to learn the details of their coverage. Pregnancy and childbirth change all that—and put your health insurance to the test.

Unfortunately, some policies flunk. One couple I know learned only after submitting obstetrical bills to their insurer that their policy provided no coverage for maternity care—doctor or hospital bills—at all! Even a couple with a comprehensive health insurance plan may be surprised to find their out-of-pocket maternity medical bills mounting to $1,000 or more. How can this happen? Because of deductibles, co-insurance, "reasonable and customary" fee limits and excluded services. Because they have a direct effect on your pocketbook, you need to understand these terms. You also need to know just what your policy covers with regard to obstetric and pediatric care. And those of you without health insurance will want to consider some of the suggestions provided here to keep your maternity medical bills down.

Who's Covered?

Nearly 85 percent of Americans have some kind of health insurance. Most of us are covered through group plans at work, although as many as 36 million Americans have individually purchased policies. While this 85 percent figure at first seems reassuring, health insurance coverage has *actually dropped* over the last decade, from nearly 90 percent, at a time when skyrocketing costs of health care have increased the need for insurance dramatically. The drop is due in part to the recession, during which more than 10 million Americans lost their insurance when they lost their jobs. It also results from the rising percentage of people employed by small (fewer than fifty employees) organizations, which tend to offer fewer benefits. Another cause for concern is that young adults are almost *twice* as likely as any other age group to be *without* health insurance. So, the picture is far from rosy—especially considering the fact that some of us *with* insurance have only limited coverage and often don't realize its limitations until we're hit with big, unreimbursed medical bills!

Components of a Comprehensive Health Insurance Plan

A comprehensive plan is made up of *Basic Protection* and *Major Medical.* If you don't have *both*, whether your insurance is through a group or is individually purchased, you don't have comprehensive coverage.

Basic Protection in its own right consists of two parts: *hospitalization* and *medical services.* Hospitalization benefits are the most widely held form of health insurance. Generally they cover costs of the hospital room (at the semiprivate rate; if you insist on privacy, you'll pay the difference), board, general nursing care, in-hospital medications, lab work, X rays, intravenous fluids, use of anesthesia equipment, the fetal heart monitor, nursery incubator, etc. Hospitalization policies are offered by commercial companies, but many people have coverage through nonprofit Blue Cross plans. Don't, however, assume all Blue Cross plans are alike. They're not! Each Blue Cross plan is the result of a specific negotiation between the buyer and the local Blue Cross. So inform yourself about the benefits provided under your plan, especially noting how many days of hospitalization are covered.

Medical services benefits are also called physician expense benefits. These are less commonly held than hospitalization insurance. These benefits cover doctor treatment fees, visits while you're in the hospital, and usually some kinds of office and home doctors' visits—generally when you're ill and/or being treated for a certain disorder. They do *not* cover routine physical checkups or related exams or laboratory work—for example, routine gynecological checkups and Pap tests. "Well-baby" visits to the pediatrician are also *not* covered.

Medical services benefits are offered by nonprofit Blue Shield, as well as by commercial companies. While many people have Blue Cross hospitalization and Blue Shield medical services, it's also common to carry Blue Cross hospitalization and physician expense benefits from a commercial company like the Travelers.

Hospitalization plus medical services make up Basic Coverage. Where Basic Coverage leaves off, Major Medical steps in. It covers hospital and medical services *beyond* the level of basic benefits—that is, when those benefits run out. Major Medical provides protection against catastrophic expenses of prolonged illness and hospitalization, and given the cost of hospitals and doctor care today, "prolonged" can be as short as a few weeks! Maximum benefits under Major Medical are generally very high—more than 80 percent of those people with this coverage have benefits of $1 million or more, and a full third have unlimited benefits.

How to Anticipate Out-of-Pocket Expenses

Even if you're lucky enough to have comprehensive health insurance, you *will* have out-of-pocket medical expenses associated with pregnancy and childbirth—and they may even be substantial. The only exception is if husband and wife each have separate comprehensive policies through their respective workplaces. In that situation, the woman would receive all the benefits due her through her own policy, leaving the unreimbursed balance available for coverage under her husband's policy. This is called *coordination of benefits*, and it sometimes results in 100 percent reimbursement of medical expenses.

Most of us, however, don't have such "double coverage," and as a result do have unreimbursed medical expenses. The first one is often the insurance *premium* itself. Health insurance premiums are obviously affected by the cost of medical care, and both are increasing at faster rates than inflation. In 1984, comprehensive family health insurance policies generally cost $1,500 to $2,600. (If your plan costs much less, chances are you don't have comprehensive coverage.) Individually purchased plans can be 15 to 40 percent more expensive than group coverage.

Obviously, if you have an individual plan, you're personally responsible for all premiums. If, however, you're covered by a group plan through work, find out if it's *contributory* or *noncontributory.* Noncontributory means your employer pays 100 percent of the premiums—lucky you. Contributory means that you and your employer *share* the payment of premiums. Given rising costs, employers increasingly opt for contributory plans requiring employees to bear anywhere from 10 to 50 percent of the premium.

Take note: even if you haven't been paying a part of the premium up to now, your plan may still be a contributory one. That's because many employers do pay 100 percent for a single employee plus one dependent (like a spouse). The contributory clause starts up for *family coverage*—that is, the addition of a second dependent (like a baby!).

Next you want to know *how* your plan pays benefits. A policy with *inside benefits* will pay only a set, fixed amount for your hospital room, no matter what the actual rates; or cover your surgical or other doctor's expenses at only a fixed limit, no matter what the actual charges. Payment is usually in cash to you. If your policy pays inside benefits, keep tabs on the going rates for hospital rooms in your area and buy supplemental coverage when the rates get appreciably higher than the inside limits of your present policy.

A better arrangement is a policy offering *service benefits*—an entitlement to receive specified hospital care rather than cash. Service benefits are the trend in hospitalization insurance, and result in "full-payment" coverage for a semiprivate room, board and in-hospital services, paid directly to the hospital. About 90 percent of people covered by employee group plans have this superior arrangement. (Many individual plans, in contrast, pay inside limits.)

Next, the *deductible. This is the dollar amount of medical expenses you must pay out of your own pocket each year before the insurance policy starts paying.* Usually the deductible applies to Major Medical, but increasingly it's being extended to physician expense benefits and to hospitalization. Deductibles under group plans are commonly in the $100 to $200 range, but experts expect them to *double* in the near future. Moreover, deductibles are applied *per person* covered by the plan—that is, you pay the first, say, $150 of medical expenses for each member of the family before insurance takes over. However, better plans offer an annual *maximum family deductible,* which allows a family to pool expenses to reach a maximum deductible that's set lower than would result from the per person rate. Also a *deductible carry-forward* feature is desirable, whereby bills incurred in the last three months of a calendar year that go toward satisfaction of the deductible can be carried forward to count for the next year's deductible. This too can be a real money saver.

The next thing that directly affects your out-of-pocket expenses is *co-insurance. This is the arrangement whereby you and the insurer share the cost of your medical treatment.* Full-service hospitalization benefits are not generally subject to co-insurance, but physician expense benefits and Major Medical are. Typically, the insurer pays 80 percent of these, *after* you've satisfied the deductible, and you pay 20 percent. The ratio of some policies is 75 to 25. This co-insurance factor can result in significant out-of-pocket expense.

Yet another feature that can result in major out-of-pocket expense is the *reasonable and customary fee* stipulation. *This is a charge for health care which, according to the insurers, is consistent with the "going rate" for identical*

or *similar services within a specific geographical area.*
Typically (after satisfaction of the deductible), a policy will
pay 80 percent (co-insurance) of up to the "reasonable and
customary" fee—*and no more.* Physician expense benefits
are the main service affected. If your doctor charges fees
in excess of what the insurer deems "reasonable and customary," *you pay the difference.*

Watch out for this stipulation! It can leave many people
stuck with large doctor's bills, especially in urban areas
where there are many doctors charging a wide range of fees
for the same service—like for prenatal care and delivery.
In Manhattan, for example, where obstetrician fees commonly ranged from $1,200 to $2,500 in 1984, while insurers
were quoting $1,800 as "reasonable and customary," I
know many women who had to pay $1,000 out of pocket
on obstetrician bills *alone*—and these were people with
comprehensive health insurance plans! (This problem will
be further explained in Chapter 2.)

Exclusions are something else to watch out for. These
are specific conditions, circumstances or treatments listed
in a policy for which it will not pay benefits. Usually, a
preexisting condition—a health problem you had before
becoming insured—is excluded from coverage, at least for
a stipulated period. (Frequently, there's an eleven-month
waiting period for coverage of a preexisting condition,
which obviously rules out pregnancy!) So, if you're pregnant
at the time of enrollment in an insurance plan, it's highly
unlikely you'll be covered for obstetrical care. Indeed, some
policies even stipulate that they won't cover a pregnancy
if conceived within a certain number of months *following*
enrollment.

Finally, better health insurance plans offer a feature that
can help *limit* your out-of-pocket expenses. Called an *out-
of-pocket maximum* or a *stop loss,* this is *the maximum
dollar amount of out-of-pocket expenses you must pay in
a calendar year before your policy steps in to pick up 100
percent of covered charges at the reasonable and customary
level.* (Charges that the insurer says are in *excess* of reasonable and customary fees are *excluded* from this out-of-

pocket limit.) Obviously, the lower the stop loss, the better for you. Usual stop losses range from $1,000 to $2,500 per person, or $2,000 to $5,000 per family, but these too are increasing as employers try to shift a bigger portion of their skyrocketing medical bills to the consumers of those services.

Checklist for Covered Maternity Services

Deductibles, co-insurance and so on are the "ground rules" of your policy. Now, let's turn specifically to what obstetrical and pediatric services are covered. Contact your employee benefits or health insurance representative and ask: "Do I have maternity coverage?" But don't stop there. To be sure of what you have, and to begin to figure what your out-of-pocket expenses will be, use this checklist:

- Do I have coverage for obstetrical fees? For both normal and Cesarean delivery? Does a deductible apply against these?
- What are the "reasonable and customary" rates for normal delivery? For a Cesarean? A pregnancy designated "high risk"?
- Genetic counseling, if recommended by my physician? Amniocentesis? Sonograms, stress and nonstress testing?
- Is anesthesia of all kinds covered?
- Do I and my baby have full-service benefits for hospitalization? Is the newborn covered from birth whether born well or ill? (Ask specifically about routine nursery care. Also ask about incubator care and use of the intensive care nursery.)
- Is circumcision covered?
- Is there an incentive for early discharge from the hospital?
- What are the stipulations and instructions about enrolling a newborn under the policy?
- How much will I be paying per month for my baby's insurance coverage? What pediatric services are covered?
- Are there any special exclusions or stipulations relating to obstetrical or pediatric care I should know about?

Leads on some of these questions. First, if you don't have physician expense benefits, it's almost certain you're *not* covered for obstetrician's fees. An exception may be if birth is by Cesarean, which might be picked up under Major Medical. Unfortunately, it's not at all uncommon for people who "have insurance" to find that they, in fact, have no coverage for obstetrician fees, because they don't have physician expense benefits.

About anesthesia—ask specifically if you're covered for a "local" anesthesia that accompanies "natural" childbirth. Under some policies, general anesthesia for delivery is covered, but you have to pay for a "local" out of your own pocket.

To reduce costs, some Blue Cross/Blue Shield plans provide financial incentives for new mothers who experience uncomplicated delivery to take early hospital discharge. They offer up to a $200 bonus to women who go home within two days, and usually will also pay for home nurse care. If the idea of early discharge appeals to you, ask your insurer if this incentive is available.

It is extremely important whether or not your newborn is covered from the moment of birth. In the past, many policies contained clauses that excluded coverage for as much as the first thirty days of life—exactly the period that some infants require the most intensive and costly care. (Intensive care nurseries can easily exceed $1,000 *a day!*) While legislation has been passed that requires *new* health insurance policies to cover infants from the moment of birth, you still cannot assume you're financially protected, because there are loopholes. Guaranteed renewable policies written in the past do not have to be altered to conform with the new statute because they are considered legal contracts. While many companies having such policies voluntarily decided to include "justborns," double-check this vital coverage. If you find your justborn will not be covered, it's smart to take out inexpensive extra insurance for the short uncovered period.

A related point. Many people are surprised to find that under their particular policies, the infant's hospitalization and care are *not* covered if the baby is born *well*—only if the baby's born ill. Policies differ, so it's an important checklist item.

To enroll a new dependent, most plans require that you notify the insurer in writing *within thirty-one days* of birth for assured continuous coverage. If you don't, you'll have to wait until the plan's next open enrollment period, which may be months away, meaning your baby is without insurance coverage for that time!

And finally, *don't* expect your health insurance to cover routine well-baby visits to the pediatrician. Nor do most reimburse for immunizations. Circumcision, too, is often excluded.

The Pregnancy Discrimination Act of 1978

My advice, then, is never to assume anything about your health insurance coverage—there are too many rude surprises for those who do. However, it *is* encouraging to report that maternity coverage has grown dramatically over the last five years. In 1977, only 57 percent of employees with medical insurance had some form of maternity protection for either themselves or their spouses, whereas 89 percent of such employees do today. *This is due in large part to the Pregnancy Discrimination Act of 1978 (PDA), which requires employers to treat pregnancy-related disabilities on an equal basis with all other medical conditions.* This means that an employer must provide the same insurance coverage for pregnancy as it provides for illnesses. For example, if the company's insurance plan pays 80 percent of the reasonable and customary surgeon's fee for one employee's appendectomy, it must also pay 80 percent of your reasonable and customary obstetrician's fee. If hospital costs are paid in full for the appendectomy, then they must be similarly paid for childbirth, or any complications from pregnancy and childbirth. (The same equality of treatment applies to employer-provided disability plans and sick leave provisions, as discussed in Chapter 14.)

This development is encouraging, but it's important to emphasize that the PDA has *no* bearing on people whose employers don't provide insurance plans. The law doesn't require an employer to provide maternity coverage for affected employees if it doesn't already have a health insurance plan for all employees. Moreover, the law only applies to employers with fifteen or more full-time employees. Taken together, these two stipulations eliminate more than 50 percent of women employees from coverage under PDA! For that matter, not all employers are in compliance who should be. One study showed that while nearly 100 percent of large firms and 80 percent of medium-size firms were in compliance with PDA, as many as 45 percent of firms with between 15 and 100 employees were not! This is something to keep in mind if you work for a small company. And finally, PDA has no bearing on individual insurance policies—you have to expressly purchase maternity coverage in such plans.

The IRS and Medical Expenses

More bad news for the medical consumer. Tax legislation passed in 1982 sharply *restricted* the amount of medical expenses that can be deducted for federal income tax purposes. The legislation eliminated the automatic deduction of up to $150 for health insurance premiums paid by an individual, and stipulated that only medical expenses *in excess of 5 percent* of adjusted gross income can be deducted. The level had been 3 percent. That means that if your adjusted gross is $30,000, your unreimbursed medical expenses plus any premium payments you make would have to exceed $1,500 before they're deductible—and then, only the amount *in excess* is deductible.

Calculation of Benefits: A Case Study

I've been emphasizing that even those of you with comprehensive health insurance may have significant out-of-pocket maternity care expenses. Let's look at an example, borrowed from a friend's experience.

Susanna M. is pregnant with her first baby. She's covered under a comprehensive group plan at work, which pays 100 percent of the premiums for her and her husband, but which requires a $38 monthly employee contribution for *family coverage.* The plan has a $150 *deductible* on medical services and *co-insurance* of 80–20. The policy provides *full-service* hospitalization benefits for her and the baby.

Susanna's obstetrician charges $1,600 for normal delivery, $1,850 for Cesarean. (The insurer, however, maintains that reasonable and customary fees for these services in Susanna's area are $1,450 and $1,600, respectively.) Her prenatal lab work costs $60. Since Susanna is thirty-five years old and a member of an ethnic group at risk for a certain genetic disorder, her doctor recommends genetic counseling followed by amniocentesis. The counseling costs $125, the "amnio" $675. Susanna also takes prenatal vitamins during her pregnancy and will continue to do so for the three months she plans to breast-feed; cost: $65.

As her due date passes, Susanna's doctor orders a series of stress and nonstress tests to be sure the fetus is still functioning well. These tests cost $120. When she finally does go into labor, it becomes prolonged, and the doctor decides to do a Cesarean. This means an anesthesia bill of $275 and a five-day hospital stay for mother and baby which mounts to $2,900. The baby is a boy, and circumcision is performed at a fee of $75. In-hospital pediatrician fees are $125.

During her son's first year, Susanna takes him to the pediatrician for seven well-baby visits and several immunizations; cost: $280. She also takes him to the doctor twice when he's sick. These visits cost $35 each.

Here's how to calculate Susanna's benefits and out-of-pocket medical expenses for pregnancy, childbirth and the baby's first year of life:

CALCULATION OF INSURANCE BENEFITS

ACTUAL EXPENSES	INSURANCE REIMBURSEMENT	
Obstetrician fee: $1,850 (Cesarean)	Reasonable & customary fee: (Cesarean)	1,600
	Deductible:	−150
	Amount available for calculation of benefit:	1,450
	Co-insurance:	× 80%
	Benefit paid by insurer:	$1,160
Prenatal labwork: $60		60
	Co-insurance:	× 80%
	Benefit paid:	48
Genetic counseling: $125	*Not covered*	
Amniocentesis: $675	Covered under medical services:	675
	Co-insurance:	× 80%
	Benefit paid by insurer:	$540
Vitamin prescription: $65	*Not covered*	
Stress tests: $120		120
	Co-insurance:	× 80%
	Benefit paid by insurer:	96
Anesthesiologist fee: $275	Reasonable & customary fee:	225
	Co-insurance:	× 80%
	Benefit paid:	176
Doctor's fee for circumcision: $75	*Not covered*	
Hospital charges: $2900	Paid by Blue Cross:	2810
Pediatrician fees: $280 (Well-baby care & immunizations)	*Not covered*	

CALCULATION OF INSURANCE BENEFITS (*Continued*)

ACTUAL EXPENSES	INSURANCE REIMBURSEMENT
Pediatrician fees: $70 (Sick-baby visits)	No reimbursement because deductible on covered services must be satisfied on baby before benefits begin

TOTAL MEDICAL EXPENSES: $6,459	TOTAL INSURANCE REIMBURSEMENT: $4,280

$$\$6,495 - 4,820 =$$
$1,675 Out-of-Pocket Expenses

Add to this the cost to Susanna of her son's first year of coverage in her health insurance plan of $456 ($38 per month), for a grand total of $2,109 in out-of-pocket medical and health insurance expenses related to pregnancy, childbirth and the first year of the baby's life. Because these expenses do not amount to 5 percent of the family's adjusted gross income, no tax deductions are available to them.

You may want to work out a similar chart for yourself.

Shopping for Health Insurance

If you're among the one in seven Americans without health insurance, shopping for it should be a top priority. Similarly, if you have insurance, but it provides only limited coverage, consider a supplemental policy. Key things to consider:

• *Buy comprehensive coverage*—Basic Protection plus Major Medical—if you can possibly afford it. Your goal should be to cover at least 75 percent of medical expenses of illness or injury. If you can't afford both, opt for the latter with maximum benefits of $250,000 or more, preferably reinstated annually.

• Try to *get coverage through a group*. If you're not eligible for a group plan at work, check out possibilities through a union, guild, fraternal organization or alumni association.

- Blue Cross has open enrollment periods for Basic Protection, when you can enroll regardless of health status. However, there will be a waiting period for coverage of "preexisting" conditions. Commercial companies don't have open enrollment—they "select" their enrollees.
- Blue Cross is usually the best buy for individual Basic Protection, but not all "Blues" offer Major Medical to individuals, so you may have to go "commercial" for that. However, if you're a young couple who can afford a premium-reducing high deductible (generally not offered by Blue Cross), you might be better off buying all your coverage through a commercial firm.
- In any case, *take the highest deductible you can manage* and co-insure 20 to 25 percent to keep premiums down.
- Remember that with an individual policy, you must *expressly* include maternity benefits. These can add several hundred dollars annually to your premium.
- Look for a policy with an advantageous *family deductible,* a *deductible carry-over* feature, and a *stop loss* limiting your total out-of-pocket expenses to a manageable level.
- Look for a policy with a *high loss ratio,* which is the percentage of premiums paid in that are returned to clients as benefits. The higher the number, the better for you. Blue Cross plans should have loss ratios of 85 to 90 percent; commercial group plans, 80 to 90 percent; commercial individual plans (overhead is much higher), 60 percent or more.
- You want a policy that's *noncancelable* and *guaranteed renewable,* without regard to a change in health.
- Choose a policy that pays *full-service* as opposed to inside-limits benefits. This is one reason not to rely on mail-order insurance as your main policy—it pays the latter. At most, use inside limits as a supplement.
- Pay your premium annually or semiannually—it's cheaper.
- When you receive a policy, take advantage of the ten-

day "free look," during which you can get a refund if you decide it's not right for you.
• Don't overinsure—it's unnecessary and expensive. The Federal Trade Commission says 3 million of us have health insurance in excess of what we'll ever need.
• Always *comparison-shop*. Get quotes from at least three companies. They should be "like" quotes—for the same benefits, exclusions, deductibles, etc.
• Expect to pay $1,500 to $2,600 for comprehensive family coverage. If your policy costs much less, it probably isn't comprehensive and warrants study for possible supplementation.
• An alternative to all this is the Health Maintenance Organization (HMO) (Chapter 7).

How to Keep Maternity Medical Bills Down if You Don't Have Insurance

If you're already pregnant and don't have insurance, you don't have a good chance of finding coverage. Consider these ways to help keep maternity costs down.

• By all means, comparison-shop for an obstetrician. In most areas fees vary. Be sure to tell the doctor you don't have insurance—sometimes doctors charge their uninsured patients less. (See Chapter 2.)
• If you have a choice between hospitals, compare their room rates and quoted charges for maternity care. Non-profit hospitals are often less expensive than for-profit ones. Teaching hospitals may not charge for your baby's in-hospital pediatric care by a resident pediatrician. (See Chapter 4.)
• Consider use of a hospital maternity ward rather than a semiprivate room. (See Chapter 4.)
• Consider use of a hospital birth center, possibly with delivery by a nurse-midwife. (See Chapter 4.)
• Less expensive still, consider an Alternative Birth Center, an out-of-hospital comprehensive maternity care unit where delivery is by a nurse-midwife. (See Chapter 5.)

• Definitely take childbirth preparation classes. Studies indicate they reduce the likelihood of Cesareans and certain postpregnancy complications that can result in extended, expensive hospital stays. (See Chapter 2.)

• If delivery is uncomplicated, definitely consider early discharge from the hospital. This will save several hundred dollars. (See Chapter 4.)

• Review your hospital bill very carefully. Audit studies show overbilling is extremely common. (See Chapter 4.)

• Save all doctor, hospital, drug (etc.) bills, including estimates of transportation costs to and from medical care, because of the tax deductibility of medical expenses exceeding 5 percent of adjusted gross income.

❖ 2

OBSTETRICAL CARE

Be Informed

More and more couples are realizing that it's a good idea to comparison-shop for an obstetrician. Couples increasingly have preferences about such things as prepared childbirth, anesthesia and the fetal heart monitor, and they want an obstetrician who shares their preferences. Moreover, with the high cost of medical care, fewer people are too shy to admit that the doctor's fee has become an element in the selection process. Just as understanding what prenatal care and lab work consist of will make you a better consumer of these medical services, so too will understanding the obstetrician's fee—what's included and what's not, "going rates," insurance coverage and payment schedule.

Preliminary Consultation

A good way to begin "shopping" for an obstetrician is with a referral from a trusted friend or associate, followed by a preliminary meeting with the prospective doctor. Make an appointment stating clearly that the meeting is not for any examination or test, but just a brief talk. (Some doctors may prefer to have an "exploratory" discussion like this over the telephone.) A doctor may balk if you call it an "interview," so just say that you'd like to meet to ask some questions about the prenatal care and maternity services provided by his or her office, and the facilities available at the hospital with which the doctor is affiliated.

When you make this appointment, ask the staff if there will be a charge. Some doctors charge for such preliminary meetings, others do not. If there is a fee, it will *not* be reimbursable under your health insurance—but it *is* a good investment nonetheless.

Have a prepared list of questions for this meeting because drawing it up can help clarify your priorities and areas of concern. It will also help you use the time with the physician most efficiently. *Don't*, however, present your list to the doctor as if it were a "list of demands." Many of the books written by and for women in recent years seem to counsel an aggressive stance vis-à-vis obstetricians (and hospitals). There should be no need for this. Just as you would like a doctor's approach toward you to be flexible and sensitive, so you should be with the doctor. Do not assume that the doctor represents "authority" or "the establishment," out to cheat you of the deeply personal and unique experience of giving birth to your baby. If the doctor's approach *does* seem inflexible, and you know that your manner and questions were reasonable, keep looking.

Some of the things you may want to discuss with the doctor at this first meeting include:

- The doctor's attitude toward childbirth preparation classes and prepared or "natural" childbirth.
- How many of the doctor's patients are Cesareans? More than 15 percent of babies are born by this method in the United States today. If a figure much higher than the national average is cited, find out why. What are the situations in which a Cesarean is *routinely* performed? Most are performed because of failure of labor to progress adequately—ask the doctor how he or she determines this.
- The presence of your husband in the delivery room. Under what conditions would your husband be *excluded?* Is Cesarean one?

• Does the doctor's hospital offer family-centered maternity and newborn care? (See Chapter 4.) An intensive care nursery?

• Does the doctor insist on full "prep," i.e., shaving of the pubic area, enema, etc.? (This approach is considered somewhat inflexible and even old-fashioned today.) Ask, too, about the doctor's preferences regarding hookup to an intravenous drip (IV) and fetal heart monitor.

• The types of anesthesia and analgesic the doctor prefers—when and why. Ask about the effect of the doctor's most frequently given analgesic or anesthetic on the fetus—and on you—both immediately and postpartum. Some physicians consider a modified paracervical block best in that when given in small doses and injected slowly, its relief effect is immediate, while side effects and fetal complications are rare. With a paracervical block, a woman's discomfort is eased, but she's still wide awake and able to actively participate in the labor and delivery. Moreover, a paracervical block can be given by an obstetrician—meaning that an anesthesiologist need not be in attendance, which can save you money. Ask the doctor what percentage of patients go without drugs.

• What percentage of the doctor's patients are induced, i.e., labor contractions started by artificial means, usually synthetic hormones? While an American College of Obstetricians and Gynecologists booklet notes that induction is a "fairly common" procedure, with some physicians using it in one in five deliveries, advocates of prepared childbirth insist even a 10 percent induction rate suggests a physician is aggressive about interfering with the natural process of labor.

• If the doctor is part of a *group* practice, you'll want to know if all members of the group have the same attitudes about childbirth, so that assurances provided by your primary physician will be honored by all members of the practice. If the doctor is in *solo* practice, ask who covers for him or her and about that doctor's procedures and attitudes on the things that most concern you.

• Does the doctor have a fetal heart monitor or ultra-sound equipment in the office? If you end up needing multiple nonstress tests or sonograms, it can save you time and money if the tests are done in your doctor's office.

• Is the father-to-be welcome at prenatal exams, at least periodically?

• Try to get a feel for how smoothly the doctor's office runs, particularly the doctor's ability to meet scheduled appointments without keeping women forever in the waiting room. This can be particularly important to a woman who works outside the home, whose schedule is tight.

• Ask at what point in labor the doctor tries to get to the hospital.

What are the right answers to these questions? While not wanting to sound equivocal, there are few across-the-board, right-or-wrong answers. Instead, there's a considerable latitude in most of these areas, which allows you some real freedom of preference and the doctor a range for professional judgment. If there's a difference in what you prefer and what he or she advises, mutually determine the possibilities for compromise, or spell out the circumstances when your way would be accepted and when the doctor's would prevail.

Don't conclude a preliminary meeting with an obstetrician without talking about the *fee*. In fact, the doctor may prefer that you discuss the fee with the office staff—that's fine, too, for they're sometimes even better able to give you a full financial rundown and detailed answers. A good office staff should take the time to talk to you about the overall fee and what it includes, the payment schedule, whether there is an additional charge if it becomes necessary to perform a Cesarean or if you become designated "medically high risk" and how much of the obstetrical fee is likely to be covered by your particular insurance policy.

Insurance Coverage of Physicians' Fees

Using the insurance checklist from Chapter 1, you already know what, if any, coverage you have for obstetrician fees. Remember that you usually need the kind of insurance called medical services (the least commonly held health insurance) to have such coverage. Don't confuse hospitalization benefits for childbirth with coverage of obstetrician fees—they're two different kinds of insurance!

Remember, too, that even if you do have coverage for obstetrician fees, it's very unlikely you'll have 100 percent reimbursement. That's because you probably have a deductible that applies against doctor fees, co-insurance of 15 to 25 percent and a "reasonable and customary fee" limit. Taken together, these can result in significant unreimbursed doctor expenses, especially if your doctor's fee is higher than what the insurer considers the "going rate." Indeed, you may want to use the reasonable and customary fee as the basis for additional comparison shopping. It doesn't hurt to telephone a few doctors' offices and ask what their fees are. If you do stick with a doctor whose fee is higher than your insurer says is reasonable and customary, when the time comes do try to negotiate with your insurance carrier for higher reimbursement. You have the right of formal review of your claim, and it sometimes works if you persist, especially if you can enlist the help of your doctor. If your doctor has been treating you as a high-risk patient, make certain the insurer understands that—it may qualify you for higher reimbursement.

If you do *not* have insurance for obstetrician fees, tell the doctor and the office staff at the outset. It's not uncommon for doctors to charge their insured patients one fee and their uninsured a *lower* fee. For example, only after she became pregnant in 1982 did my sister-in-law learn that her health insurance plan provided no maternity insurance coverage. When she told her obstetrician she was "uncovered," the doctor quoted her a fee of $700 versus his usual $800 for insured patients. Some doctors also charge their less affluent patients a lower fee.

What the Fee Includes

Make sure you understand from either the doctor or staff what is included in the fee you have been quoted. Generally it includes:

- Prenatal office visits. Generally twelve to fourteen: once a month in the first seven months, two in the eighth, weekly in the ninth, biweekly or more frequently if you become overdue.
- Usual (vaginal) delivery.
- Postpartum visits each day you're in the hospital.
- Postpartum office visit at six to eight weeks.

Not generally included in the "regular" fee:

- Prenatal lab work.
- Prenatal use of advanced obstetrical technology (ultrasound, fetal heart monitor).
- High-risk pregnancy.
- Vaginal birth after a Cesarean.
- Cesarean delivery.
- Circumcision.
- Anesthesia services.

Most doctors charge extra for a *Cesarean.* The average such charge nationwide is about $175 to $200. However, in medium-size cities and their suburbs, expect a $175 to $350 differential, while in the largest cities $500 or more for Cesarean is common. So be sure to ask about Cesarean fees. In fact, also ask if there is a difference in the fee charged for a *scheduled* Cesarean (i.e., when you know sometime in advance that you'll be having a C-section) versus an "emergency" Cesarean (one which becomes necessary during labor). You may find that your doctor charges more for the latter than the former. Doctors also often charge more than the regular fee for a vaginal delivery following an earlier Cesarean. This is justified because of the extra care necessary during such a labor and delivery. For example, one New York City doctor I know charges

$1,800 for ordinary obstetrical care, $2,400 for Cesarean and $2,100 for vaginal delivery of a previous Cesarean patient.

If you're judged *high-risk* for any reason—diabetes, hypertension, complications of previous pregnancy, whatever—many doctors will quote you a higher fee than that charged to their low-risk patients. This is understandable, because a high-risk patient requires more office visits, often more tests and sometimes special hospital procedures. Remember that you can be designated high-risk at any stage of your pregnancy.

While some doctors who have ultrasound equipment or a fetal heart monitor in their office may also include in their standard fee one or more sonograms or nonstress tests, should you need them, these are generally extra, as you usually must go to another doctor's office or a lab for them. These procedures are discussed in the next chapter.

Payment Schedule

Next ask the staff about payment *schedule,* as procedure varies considerably from one obstetrician's office to the next. *Some doctors require payment in full by the thirty-fourth week* of pregnancy. Usually three installment payments are acceptable. Others bill a set percentage of the total fee on a monthly basis, also to guarantee payment in full prior to delivery. However, other doctors will ask for only one-third or half payment prior to delivery. Payment in full prior to delivery is more prevalent in large cities. Doctors in the suburbs and in small towns more frequently bill part before, part after your baby's birth. If you demonstrate need, chances are that your doctor will exhibit some flexibility in the payment schedule.

Note that even if you have excellent maternity coverage that includes substantial coverage of the doctor's fee, you'll not be reimbursed by the insurer until sometime *after* you give birth. Hence, *on a cash-flow basis, you'll have to put up that money for a period of time, and you should plan accordingly.* Say, for example, your obstetrician's fee is $1,600 and must be paid in full by the thirty-fourth week of pregnancy. The office practice is to bill monthly a straight percentage. In this situation, you would be getting a doctor's bill for $200 each month. On top of mortgage or rent, car payments, food, commuting expenses and all the other myriad monthly expenses—coupled with baby-related purchases!—chances are, that $200 needs to be planned for. For the earliest reimbursement, file your claim from the hospital.

Obstetrical Fees Across the Country

The key determinant of what you'll pay for obstetrical care is where you live. In January 1983, the Health Insurance Association of America (HIAA) published the results of a 1982 survey on the medical costs of having a baby in the United States. While the data are now somewhat old given inflation in the medical industry, the HIAA findings nevertheless provide a useful starting point. The HIAA findings are summarized on the maps on the opposite page.

As you can see, the cost difference between urban and rural *within* each region is as marked as the cost differences *among* geographical regions. Physician fees are consistently lower in rural areas. The greatest distinctions between urban and rural costs are in the West and Northeast. The West has the highest *average* doctors' fees for obstetrical care. Doctors' fees for Cesareans are, for the most part, at least $175 higher than for usual delivery.

Once you've located yourself on the map, do some mental addition for the time elapsed since the HIAA survey was conducted. Doctors' fees on rough average increased about 10 percent in 1983 and 5 percent in 1984. Also, bear in mind that numbers given on the map are *averaged* from the *range* of fees that exist over your entire geographic area. That's covering a lot of territory. And a lot of doctors in various situations! Say you live in Dallas and know you're having a Cesarean and your obstetrician is charging $1,600. You look at the map and see that the average physician fee for Cesareans in the urban South was $785 in early 1982—about half your doctor's fee!

Don't automatically conclude from this that your doc-

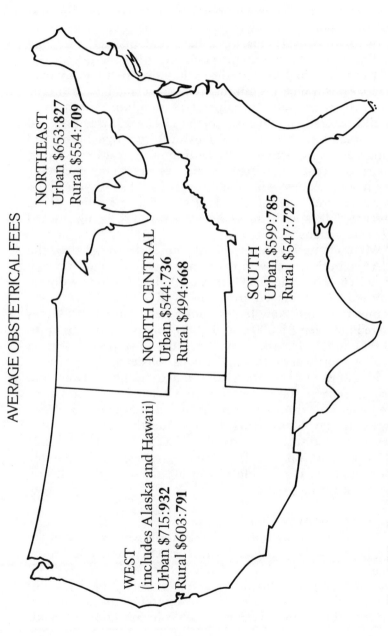

AVERAGE OBSTETRICAL FEES

NORTHEAST
Urban $653:**827**
Rural $554:**709**

NORTH CENTRAL
Urban $544:**736**
Rural $494:**668**

SOUTH
Urban $599:**785**
Rural $547:**727**

WEST
(includes Alaska and Hawaii)
Urban $715:**932**
Rural $603:**791**

NOTE: Boldface figures are for Cesarean delivery.

SOURCE: Health Insurance Association of America. Survey conducted in 1982.

tor's fee is too high. Remember to figure in not just inflation, but also, and more important, that your doctor is in downtown Dallas, in a high-rent district, probably serving a relatively affluent clientele. Also the doctor has probably just had yet another whopping increase in malpractice insurance premiums. (Obstetricians have suffered about the worst rate of malpractice premium rate increase of all doctors.) In contrast, the $785 is a 1982 figure, and it has factored in obstetrical fees in Biloxi, Lynchburg and hundreds more small and medium-size southern cities, where the cost of living—as well as practicing medicine and having babies!—is much lower. So those of you living in or around one of the largest cities may find these "average" fees as little as *half* what you're being quoted by obstetricians.

My own survey, more recent (but less formal) than the HIAA's, indicates that in major metropolitan areas like San Francisco, Los Angeles, Denver, Dallas, Boston, Atlanta, Chicago and their environs, as well as the New York, Connecticut and New Jersey commuter suburbs, 1984 fees ranged between $1,000 and $1,800, and occasionally up to $3,000 in New York City for usual obstetrical care. In smaller Northeast cities and towns, obstetrician fees generally fall in the $760-to-$1,000 range. In the Midwest and North Central states fees are somewhat lower, and they are lower still throughout most of the South. In the West, expect to pay $800 to $1,000 outside the big cities. If a Cesarean section is performed, expect an additional fee of $175 to $300 (up to $500 in the big cities). A comparable additional fee is possible if you are designated medically high-risk for any reason.

"Comparison Shopping"

Besides location, another key determinant of how much you'll pay an obstetrician is how much you are, in effect, "willing" to pay. This sounds curious, so let me explain: *Even within your immediate area, you will find that there is a range of prices doctors are charging for obstetrical services.* This range is *considerable* in and around major cities and suburbs, less so in smaller towns. But in general, it's safe to say that if you think all obstetricians in your area charge the same fees, you probably haven't checked.

For example, in New York City within the same three months in mid-1984, I found women paying between $1,500 and $3,000 to their obstetricians for usual delivery—all within a twenty-block radius. In neighboring towns in the New Jersey suburbs, one woman paid $1,450, another paid $900 and a third paid $1,100—all within three months of one another. Within the same two months in 1984, a woman living in Oakland, California, paid her obstetrician $1,250, her neighbor paid $1,600 and three miles away in Berkeley a third woman paid $1,000! What does this mean to you? It means that practically no matter where you live, you probably have a choice—should you choose to exercise it—to comparison-shop for an OB on a *price* basis. Don't be embarrassed if you decide that the fee charged is *one* of the criteria on which you will base your selection of an obstetrician. This is perfectly understandable—especially if you don't have medical insurance that will substantially defray the fee. Pregnancy, childbirth and the first few years of baby's life are a time of substantial expense and whole new patterns of expenditures. It makes sense not to spend more money than an "informed you" thinks is necessary in *any* area of your life—including doctors' fees.

What About the Fee if You Change Doctors?

If you start out with a physician with whom you later become unhappy, look for a new doctor. It's not uncommon to do so. One friend of mine did so when her OB insisted that *all* her patients had to have a "full prep"—including enema—upon admission to the hospital. And my sister-in-law changed doctors because she couldn't establish a rapport with him and because she heard previous patients complain about the care they had received. Although no one relishes the task of informing a physician you'll be leaving his care, it's far better to do it and get it over with than to wish you had over the next several months.

What about the fee when you change? This is simpler,

if you've made just one or two visits, because you'll probably not have made a major installment payment on the overall fee. When you inform the doctor (or staff) of your decision to leave, simply ask that a bill for the visit(s) to date be sent to you. Charges will probably be in the range of $35 to $65 per office visit (higher if the physician's fee is at the high end of the scale) and more for the first prenatal visit when the doctor performed a thorough physical and examination. If you've already made a major installment payment, you'll have to discuss whether a reimbursement is due. Most doctors will be fair to you. If you have carefully satisfied yourself that a reimbursement is due but not forthcoming, you have the option of writing a letter to the Medical Ethics Committee of the County Medical Association, and the Chief of OB-GYN of the hospital with which the physician is associated. Inform the doctor's office that you're doing so, and chances are you'll get your money refunded promptly. Let me stress, however, that you probably won't have a problem like this—the doctor will probably refund the fair amount, promptly.

Having covered obstetrical fees, let's turn to the lab tests and expenses of routine prenatal care which are *not* generally included in the OB fee. Usually, if a blood or other sample is sent to a laboratory for analysis, you will be billed directly from that lab and you'll pay the lab directly—although test results are provided to your physician, rather than to you, in most instances.

Pregnancy Tests

Your first medical costs will probably be for tests to confirm your pregnancy. Tests can be performed on a sample of urine or blood. They are looking for the presence of the pregnancy hormone—human chorionic gonadotrophin or HCG—secreted by the early placenta. Today, many couples who suspect a pregnancy try one of the at-home pregnancy test kits on the market. (About $60 million worth of these tests were sold in 1983!) These are a variation of the standard urine pregnancy test and are easily administered by yourself. They can be purchased at any pharmacy *without a prescription* and cost about $10. Of course, your doctor's office staff can do a quick urine pregnancy test—sometimes without a charge. If there is one, expect to pay $10 to $15. Ditto if you go to a medical lab. Some women's health clinics will do the test for free. The same is true if you work for an employer with on-site medical facilities.

However, because of accuracy limitations with the urine pregnancy test, many obstetricians prefer the more precise blood analysis. One such test is a radioreceptor assay blood test, or *RRA*, also known as *Biocept-G*. The Biocept-G is extremely accurate, and its greater sensitivity to smaller amounts of HCG also can help a physician make an early diagnosis of some abnormal pregnancies—for example, an ectopic one. Test results are usually available on a same-day basis, and cost $20 to $30, billed directly to you from the lab.

The most accurate of all pregnancy tests is called a radioimmunoassay or *RIA*. This blood test measures a tiny component of HCG called a Beta-subunit and can detect a pregnancy as early as eight or nine days after ovulation. It will rarely miss an ectopic pregnancy or threatened miscarriage. This test, however, is more time-consuming and expensive. Results are usually available to your physician in thirty-six hours. You'll be billed directly from the lab, for about $40. However, a less expensive RIA test kit is becoming commercially available to labs, with the added advantage of same-day results. All pregnancy tests are reimbursable under a health insurance plan providing coverage for diagnostic tests.

Prenatal Lab Work and Vitamins

At the first prenatal visit, your doctor will perform several procedures for laboratory analysis. Few books or doctors bother to tell you anything about these procedures— you just get a bill for them, lumping the various analyses together as "prenatal lab workup." I think you'll be interested in knowing what the tests are for, and what they cost.

First, the doctor will withdraw a sample of blood for typing. Your blood will fall into one of four groups—A, B, AB or O—and will be either Rh positive or negative. About 85 percent of white people and 93 percent of black people have a substance in their blood called the Rh factor, which makes them Rh positive. Those lacking the factor are Rh negative, and while this in no way affects their own well-being, it can (although it need not today, thanks to an effective vaccine) put future offspring at risk, as described in the next chapter.

The blood sample taken at this first prenatal visit is usually a few vials, because other tests are done, too. Two of these are the *hemoglobin* and *hematocrit* tests. The hemoglobin test measures the amount of iron pigment in the blood—hemoglobin is, in effect, what makes the red blood cells red, and transfers oxygen to the body cells. The hematocrit count is the percentage of red blood cell mass to whole blood fluid. Most *non*pregnant women have a hemoglobin level of 13 or 14 milligrams, and a hematocrit of 40 percent. Although most pregnant women have somewhat lower levels, a diagnosis of anemia is made if your hemoglobin is 10 milligrams or lower, and hematocrit 30 percent. These tests are repeated during pregnancy—usually at midterm, in the month prior to delivery, and at hospital admission—to make sure that your iron reserve hasn't been depleted. It's quite possible for this to happen, as pregnancy is a major drain on your iron reserves. Because anemia caused by lack of iron is one of the most common medical problems of pregnancy, let me digress for a moment from prenatal lab work to talk about the pregnant woman's iron and vitamin needs.

A pregnant woman uses up to twice the normal amount of iron, to meet both the needs of her unborn baby and to compensate for the additional fluid in her bloodstream. For this reason, all pregnant women should receive daily iron supplements during the second and third trimesters and until a nursing baby is weaned. (Iron therapy is normally not required in the first trimester, which is fortunate, as it can exacerbate "morning sickness." But doctors do vary as to whether they prescribe iron during the first trimester.) The usual supplement is 60 milligrams, but your doctor will prescribe the proper dosage for you. It's usually taken in pill form, preferably after meals to reduce stomach distress. Don't take iron pills with a soft drink, because the phosphates in soft drinks interfere with the body's ability to absorb iron. Instead, take the pills with a glass of milk or citrus juice, because calcium and vitamin C enhance iron absorption.

Your doctor will also prescribe *vitamin supplements.* Even if you're extremely conscientious about eating nutritiously during pregnancy, you will need additional folic acid (a B vitamin), vitamin A, B complex vitamins and vitamin C. A calcium supplement is also essential during pregnancy and lactation. These prenatal vitamins are not cheap, and are an expense that many first-time pregnant women haven't anticipated. Expect to pay between $12 to $15 for a bottle of 100 pills—approximately a three-month supply. Often the vitamins, iron and calcium supplements are all in one pill, and these are usually the better buy. The costs can add up—if you breastfeed for six months, vitamin and iron supplements could cost $75 or more. Go to a discount pharmacy for the best price. If you're lucky, this item may be reimbursed under your medical insurance, so save the prescription number and receipts, and submit a claim—but *don't* spell out the fact that this is a claim for vitamins.

Returning to the prenatal lab workup, your blood sample will also be used for a *serology* test (sometimes listed as Wasserman or VDRL) to screen for syphilis, as required by law in most states. Another test determines if you have immunity to *rubella* (German measles). Ideally, this test should be done several months *before* you get pregnant. That way, if you're found *not* to have immunity, you can take the rubella vaccine, then wait three months before attempting conception (because the vaccine itself presents some risk to an early fetus). However, if you're already pregnant and your prenatal blood workup shows no immunity, it's too late for the vaccine. Instead, you must take special precautions about coming into contact with anyone having the disease, which, by and large, means children, because in most parts of the country (the Far West excepted) most adults have immunity.

Some doctors also make the test for *toxoplasmosis* part of the routine prenatal blood workup. In fact, some states require it by law. Toxoplasmosis is the most common of all parasitic infections. In adults it often has no symptoms or only very mild ones, such as headache or swollen glands, and may be mistaken for flu. However, during pregnancy, the parasite crosses the placenta in 45 percent of all cases, with severe fetal damage or death resulting. About one baby in a thousand in the United States is born with congenital toxoplasmosis each year.

Unlike with rubella, there is no vaccine to prevent toxoplasmosis. Rather, if the antibody blood test shows that you're in the two-thirds majority with *no* immunity, you can only use that knowledge to take precautions against contracting the parasite. Most cases of toxoplasmosis are caused by eating infected raw or rare meat, so they should not be eaten during pregnancy; wear gloves when handling raw meat and wash hands and counter surfaces thoroughly afterward. Secondly, if you have a cat, avoid its litter box. Cats can become infected with the parasite fairly easily (and will appear perfectly healthy, giving you no hint of it), and when they do, will pass the toxoplasmosis organism daily in their feces. So let someone else clean the litter box, while wearing gloves. Also, ask that the box be cleaned *daily*, because the toxoplasmosis organism in the cat's feces is not infectious for the first twenty-four hours.

Cost of Prenatal Lab Work

Not all obstetricians routinely perform all the tests just described. In part it depends on state laws. On the other hand, some doctors routinely perform all the tests described and more. For example, some obstetricians require their patients to have a blood test at sixteen weeks, which can help determine whether the fetus has a *neural tube defect* by measuring a substance in the maternal blood called alpha-fetoprotein (AFP). Another procedure that many doctors routinely perform is the *glucose tolerance test*. It determines if your blood sugar has been affected by the hormonal stimulation of pregnancy to abnormal levels, which can affect the pregnancy.

The larger point is that depending on your physician, on the state you live in and, of course, on your personal health background, you may not have all the tests described here, or you may well have all of them and more. Nearly always, however, the *initial* and *routine* prenatal lab workup includes blood typing and Rh antibody screening, hemoglobin and hematocrit, rubella immunity, the syphilis test and a Pap test. The Pap test is sometimes billed separately at about $10 to $15. For the other tests, expect to receive a lab bill for between $45 to $65. If your doctor takes additional tests, the cost can rise to more than $100 for lab work performed at the first prenatal visit alone. In addition, prenatal vitamin, iron and calcium supplements prescribed by your physician may easily run $36 to $75 or more, depending on how many months following delivery you take them. Good health insurance will reimburse for the lab work under the bailiwick of diagnostic tests, but usually will not for the vitamins, despite the fact that they're a doctor's prescription.

Prepared Childbirth Training

Another health-related expense of pregnancy is prepared childbirth training, the best known being Lamaze. Essentially, these classes teach you how to prepare for and partially protect yourself from pain, via a system of conditioned reflexes or other such trained responses to pain. Your husband or other support person plays an active monitoring and coaching role. The training aims to break the cycle of fear–tension–pain, by providing you with a thorough understanding of the labor and birthing process and with techniques of systematic muscular relaxation (tension reduction) coupled with "cognitive control." Cognitive control means a vigorous focusing of concentration away from the pain, which enables you to moderate the brain's reception of pain stimuli. This is done via several controlled breathing techniques in tandem with a "concentration point" on a distant wall.

Several studies have documented the medical value of prepared childbirth training. Fear of labor can intensify pain by stimulating the release of certain chemicals which cause a constriction of blood vessels carrying oxygen to the fetus and placenta. This can slow labor and exacerbate fetal distress. One study showed that the length of labor was shortened for trained women by as much as four hours. More specifically, *a 1978 study conducted by Northwestern University showed that Lamaze-trained women had significantly fewer Cesareans, significantly lower incidence of fetal distress, less maternal infection and fewer infant deaths.* Of course, researchers recognize that Lamaze-trained women are a biased group, in that they tend to be better informed and more actively, positively oriented toward caring for themselves during pregnancy. Nonetheless, few informed physicians dispute the medical value of prepared childbirth training.

But the highest marks for such training come from the couples who have taken it and used it. They are *overwhelmingly* enthusiastic. One Massachusetts woman wrote, "Prepared childbirth classes are the best investment in preventive medicine you can make!!"

The training is not usually expensive. Red Cross, "Y" and hospital classes are usually cheapest—indeed, sometimes they're free. When not, the range is usually $25 to $35. Doctors' office classes are also sometimes free. When not, they can be up to $50 to $65. Most expensive are the private classes, but many couples happily pay extra for the special attention these provide. In contrast to hospital classes, where fifteen to twenty or even more couples may be in attendance, private organizations try to confine class size to six to ten couples, so each is given specific, individual attention in an informal atmosphere that encourages questions about all aspects of pregnancy, birth and postpartum care. The instructors in these classes are also likely to be graduates of the rigorous training program of the American

Society for Prophylaxis in Obstetrics (ASPO)—the official name of the Lamaze organization. An ASPO certification represents quality control. These private classes cost $50 to $75, although they can go up to $150 in large cities. (Don't confuse prepared childbirth training with special pregnancy exercise classes. These can cost anywhere from $35 to $225 or more.)

"Refresher" classes for women who have taken the training for an earlier baby usually involve two sessions and run in cost from free to $35. I loved the note I received from a friend and mother of four from Southington, Connecticut, on this subject of "refresher" Lamaze training. She wrote:

> Lamaze classes, first time—$35
> for #2 refresher classes—$12
> #3 refresher classes—$12
> #4—$0 (guest lecturer!)

While these classes are not reimbursable under health insurance—despite their value as "preventive medicine"!—if you work for a large company or a government agency or are a member of a union that has a program for the reimbursement of educational costs, check to see if prepared childbirth classes are included.

Dental Care During Pregnancy

A final health-related expense of pregnancy that many women don't anticipate: special dental care. It's often required because hormonal changes in pregnancy can cause your gums to develop an exaggerated response to oral irritants like plaque. In fact, this condition—called "pregnancy gingivitis"—affects at least half of all pregnant women. It's an inflammation of the little triangular wedge of gum tissue between the teeth. You'll know it if you develop it—your gums will be puffy-looking and red or bluish red and will bleed easily when you brush or use dental floss. Pregnancy gingivitis can begin as early as the second month and can continue through pregnancy and even a month or two afterward. If you have a tendency to sensitive, bleeding gums, you'll have to be especially careful.

With strict attention to oral hygiene and correct brushing, flossing and gum massaging techniques, pregnancy gingivitis can be prevented. *So, as soon as you know you're pregnant, make an appointment with your dentist for an examination and thorough cleaning.* The dentist or dental hygienist will remove all the plaque and calculus from your teeth. If your home care keeps your mouth plaque-free, you'll not develop pregnancy gingivitis. If you already *have* the condition, the treatment is the same, but it will be more uncomfortable for you. Because of this heightened sensitivity of the gums during pregnancy, your dentist will probably suggest an office visit for cleaning every three, rather than six months. Some women have to go as often as once a month during pregnancy. If you have a dental insurance plan, submit the bills as you usually do, and once your deductible is satisfied, you can expect reimbursement for these visits.

❖ 3

THE LESS ROUTINE MEDICAL TESTS AND EXPENSES OF PREGNANCY

By "somewhat less routine" prenatal medical tests, I mean just that. By and large, the tests and procedures described here are not exotic or reserved only for high-risk pregnancies. In fact, procedures like sonograms and nonstress testing verge on the routine today. So, read on. Even if you have every reason to expect a normal, low-risk pregnancy, there's still a good chance that you'll undergo one or more of these procedures.

Rh Incompatibility

If your prenatal blood workup (Chapter 2) shows you're Rh-negative, your pregnancy will require special medical supervision. This is because a problem can potentially arise when you're Rh-negative, your mate is Rh-positive (this happens in about 13 percent of Caucasian marriages, and 5 percent of marriages between U.S. blacks), and you conceive a baby with Rh-positive blood. Primarily during the last trimester and especially at delivery, some of the baby's Rh-positive blood may enter your bloodstream. Because these Rh-positive blood cells are "foreign agents" to your system, your body may attack them by developing immune antibodies—just as the body attacks and protects against a virus or bacterium. These "anti-Rh" substances destroy the Rh-positive cells circulating in your system, and you thus become "sensitized" to the Rh factor.

In a first pregnancy, the risk to an Rh-positive baby is low, because the baby is usually safely born before your system produces the antibodies. *The potential danger is with subsequent pregnancies.* If you're Rh-sensitized by your first pregnancy, your body will have set up—and will *always* maintain—an "anti-Rh" defense mechanism. These antibodies can cross the placenta and attack an unborn Rh-positive baby's red blood cells. (If the fetus is Rh-negative like the mother, there's no problem.) The result can be jaundice, anemia, severe brain damage and even fetal death.

Happily, there's an effective vaccine against Rh sensitization. Developed in 1968, the vaccine is known by the trade name Rhogam. Properly administered, it's completely effective and has dramatically decreased the number of newborns affected by Rh disease. However, about one in five women who need the vaccine still don't get it, with the tragic result that 5,500 affected infants are born each year.

To be effective, the vaccine should be injected into the Rh-negative mother within seventy-two hours of *every* delivery of an Rh-positive infant. (The same is true after a miscarriage, abortion, ectopic pregnancy and even in some cases amniocentesis.) This done, the mother's system will not develop antibodies and her next pregnancy will not be affected. *While only about 10 percent of Rh-negative women with an incompatible pregnancy become sensitized, there's no way to tell who will or will not, so all of them must receive the vaccine.*

For the additional lab work and vaccine her pregnancy requires, the Rh-negative woman will pay at least $150 to $250. Many hospitals also require that a woman's blood be cross-matched with the vaccine—a time-consuming and additionally expensive lab procedure. Good maternity coverage in a health insurance plan will reimburse for these costs.

Genetic Counseling

The purpose of genetic counseling and testing is to determine the presence of genetic disease and a pattern, if any, of inheritance of such disease. Genetic counseling can determine the *probability*—the mathematical odds—of an individual couple producing a child with a particular genetic or chromosomal disorder. A genetic counselor is a person specifically trained in medical genetics. He or she can be a physician—often a pediatrician or internist—or a Ph.D. in genetics with special training in genetic counseling. There are also an increasing number of genetic counselors who have M.S. degrees in medical genetics.

Who should seek genetic counseling? Many more people than currently do. While as many as 15 million Americans might benefit from it, 90 percent of these don't receive it, partly because they're not aware of its importance and availability. Fortunately, this situation is changing because of the public education efforts of the March of Dimes, the National Genetics Foundation and the increased efforts on the part of physicians to inform their patients about genetic counseling.

As the experts often emphasize, *there is no immunity from genetic illness*. With the vast number of genes within each chromosome of each cell of our bodies, a few are likely to be faulty. In other words, we all carry some abnormal genes, but most of the time these are "overshadowed" by normal ones. These remarks aren't meant to frighten you—obviously, the vast majority of babies are born normal and healthy and grow up that way. However, medical science has determined that there are certain categories of people who may be more at risk than others of bearing a child with a genetic or chromosomal disorder. According to the experts, *you should see a genetic counselor if:*

• You or your mate (either together or with previous partners) have already given birth to a child with a genetic or chromosomal disorder.
• You or your mate have a family medical history of genetic disease.
• You and your mate are from an ethnic or racial group at high risk for specific genetic disorders.
• You or your mate have had X rays, taken drugs, or been exposed to a virus like German measles at or near

the time of conception of a baby you're now carrying. (Although these are "external" rather than "internal" or genetic factors, a genetic counselor can help you.)

• You're a pregnant woman over thirty-five years old. You have an increased risk of bearing a child with a chromosomal disorder, the most common of which is Down's syndrome ("mongolism").

• You are a pregnant woman whose mate is over 55 years old. Recent evidence suggests that babies fathered by men of this age have an approximately doubled risk of Down's syndrome regardless of the mother's age.

• If you have had repeat positive blood tests indicating high levels of alphafetaprotein (AFP), which may indicate a fetus with a neural tube defect.

• If you have already had three (some doctors say two) miscarriages, or stillborn births. (Also if you're married to a man whose *previous* wife had three miscarriages or stillbirths.)

Genetic counseling begins with a thorough family medical history—usually at least two generations back—from both members of a couple. In addition, when they exist for a specific disorder, *lab tests* are used to establish or confirm a diagnosis. For example, a skin test or a blood sample may be taken to study your chromosome pattern, or to determine whether one or both members of a couple are "carriers" for certain genetic disorders suggested by your family histories or your racial or ethnic groups. A "carrier" of a genetic disease carries one "dose" of the defective genetic material in question. Unless you're tested—or "carrier screened"—you won't know whether you're a carrier, because a *carrier does not exhibit or "have" the disorder*. You may look, feel and truly be fine, but still carry a genetic dose for a certain disease that could place your baby at risk.

Currently, carrier screening exists for some of the better-known genetic diseases including *Tay-Sachs*, a fatal disorder of the nervous system primarily affecting people of Eastern European Jewish ancestry (about 1 in 25 Jews is a carrier);

sickle-cell anemia, a painful, sometimes fatal blood disorder primarily affecting blacks and Hispanics (at least 1 in 10 blacks is a carrier and 1 in 625 black newborns has the disease); and *thalassemia,* a blood disorder mainly affecting people of Mediterranean descent (of whom 1 in 25 is a carrier) and to a lesser extent, blacks and Asians. *Both* parents must be carriers for their baby to have a *25 percent* chance of being born with these diseases. The point here is that when an accurate carrier-screening test exists, that's where diagnosis begins. In these examples, the screening is a simple blood test, costing between $10 to $35 and widely available at medical centers across the country. If you're a member of an at-risk group, your obstetrician will probably routinely suggest you, as a couple, go for a screening test. If the tests come back positive, you'll need to go to a genetic counselor. The job of the counselor is then to discuss with you the odds of your baby having the disease for which you are carriers; whether or not a definitive prenatal diagnostic test exists for the disorder, the characteristics of the disease itself (including an affected child's life expectancy and potential); your various medical options and availability of community resources for help in caring for an affected child.

Unfortunately, accurate carrier-screening tests don't yet exist for many genetic diseases—for example, cystic fibrosis, the most common genetic disorder among Caucasians (an estimated 10 million Americans are carriers). When no screening test exists, the diagnostic job of the genetic counselor is obviously harder, with the family medical history the only real key. The cost of these counseling services is generally $100 to $200, the latter if the diagnosis is very complex.

As for insurance reimbursement for genetic counseling and carrier screening—some policies will cover for them, others won't. It does seem ridiculous that some policies won't—it's so obviously in the interest of the insurer to learn if a couple has a high probability of bearing a child with a particular genetic disorder. As genetic counseling and screening become increasingly widespread, insurers are bound to respond and reimbursement will become more routine. In the meantime, if you find your insurer does *not* reimburse for genetic counseling and testing, complain, preferably in writing, to both your employer and the insurer. Consumer complaints will help speed the process of "enlightenment."

Whatever the policy of your insurer, if you fit in the risk categories discussed earlier, *get the help you need.* Concern about the cost should not stop you. This is not the place to economize—although many organizations and people will try to help if cost is a major problem. Medical centers, for example, may work with you to reduce the cost to a more manageable level, or may arrange for deferred payment. Moreover, blood and tissue samples can usually be sent by mail to a genetic center if you don't live near one, sparing the expense of extensive travel. In some instances, a center that's doing research on a particular genetic disorder will not charge for counseling and testing involving that disease. The National Genetics Foundation (NGF) in New York City is able to advise you of any medical center doing research on the specific disease for which you're at risk. Advisory and referral services provided by the NGF are free.

Prenatal Diagnosis by Amniocentesis

If it sounds to you that genetic counseling is no panacea—you're right. Since many genetic diseases don't yet have accurate carrier screening tests, a counselor can't even diagnose with certainty whether a person is a carrier. And even when a screening test exists, and both parents-to-be are found to be carriers of a genetic "dose" for a certain disease, the counselor can still only deal in the *probabilities* the baby will be born with the disease—unless, that is, there's an accurate *prenatal diagnostic test* for the disorder.

Today, with the procedure called *amniocentesis*, medical specialists can often go that next step of prenatal diagnosis. That is, your baby can be tested and diagnosed *in utero* for many disorders. Amniocentesis can provide accurate diagnosis of *all* chromosomal abnormalities (of which Down's syndrome is an example), many biochemical disorders (like Tay-Sachs) and certain developmental or structural abnormalities (neural tube defects like spina bifida). All together, more than one hundred different genetic disorders can currently be diagnosed by amniocentesis—a wonderful advance in medical science.

Amniocentesis involves withdrawing a small amount of amniotic fluid from the amniotic sac surrounding the fetus. It's performed during the period between the fourteenth and the eighteenth weeks of pregnancy, calculated from the first day of the last menstrual period. The importance of accurate timing is this: until the fourteenth week, there's not sufficient amniotic fluid to safely withdraw even the small amount needed for testing. If you wait much *after* the eighteenth week, by the time you get the test results, it may be too late for you to have a therapeutic abortion of a fetus determined to have a severe genetic disease like Tay-Sachs. (This is probably the place to note that if you would absolutely *not* have an abortion, even of a severely damaged fetus, there is little point in having amniocentesis for genetic diagnostic purposes.)

Briefly about the procedure: "Amnio" is done on an out-patient basis, in a hospital, a specialized laboratory or even a doctor's office. It's performed by a physician who specializes in the procedure. (Many facilities and physicians will allow your husband to be with you.) The procedure begins with an *ultrasound* examination, or *sonogram*. A sonogram uses sound waves (rather than X rays) to locate the fetus and placenta, which then appear as a "picture" on a TV-like monitor. Following the sonogram, the physician numbs your abdomen with a local anesthetic. Then, guided by the sonogram away from the fetus and placenta, the doctor inserts a long, thin, hollow needle through your abdomen and into the uterus. (You must lie *very* still and if you're nervous about needles, don't look at this one—it *is* big.) The physician then withdraws about four teaspoons of the amniotic fluid, the needle is removed, and the baby's heartbeat is checked. It takes only a few minutes, and your body will replace the lost fluid in a short time.

Some women are quite nervous with the *idea* of amniocentesis, but in fact most don't find it particularly painful.
They usually describe the needle insertion as a firm pressure.
About 2 percent of women undergoing it do report some
minor cramping and bleeding afterward. Many medical
organizations have conducted research on the safety of
amniocentesis, and have concluded that in the hands of an
expert and immediately preceded by ultrasound, it's safe
for mother and baby. The National Institute of Health, the
American College of Obstetricians and Gynecologists, the
National Institute of Child Health and Human Development and the National Genetics Foundation, among others,
report that the risk of miscarriage caused by amniocentesis
is less than 1 percent. Most couples conclude that if the
test is medically warranted in their case, this risk is worth
taking. It's also good to know that in the unusual instances
when the needle has touched the fetus, serious effects have
been rare—usually there's just a skin dimple. *However,
you should know and assess the fact that serious after-
effects have on occasion been reported, including rupture
of the amniotic membranes, uterine and amniotic fluid
infections, placental hemorrhage and premature labor resulting in fetal death.*

Usually the hardest part of amniocentesis is waiting for
the results. The fluid withdrawn during the test contains
cells naturally shed by the fetus. These cells are collected,
then cultured and grown in a lab until there are enough
for analysis. The analysis is complex, and can take up to
four weeks.

It's essential to realize that *amniocentesis cannot guarantee your baby will be normal.* Rather, it can rule out
certain *specific* problems for which you've been determined
to have a greater risk than the average expectant couple.
You, your genetic counselor and your physician tell the lab
which disorders to look for, which tests to run. Many
couples ask, "Why can't the lab run *all* the tests?" This
would be impossible—far too time-consuming and enormously expensive. However, when a competent physician
and lab perform the procedure and analyses, amniocentesis

can provide assurance at greater than 98 percent accuracy that your baby will not have the disorders for which he or she has been tested.

The most common use of amnio is by mothers-to-be thirty-five years old and older, who want to assure themselves that their babies won't have *Down's syndrome* or another chromosomal disorder. Indeed, more than three-quarters of all the women who undergo amniocentesis are thirty-five and up. Testing has become so widespread for this age group that today women over thirty-five are having only 30 percent of the infants born with Down's syndrome! As women increasingly delay their pregnancies for career or other purposes later into their thirties, more and more of them will be having amniocentesis—it's not the "exotic" test it was just a few years ago.

It's good news that *96 to 97 percent of the women undergoing amniocentesis find that their baby is free of the suspected genetic, chromosomal or structural defect.* Because of "amnio," many couples who formerly would not run the risk of having a baby because of suspected genetic problems can now plan a family with the same confidence as other couples. And in the unusual situation that a defect *is* identified by amniocentesis, a physician learning of it early in pregnancy is able, *in some instances,* to minimize damage through treatment *in utero* or by prompt action at or near birth. If a disorder is not treatable (like Down's syndrome or Tay-Sachs), the couple at least has the opportunity to make an informed decision as to whether they wish to continue the pregnancy.

A final word about the diagnostic capabilities of amnio: The procedure reveals the sex of your baby—so be sure to tell the doctor if you *don't* want the news ahead of the big event.

Amnio generally costs from $500 to $1,000 for the doctor's fee plus lab analyses. If you're quoted a fee in the higher end of this range, it probably includes the cost of a genetic counselor's services, too. Most health insurers will reimburse for amnio as a diagnostic test. It's usually subject to a deductible and co-insurance.

Late-Pregnancy Amniocentesis

Up to now I've been talking about *mid-pregnancy am-niocentesis for genetic diagnostic purposes.* At or about term, your doctor may recommend amniocentesis to help determine the health of your baby. Late-pregnancy amnio can, for example, tell if the baby is postmature and should be delivered; or alternately, if the baby is mature enough to be safely delivered, if there are other medical reasons to induce labor or schedule a Cesarean. It can also reveal the amount of oxygen a baby is receiving, to help determine if the baby is at risk and should be delivered. Amnio can detect the presence of meconium in the amniotic fluid, too. This is the baby's waste material, and its release into the fluid *may* indicate fetal distress (although there is some debate about this currently in the medical community), and may suggest the need for rapid delivery. Amnio can tell when an Rh-negative baby needs an intrauterine transfusion.

Because time is crucial in these cases, and because the analyses conducted are different from those done with mid-pregnancy amniocentesis for genetic diagnostic purposes, lab results are available in a matter of hours for late-pregnancy amnio. Physician fees for amniocentesis at or near term run about $50 to $200. If you require *repeated* amniocentesis during the last few weeks before delivery, the doctor may reduce the per procedure charge.

Chorionic Villi Sampling (CVS)

This is a new prenatal diagnostic procedure, which can perform the same functions as mid-pregnancy amnio. It's an advance over amniocentesis, however, in that it can be done with accurate results as soon as the *fifth* week of pregnancy. If test results—which are available overnight, in another advantage over mid-pregnancy amnio—indicate the fetus has a severe genetic disorder, the decision to have a therapeutic abortion may be less wrenching for a woman six weeks pregnant, rather than twenty.

The procedure isn't painful and will eventually be performed in doctors' offices. A woman is hooked up to an ultrasound machine, and an obstetrician inserts a thin, long needle through the vagina into the uterus. A second doctor follows the procedure via the ultrasound monitor, and directs the first physician to position the tube correctly between the lining of the uterus and the chorion. The chorion is the early placenta—the sac or layer of tissue surrounding the embryo in the first two months. The purpose is to obtain a few samples of the chorionic villi, the tiny projections of tissue which transfer nutrients, oxygen and embryonic waste between mother and embryo. The chorionic villi are withdrawn and sent for lab analysis for the suspected genetic or chromosomal disorder. Since the sample is composed of the same cells as the fetus, any genetic defects that show up in it presumably would affect the fetus, too.

Because the test is so new, its risks have not been fully substantiated by experience. Many experts anticipate, however, that they'll be about the same as those of amniocentesis—less than 1 percent of CVS testing will result in miscarriage. However, some obstetricians disagree. One I spoke with felt CVS was significantly more "invasive" than amnio and would prove to be higher risk. By early 1985, CVS was available at about fifty hospitals across the country, but availability is expected to grow quickly. CVS costs about the same as amniocentesis. However, because it's such a new procedure, you may have a harder time getting insurance to reimburse for it, as insurers generally won't cover "experimental" procedures. So check with your insurer in advance of undergoing CVS.

Ultrasound Testing

The ultrasound exam, or *sonogram*, is a diagnostic procedure with many uses in obstetrical care. It uses sound waves of very high frequency (you can't hear them) sent out by a scanner. The sound waves reflect or "echo" back from the object of study, creating a "picture" of that object that is displayed on a TV-like monitor. Before its use as a medical procedure, ultrasound in the form of sonar was used to locate submarines below the surface of the water.

It's easy to see how medical science made the creative leap to using it as a way of locating and picturing a fetus in the womb!

A common use of the sonogram is when date of conception is unknown, and hence gestational age of the fetus and due date are uncertain. With a sonogram, a doctor can measure the fetus crown to rump, and correlate the size to age. Performed during the first fourteen weeks of pregnancy, this measurement can usually pinpoint date of conception within a week, with 95 percent accuracy. In the second and third trimesters, some physicians use the sonogram to get a measurement of the fetal skull, or even the fetus's femur (thigh bone), the longest bone in the body, for the same purpose of determining gestational age. However, at these stages of pregnancy, the procedure is less accurate.

A sonogram can also be used to confirm a pregnancy at four or five weeks, when the fetal sac becomes visible. A version of ultrasound called "real-time" can detect fetal heartbeat as early as seven weeks and fetal movement by about the same time. (The absence of fetal movement at or after seven weeks is frequently a reliable predictor of an impending miscarriage.) A sonogram can identify a multiple pregnancy. If you have bleeding during your pregnancy, the test may be advised to help determine the cause. And a sonogram can also reveal an ectopic pregnancy—one that has occurred outside the uterus, most likely in the fallopian tube.

Other important uses. In the second trimester and later, many placental abnormalities that might place the fetus at risk can be diagnosed with the help of ultrasound—for example, placenta previa, in which the placenta obstructs the birth canal. (A pregnancy characterized by placenta previa can develop otherwise normally and culminate in delivery of a healthy baby by C-section.) Ultrasound can identify ovarian cysts, which might complicate a pregnancy, and an incomplete or missed miscarriage. It can also identify certain fetal complications or disorders like hydrocephalus—fluid on the brain. If you have high blood pressure, following the baby's development with ultrasound can help determine what treatment is needed to protect the fetus. Sonograms can also help doctors diagnose a variety of fetal heart malformations and malfunctions. In addition, ultrasound can detect the presence of meconium in the amniotic fluid. It can also help in diagnosing problems that may arise with mothers who have an Rh incompatibility, described earlier.

Since more than half of all pregnant women in the United States have sonograms these days, you'll want to be prepared for the possibility by knowing what the procedure is like. First of all, it doesn't hurt and it's fairly quick—about thirty minutes. It can be performed in a hospital on an out-patient basis, or in a special clinic or laboratory facility. Some physicians have ultrasound equipment in their offices, which can be very convenient. The procedure is performed by a doctor or an ultrasound technician. In preparation for the exam, you drink several glasses of water because a full bladder helps the doctor "read" the pattern of echoes. Other than the water, no diet restrictions, medications or injections are involved. You lie on an examining table, your abdomen is exposed and covered with mineral oil, which helps the "microphone" glide across your belly and improves penetration of sound waves. The doctor then moves the "microphone" across the abdomen to a variety of positions. All the while, the instrument emits high-frequency sound waves, which are reflected at different intensities as they strike the various body (and baby!) structures. The returning echoes are transferred into a picture on a TV-like screen for the doctor and you to see.

How much *you* (not the doctor) can really see and interpret depends in large part on when during the pregnancy you have the sonogram. Early on, you may on your own just be able to discern a pulsing (from the fetus's heartbeat) mass. The doctor will have to point out which is the head, which the placenta, and so on. Later in a pregnancy, however, women can make out their babies much more clearly. For most women, this first "meeting" with their baby is a highly emotional experience. Many doctors will allow your husband to be present, and give you a picture of the baby afterward.

Is ultrasound safe? Yes, according to the American College of Obstetricians-Gynecologists (ACOG) and many other sources. Ultrasound has been extensively studied for more than twenty years, and no damage has been reported to mother or unborn baby. However, ACOG does feel the responsibility to note that while extensive use and tests don't show any danger, as ultrasound is still a relatively new procedure it cannot be said with 100 percent certainty that it's 100 percent safe. In this regard, I must note that there is currently a study under way in England by the Oxford Survey of Childhood Cancers. The U.S. government has helped to fund the study, which is trying to determine if there's any correlation between obstetric ultrasound and childhood cancers. Study results are not expected before 1986. Certainly, ultrasound should only be used when medically indicated, and conservative physicians might especially emphasize this during the first trimester—the period of especially rapid embryological growth. Some doctors will make a pointed effort to confine a patient to no more than one sonogram throughout her pregnancy.

Nonetheless, the vast majority of medical opinion is that the risk, if any, for mother or baby from ultrasound is very slight indeed. *If the procedure is required to diagnose a problem which you or your unborn baby have, you'll be medically advised that the benefits obtained from this information far outweigh the slim possibility of risk the procedure might involve.*

The cost of ultrasound ranges from $70 to $150, with most women reporting payment of between $85 and $125. Sometimes the cost is lower if your own obstetrician has the equipment in the office and will perform it there for you. For example, I know an obstetrician in Manhattan who charges $55 for in-office sonograms—and he's on Park Avenue! There is sometimes one fee for the procedure performed by a medical technician, and an *additional* fee if the sonogram is also "read" by a physician. Note too that if you have or are suspected of having a condition that warrants a sonogram, even if that "condition" is simply an uncertainty about gestational age and hence due date, you may require more than one such test. Jane D., for example, of St. Louis, Missouri, told me she had seven sonograms performed by a technician during her difficult second pregnancy, at $100 each. She was charged an additional $50 when a doctor "read" them!

Most good health insurance policies cover sonograms under the bailiwick of diagnostic tests.

Fetal Nonstress Testing

This is the most frequently used method of assessing fetal well-being in the last trimester. The nonstress test (NST) makes use of the fetal heart monitor (FHM) to measure the *normal acceleration* of the baby's heartbeat in response to a distinct fetal movement. Normal fetal heart rate is 120 to 160 beats per minute (although deviation of as much as 20 beats per minute outside this range doesn't necessarily indicate fetal distress). An NST is normal if *the fetal heartbeat accelerates at a rate of at least 15 beats per minute (held for at least fifteen seconds), following at least two fetal movements within a twenty-minute period.* (This will become clearer with the description of the procedure.) A normal NST is called a *reactive NST,* meaning your baby's nervous and cardiovascular system has normal reactive capacity. In short, it means your baby is not in distress at the time of testing, and more important, it means that there is an approximately 99 percent chance that the fetus is healthy enough to survive at least one more week *in utero.*

Many doctors routinely order an NST as a woman's due date comes and goes. (However, some members of the medical community think that the initial test for fetal condition in a prolonged pregnancy should be the stress test, discussed below.) NSTs can be especially useful in the management of high-risk pregnancies complicated by diabetes, toxemia, hypertension, Rh incompatibility and other problems. In these cases, weekly NSTs often begin as early as two months prior to due date. These NSTs are one way a physician determines the appropriate time for delivery.

The procedure is simple and painless. No special diets or injections. It will take at least a half hour and is performed by a medical technician or physician. It can be done on an outpatient basis in a hospital, a special lab or a doctor's office.

A comfortable two-piece outfit is a good thing to wear, as you needn't completely undress. You lie on a table with your abdomen exposed and get connected to an FHM. Jelly may be put on your abdomen to improve conduction of the sensing devices. The FHM will pick up and begin recording the fetal heartbeat on a piece of graph paper. The beat rate may read out in digital numbers for you to see, too. They'll flash every second and will represent a compilation of the baby's heartbeat *per minute*.

Then, each time that you feel a fetal movement, you'll immediately press a button you've been given to hold, so that the movement gets recorded on the same paper as the heartbeat. The technician or doctor can then see if there's a *normal acceleration* of at least 15 beats per minute rate, held for fifteen seconds, in response to the fetal movement. So, if your baby was beating away at 150 beats per minute, then gives a big kick, you'll want to see the graph jump up to at least 165 and hold there for fifteen seconds. If this is accomplished twice within twenty minutes, you have a normal, reactive NST.

If your baby doesn't want to move during the test, a way will be found to "encourage" him or her. Sometimes auditory stimulus is used. Sometimes simply jiggling your abdomen will get the baby to kick. On occasion, you might be asked to drink a glucose solution, which within twenty minutes will work through your system and to the baby to elicit a response that can begin the NST.

Contraction Stress Testing (CST)

If there is no heartbeat acceleration associated with a fetal movement, you have an NST that is *nonreactive* or *not normal*. This *may* mean that the fetus is in distress, and assuming other tests indicate that the baby's lungs are mature enough for survival, your doctor *may* decide to arrange for prompt delivery. First, however, he or she will probably double-check by ordering a contraction stress test (CST), or more simply, a stress test. A CST is usually not the initial test for determining fetal well-being or distress, because it is a more complex procedure than the NST. An exception may be in the instance of known postmaturity, where recent medical studies indicate that CST provides a more consistent, accurate assessment of fetal conditions than the NST. However, a CST is far more likely to be ordered if the doctor already has reason to suspect the fetus may be in jeopardy by virtue of a *nonreactive* NST.

A CST—at least as the test was originally devised—is usually performed in the hospital. Like the NST, a CST makes use of the fetal monitor. However, instead of measuring changes in the beat rate associated with fetal movement, the CST measures any changes associated with a *maternal uterine contraction.* These are recorded via a second strap or sensor on your upper abdomen. The test is done in the hospital because while some women will spontaneously experience a sufficient number of measurable contractions (known as Braxton-Hicks) during the last trimester, most will require an external "stimulant" to incite these contractions for the test. This "stimulant" is a very dilute solution of the hormone oxytocin (commercial name, Pitocin), which is administered by an intravenous drip. (For this reason, the CST is also known as the oxytocin challenge test.) This oxytocin will trigger the necessary uterine contractions. The doctor will want to see three strong contractions in a ten-minute cycle and will carefully watch for any changes in the fetal heartbeat.

Under normal conditions, the fetal heart rate will *not* change following a contraction. Hence, if the heartbeat stays as strong as before the contraction, the test is negative. *A negative CST is good* and, like a reactive NST, means that placental function is adequate to maintain the fetus *in utero* for at least another week. A negative CST "predominates" over a nonreactive NST. In other words, if a nonreactive NST is what prompts you to have a CST and that CST is *negative,* you can relax.

If, however, the heart rate consistently *slows* following uterine contractions, this may be indication of fetal distress, probably due to placental deficiency. This is called a *positive CST.* The fact that the heartbeat slows following these mini-contractions suggests that the baby may not respond well to the rigors of real labor. Assuming fetal lung maturity has been previously determined, your doctor will probably schedule a prompt Cesarean.

Many women express concern that the hormone administered during the CST will trigger real labor to begin. In fact, such small quantities of it are used and the drip is so carefully controlled that in the majority of cases there's no danger of this. However, if you have a history of premature labor, or the doctor has other reason for concern of a "too early" labor, you'll not be given a CST. Moreover, if you have excess amniotic fluid (hydramnios) which has overly stretched the uterus, the doctor may not give you oxytocin. The same may apply if you're carrying more than one baby. Other placental abnormalities like placenta previa can be a contraindication for oxytocin, as can unexplained bleeding.

In any case, today there's a new and welcome version of the CST which avoids the use of the intravenous hormonal drip. Instead, to get the uterus to contract, the woman is simply asked to massage her nipples—this will nearly always result in an immediate uterine contraction! Apparently this method works quite well, and has the obvious advantages of being faster, cheaper and far less "invasive." This simplification of the CST also makes it easy to do an NST and CST one right after the other. First fetal movement–heartbeat acceleration is measured. Then the woman stimulates her nipples to initiate a uterine contraction for a CST. So today, many women will have both tests in one "sitting."

Nonstress tests cost between $25 and $50. This doesn't sound too bad, but remember that multiple testing is very common—particularly in a high-risk pregnancy, but also sometimes in postterm pregnancies. Many women report having as many as five NSTs. Contraction stress testing is usually somewhat more expensive. A possible exception is if the CST is done in your doctor's office. The CST is particularly more expensive, of course, when it is done by the intravenous drip method, which requires very close monitoring by a medical professional and is usually done in the hospital. Going rates for the less "invasive" CST are in the $40 to $75 range. Once again, repeat testing is not uncommon, especially in postterm pregnancies. One woman living in St. Paul, Minnesota, wrote to me of having eight CSTs, at $69 each—$552 in stress test bills! And one New York City friend had eleven combination NST and CSTs over a three-week period. She had them done on an out-patient basis in a city hospital, which charged a weekly, sliding scale for them: $70, $50, $40 for tests done within a single week, starting again at $70 for tests in the second week, and so on.

Genetic counseling, amnio, ultrasound, NSTs, CST—no doubt, some couples will regard the advanced obstetrical technology and tests described here as an alienating and frightening intrusion into the natural process of pregnancy and childbirth, an intrusion that depersonalizes the experience, and adds intimidating extra expenses. What with all these procedures, the original meaning of obstetrics—"standing by"—does seem forgotten. Instead, obstetrics seems to mean "intervention."

However, there's another and, I believe, more valid way of looking at advanced obstetrical technology: It can save lives, and thereby prevent untold anguish. In less dramatic instances, it can relieve unnecessary anxiety on the part of expectant parents. Just think of the woman who learns from amniocentesis that her baby does not have Tay-Sachs disease, despite the fact that both she and her husband are carriers. Or the woman for whom Rh sensitization is prevented by a simple injection following the birth of her first baby. Or the baby who is saved by an early delivery, following determination by stress testing that the placenta is deteriorating. Of course, this technology must be carefully and selectively utilized—far from every couple will need it. But if you do, be glad it's there. Yes, it may add substantially to your medical bills; particularly if you have no health insurance, it may strain your overall family budget. But when it comes right down to it, who's counting, if good health is at stake?

❖ 4

HOSPITAL COSTS

Hospitals consume 41 cents of every dollar spent on health care in the United States. In fact, the component of health care costs that's risen most dramatically is the semiprivate hospital room—up more than 400 percent since 1967, to an average of more than $200 a day in 1984! (However, the rate of increase slowed dramatically in 1984, when hospital costs rose "only" about 5 percent from 1983.) Room costs are even higher in the largest cities—about $250 to $325 in New York, for example. That's for room and board alone, mind you. If both you and your justborn have full-service hospitalization insurance, you'll be fairly well insulated from the considerable costs of your hospital maternity stay. If, however, your insurance is limited or nonexistent, these are bills that will need planning for, although there *are* ways to cut costs.

State-by-State Hospital Charges

The cost of a semiprivate hospital room varies significantly across the country. It's much lower in most southern states, highest in the Northeast and West. What state averages don't show is the difference between urban and rural areas within each state. Urban hospitals average $50 or so a day more for a semiprivate room than rural hospitals, although in the largest cities in the Northeast and West, the difference is often much greater.

STATE-BY-STATE COST OF SEMIPRIVATE HOSPITAL ROOM

State	Semiprivate Daily Charge	State	Semiprivate Daily Charge
Alabama	$159.21	Missouri	181.45
Alaska	237.17	Montana	185.47
Arizona	185.97	Nebraska	150.74
Arkansas	139.25	Nevada	236.10
California	275.57	New Hampshire	201.04
Colorado	207.38	New Jersey	178.85
Connecticut	198.33	New Mexico	187.81
Delaware	216.94	New York	203.14
District of		North Carolina	144.59
Columbia	284.62	North Dakota	157.08
Florida	174.91	Ohio	225.11
Georgia	164.36	Oklahoma	165.07
Hawaii	224.31	Oregon	233.10
Idaho	180.86	Pennsylvania	243.25
Illinois	233.18	Rhode Island	198.08
Indiana	181.28	South Carolina	136.36
Iowa	171.24	South Dakota	159.95
Kansas	179.68	Tennessee	137.38
Kentucky	165.50	Texas	152.72
Louisiana	153.47	Utah	176.67
Maine	207.51	Vermont	201.54
Maryland	182.16	Virginia	164.09
Massachusetts	208.21	Washington	221.96
Michigan	248.30	West Virginia	168.72
Minnesota	178.91	Wisconsin	162.03
Mississippi	108.39	Wyoming	154.34

MEAN UNITED STATES CHARGE   203.03

NOTE: Daily charges as of early 1984.
SOURCE: Health Insurance Association of America.

The difference in cost of a semiprivate room (which in some city hospitals "houses" up to four people, although the usual is two) and a private room varies enormously— from as little as $5 a day in some rural and suburban hospitals, up to $60 to $225 a day in major cities. *Remember that if you insist on privacy, you'll pay the difference between the cost of the private room and the insurer-reimbursed semiprivate rate.*

Daily charges for routine nursery care vary a lot, too. Data is hard to come by on a state-by-state basis, but here it is regionally:

	AVERAGE DAILY NURSERY COSTS, 1982			
	Northeast	*South*	*North Central*	*West*
Urban	$103	$84	$110	$127
Rural	$112	$78	$ 95	$ 90

SOURCE: Health Insurance Association of America.

Shopping for a Hospital

Why not, if you have a choice? If you've committed to an obstetrician, find out where he or she has admitting privileges. Contact the hospitals and ask about the kind and extent of family-centered maternity care offered—whether there's an advance tour of the maternity facilities and preregistration, emphasis on multiple support techniques (husband, nurse-midwife and/or monitrice) and prepared childbirth, a birthing room, newborn rooming-in, breastfeeding on the delivery table and subsequently on demand, etc. You'll also want to know if there's an intensive care nursery.

Then ask about costs. Even in the same city or town, hospitals charge very different room and nursery rates. I called three Manhattan hospitals and was quoted semiprivate rates ranging from $250 to $332 (and private rates from $311 to $547!). Consider starting with a nonprofit hospital. Although there are exceptions, several studies suggest for-profit hospitals are substantially more expensive—I've seen estimates of between 17 and 24 percent more—than nonprofit hospitals.

Of course, room, board and nursery are only a part of the overall maternity hospital bill—very roughly half. So, *ask the hospital to provide you with an estimate of the total maternity bill for both uncomplicated delivery and for Cesarean.* Because the hospital won't break the estimate down for you, I've provided here approximate cost ranges for the various hospital facilities and services that make up the total bill. Your estimate should be at the lower end if you live in the South and/or a rural area, at the high end if you live in the Northeast, the North Central states or the West. These approximations are for usual, *uncomplicated* delivery.

(You should understand that complications can lead to radically higher hospital bills—which speaks directly to the necessity of good health insurance, at least a Major Medical policy. During my research, I heard from women whose hospital bills were $15,000 and more because of complications like toxemia and premature birth. Even in Mississippi, for example, where hospital costs are the lowest in the land, an intensive care nursery can cost $1,000 a day.)

ESTIMATED COST OF MATERNITY HOSPITAL STAY*
UNCOMPLICATED USUAL DELIVERY

Room and board	
3.3 days ($150–300 per day)	$ 495–990
Nursery	
3.3 days ($125–160 per day)	412–528
Labor room	150–250
Delivery room	200–375
Birthing room†	275–550
Anesthesia	
equipment and supplies	55–100
Circumcision setup	25–45
Central supplies	75–175
Laboratory	100–175
Pharmacy	50–120
TOTAL (using labor and delivery rooms)	$1,637–2,933
TOTAL (using birthing room)	$1,562–2,858

---

* This chart is adapted in concept from the Health Insurance Association of America booklet *The Cost of Having a Baby*.
† Alternative to labor and delivery rooms.

To emphasize a few points relating to this chart. As it suggests, a hospital that offers the *birthing room alternative* to the traditional labor and delivery rooms may demonstrate a commitment not just to personalized, family-centered maternity care but also to cost containment. A birthing room can lower the cost of your hospital maternity stay by $100 or so—perhaps more in the Northeast and in rural areas.

Understand that these estimated hospital bills are *exclusive* of any doctors' fees whether obstetrician (see Chapter 2), pediatrician (see Chapter 6) or anesthesiologist. The reference in the chart to anesthesia is for equipment and supplies, not professional services. Ditto for circumcision. For anesthesia associated with uncomplicated usual delivery, expect to pay about $200 (as always, more in big cities). This is also the place to note that frequently a woman will be charged for an anesthesia setup she does not use ($45 to $75) because an anesthesiologist is required by hospital regulations (the hospital's obstetrical license may depend on it) to be present on "standby." This obviously takes up a lot of valuable professional time. Ask the hospital about its practice in this regard in advance. It's not likely to happen if you opt for a birthing room because an anesthesiologist is usually not required to be present there.

Hospital bills—indeed total maternity medical expenses—for uncomplicated Cesarean delivery will be *at least* 50 percent higher than for usual delivery, because of the longer hospital stay, use of an operating and a recovery room, higher anesthesia, lab, pharmacy and central supply bills, and higher doctor fees. Anesthesia for an uncomplicated Cesarean, for example, can easily cost $350. In some instances and locations, the total medical cost for Cesarean delivery can be almost *double* that for usual delivery.

After getting estimates from the hospital for both usual and Cesarean delivery, ask about *payment schedule.* Many couples are surprised to learn their hospitals require a substantial *advance deposit,* and in some cases, advance payment in whole of the estimated bill! Ask, too, if payment at the time of checkout has to be in full. Some hospitals allow installment payments. Credit cards are also accepted by many hospitals, which can help in pacing your payments. (Did you ever imagine "Don't leave home without it!" might apply equally to a hospital stay as to a Caribbean vacation?)

Length of Stay

This clearly has a major effect on the bill. There's no rule that says you have to spend the average 3.3 days in the hospital following an uncomplicated usual delivery. In fact, length of maternity stays varies across the country.

	AVERAGE DAYS OF MATERNITY HOSPITAL STAY			
	Northeast	*South*	*North Central*	*West*
Urban	3.2	3.1	3.3	2.4
Rural	3.3	2.9	3.2	1.9

In contrast, delivery in an in-hospital birth center under the care of a nurse midwife generally results in stays of less than two days—and so lower hospital bills—in all parts of the country. Cesarean stays range from 4.4 days in the rural West to 6.2 days in the urban Northeast. Assuming your delivery is uncomplicated, you might tell your doctor you'd prefer an *early discharge.* In fact, check if your insurance policy offers a financial incentive for early maternity discharge (usually defined by insurers as within two days of delivery). By year end 1983, as many as thirty-four Blue Cross/Blue Shield plans offered such incentives, providing up to a $200 bonus, home care or both. Private insurers and employers are starting such incentive plans too. And there are reasons other than financial that early discharge appeals to many new mothers—such as getting away from hospital routine and noise and being in the comfort of one's own home, which allow for, as one Rochester, New York, woman told me, "more intimate bonding" with the newborn. A St. Paul, Minnesota, study showed that 79 percent of mothers who'd elected early discharge were happy they'd done so and would do it again.

Ways to Cut Your Hospital Bill

Some of the potentially most significant of these have been discussed: choosing a lower-cost (perhaps nonprofit) hospital to begin with, using a birthing room or, more cost-effective still, an in-hospital birth center where delivery is by a nurse midwife, and particularly, electing early discharge.

You might also want to consider a *maternity ward* rather than a semiprivate room. Don't let the word "ward" conjure up an image of nineteenth-century gloom. Maternity wards today are often bright and cheerful places and the scene of lively exchanges between new mothers. Anyway, you're not there for very long, so why not check one out? It can save a few hundred dollars. And look for special deals. Because of a surplus of hospital beds in many parts of the country, and underutilized maternity beds in particular, some hospitals have established and then cut "set prices" for uncomplicated maternity care. In Las Vegas, for example, one of the city's major hospitals cut its charge for a forty-eight-hour maternity ward stay 46 percent in 1984, to $1,000 from $1,850, in hopes of luring patients from other city hospitals. (One catch: the $1,000 must be paid in advance.) Even some for-profit hospitals are doing this: In 1985 Humana hospitals in Houston advertised a special set rate of $750 for a one-day maternity stay, $950 for two days, and $2,200 for a five-day Cesarean delivery— plus they throw in free Lamaze classes and a car seat!

Another way you might save: some *teaching hospitals* don't charge for pediatric newborn care conducted by staff pediatric residents.

If your insurer has developed special arrangements with a *Preferred Provider Organization* (Chapter 7), by all means use a hospital that's part of the PPO. There will be financial incentives for you to do so—perhaps 100 percent reimbursement with no deductible—and financial disincentives for you to use other than a PPO hospital.

If you're scheduled in advance for a Cesarean, see if arranging for *preadmission testing* (blood and urine work, etc.) can save you a night in the hospital. Also discuss with your doctor beforehand your desire to have *only* the tests that are definitely medically necessary. Frequently, hospital "routine" results in extra tests and retests—and so extra bills. For example, one maternity hospital bill I studied had three separate syphilis tests (of all things) in a two-day period! Don't be afraid to ask of hospital staff, "Is this test really necessary? Have I had it before?"

And, as a St. Louis, Missouri, woman wrote to me, "In the hospital, ask about everything that's brought to you. How much does it cost? Do *not* assume that it's free— nothing is. I was brought Massé breast cream, 'tucks,' some kind of dermoplast spray—all of which I assumed were free, none of which I used, and all of which were on my hospital bill at checkout time!" Such items fall under "central supplies" in the estimated hospital charges provided earlier, and you can see how that category adds up.

Finally, at checkout time, *review your bill very carefully.* It should be fully itemized. Here are abbreviations often appearing on hospital maternity bills to help in your review:

FACILITIES

SP—Semiprivate room
NURS—Nursery
W—Ward
ICN—Intensive Care
  Nursery
OR—Operating Room
R/ROOM—Recovery
  Room
FHM—Fetal Heart
  Monitor

LABS AND SUPPLIES

VDRL—Syphilis Test
CBC—Complete Blood Count
HBG—Hemoglobin
UA—Urinalysis
PTT—blood clotting factor
  test
ANE or ANEX—Anesthesia
IV—Intravenous
IVADD—Intravenous
  Additives
MED/SURG—Medical and
  Surgical
SUPPLIES—Supplies
CATH—Catheter

Anything that you don't understand, *ask about.* Look for charges for X rays not taken, charges for a longer time than you spent in OR or R/ROOM, several of the same lab tests on the same day, and of course, incorrect number of days for room and board. Hospital bills are frequently rife with errors like these! Indeed, one hospital auditing firm has reported that 93 *percent* of hospital bills contain errors! Given the savings potential of hospital bill auditing, a number of companies today have incentive bonuses to encourage employees to question items on their bills. One large Midwestern firm, for example, introduced a hospital refund program in 1984 that gives employees 100 percent of the first $100 they save the company on a hospital bill error. Uniroyal, Inc. of Connecticut is even more gener-ous—employees who discover errors get 50 percent of the overcharge up to a maximum of $1,000 per bill. Find out if your employer or insurer has instituted such a program. And if you're uninsured, every dollar of overcharge you find is a dollar less out of your pocket.

Finally, ways to avoid maternity hospital bills altogether: Join an HMO (see Chapter 7) or go to an Alternative Birth Center (see Chapter 5).

❖ 5

THE ALTERNATIVE BIRTH CENTER

What Is It?

For many women today there's a safe, satisfying and low-cost alternative to conventional obstetrical care and hospital delivery of their babies. This option is provided by more than one hundred out-of-hospital Alternative Birth Centers (ABCs) across the United States.

An ABC is the "in-between" of a hospital delivery and a home birth. It's a short-stay (new mothers and babies go home within twenty-four hours), homelike facility providing comprehensive prenatal, birth, newborn and postpartum services for women who are "medically low-risk"—those anticipating a healthy, normal pregnancy and birth. Care at an ABC is provided by highly trained, licensed and certified nurse-midwives (CNMs), in collaboration with obstetricians and pediatricians. Birth itself is attended by the nurse-midwife. That is, while all licensed ABCs have staff obstetricians providing around-the-clock emergency backup, a physician is *not* present during your birth center delivery. A pediatrician comes after the birth to check the baby, but one is also on call at all times. In addition to on-call obstetrical and pediatric coverage, ABCs normally have an active working relationship with, and "quick access" to, a nearby hospital providing acute-care obstetrical and newborn services, for the unusual occasions when an emergency arises or transfer of the mother-to-be or baby is otherwise warranted. However, a freestanding or Alternative Birth Center should *not* be confused with a birth room or birthing suite in a hospital, or even a birth center staffed by nurse-midwives that is located in a hospital maternity unit.

Philosophy

At ABCs, the emphasis is on the naturalness, the enjoyment, the "celebration" of pregnancy and birth, and the active responsibility of both parents-to-be in managing the process. For example, many ABCs encourage you to learn to test your own urine and note results in your chart, as well as to graph your weight gain. Fathers or other support persons are often taught blood pressure estimation, abdominal palpation, fundal height measurement and the checking of fetal heart tones. (The CNMs review, supervise and, if necessary, check findings.) The philosophy behind all this is that families, when provided with principles and guidance, can go a long way in caring for themselves. Eventually, they must care for the baby; birth centers believe that learning to care for the fetus is the best preparation for this responsibility.

The philosophy of the "naturalness" of birth translates into a commitment to minimize "obstetrical intervention" in the process. Birth centers adhere to the original meaning of the word obstetrics—"to stand by," not to intervene unless warranted. For example, there's no routine "prepping"—enema, shaving of the pubic region, etc. Nor will you be hooked up to a fetal monitor, or an intravenous drip. You are encouraged to walk around during early labor, and light food and drink is usually allowed. Many ABCs permit you to bring pictures or favorite objects, to have music, to take photographs or even videotape. Medications are available at most (but not all) birth centers if you want and need them, but are not routinely given. There is no mandatory position for birth—whatever is both safe and most comfortable is acceptable. Stirrups and restraints are not used, and episiotomies are done *far* less frequently than in hospital. Forceps are not often used. The birth rooms look more like a bedroom than a hospital room. Fathers play a very active part in the birth itself, and many even "catch" the baby and cut the umbilical cord, if they wish (under the supervision of the CNM, of course). Parents and healthy babies are never separated after birth; breastfeeding can begin immediately and continue "on demand," and the newborn's examination by a pediatrician is conducted in the presence of the parents. Obviously, then, there is every opportunity for parent-infant bonding. Hence, within the limits of safety, centers encourage you to make the entire experience as personal as you desire. Indeed, the impetus for the birth center movement in the United States over the last decade was the desire by parents to gain a new level of participation in and control over pregnancy and childbirth.

When parents who have chosen an ABC are asked why, an overwhelming majority cite the "philosophy," or simply the "attitude" toward pregnancy and birth, that the centers represent. One woman wrote to me, "The philosophy prevalent at the birth center was, you're not sick—you're pregnant. You're healthy and smart enough to be in control of your body!" Parents also emphasize that ABC staffs seem to have so much more time to spend with individual clients—they never felt rushed. Several people also told me that they had chosen the birth center because they were made anxious or intimidated by hospitals. Suzanne M., for example, said, "I'm terribly nervous in hospitals—even just visiting someone. I didn't *want* to be intimidated when I was having my baby. I wanted to be on top of it. I can't speak for others, but I felt that *I* had a better chance at that in a birth center." Many other couples cite concerns that hospitals present unnecessary infection risks, and more generally, "are not the right places for healthy people."

To convey what the birth center experience can be like, read what Maryann Brinley, a New Jersey author of motherhood books, had to say about her own happy experience at a New Jersey ABC:

The Childbirth Center, which operates under the firm, loving direction of Lonnie Morris, a certified nurse-midwife, is a marvelous alternative for women who want a delivery outside the hospital but would prefer to be under the watchful eye of a loving professional with excellent backup medical support always at the ready.

For me last year, already the mother of a healthy little boy who was born at a Manhattan hospital, the Childbirth Center was cheaper for every step of care; more comfortable (no one told me that laboring while on my side would ease tremendously the pain of a long, long labor); and easier on every member of my little family. Zach, my three-year-old, arrived about two hours after my daughter's birth to share breakfast in bed with me and meet his new baby sister. Bob, my husband, was very much a part of the team of professionals at my side and still says he witnessed "the best bedside manner in the world." I went home that first night—Maggie was born at 8:14 in the morning—to sleep soundly in my own bed with no midnight, routine hospital interruptions to upset my deep slumber. And, best of all, my infant daughter, who never knew the bright lights of a hospital or the cry of neighboring babies in a nursery or the insistent touch of strange hands, slept all night on her birthday in her bassinet by my side. (I consider a midnight-to-five A.M. shift all night!) Meanwhile, she continued on that very comfortable shift for six months—until teething turned our wonderful routine upside down.

Who Is Eligible?

Not every couple interested in the birth center alternative is necessarily eligible for enrollment. Only healthy, medically low-risk women anticipating normal delivery can be accommodated. All centers have preliminary health requirements that a woman must first meet even before she can proceed to a careful medical screening that includes a lengthy family medical history, a physical examination by an obstetrician and/or midwife, and laboratory work. (Most ABCs have *at least* one physical exam conducted by an obstetrician.) Preliminary requirements are rigorous, starting with good general health, no history of prior Cesarean section, or any complications of previous birth (often including prolonged labor), and proceeding at some ABCs to more than forty conditions or combinations of conditions that preclude admission. At some ABCs, for example, a woman can be no more than forty years old if having her first baby, or forty-five for any subsequent baby. Other birth centers set the limits at thirty-five and thirty-nine, respectively. Some birth centers require that appropriate genetic screening studies be conducted with negative results for all women over thirty-five. Heavy smokers who do not promise to cut out or down to five cigarettes a day are not admitted to many ABC programs, and some ABCs exclude women who will not pledge to give up alcohol for the duration of their pregnancies.

Prior to the initial, comprehensive medical screening, ABCs also require that the mother-to-be (preferably with the support person to be present at birth) attend an on-site orientation session, usually conducted by a nurse-midwife. At these sessions, the mutual expectations of both parents-to-be and center professionals should be fully discussed. Discussions revolve around the ABC concept and philosophy, services provided by the center and accompanying responsibilities of the client (a word which is preferred in the ABC milieu over "patient"), the potential risks of childbearing to mother and baby, costs and financing arrangements. *In particular, the differences between hospital and ABC procedures are emphasized.* You'll be told what medical equipment is available at the birth center, and what's not. The birth center's relationship with its backup hospital should be fully discussed. Couples will also be able to tour the center's facilities, seeing the early labor and birth rooms.

Another stipulation: *Many birth centers will not enroll a woman who is more than twenty-two weeks pregnant;* others will stretch it to twenty-four. This is because ABCs place such a strong emphasis on continuity of full prenatal care, on health education and birth preparation. At the prominent Manhattan Childbearing Center, for example, a woman and her support person are *required* to participate in a basic program of two-hour, once-a-week classes lasting eight to ten weeks. Moreover, an early series of classes is offered in advance of the basic program. In many centers, in fact, a woman is not permitted to continue in the program if she fails to attend these educational classes.

Once the preliminary requirements are met, and the first medical screening turns up nothing that would indicate other than a normal, healthy pregnancy and birth, you're eligible to enroll in the ABC program. Throughout the pregnancy, medical screening continues on a regular basis. In the course of prenatal visits you will meet and be cared for by all the center's CNMs. The CNM who is on duty when you go into labor will be the one who is with you at birth.

Later, if ongoing screening indicates the pregnancy is no longer developing in a routine way, the birth center will assist you in finding alternate obstetrical care. Conditions that usually cause transfer out of a birth center program include multiple gestation, abnormal weight gain, sometimes apparent small-for-date fetuses, unexplained vaginal bleeding, nonvertex presentation persisting past the thirty-seventh week of gestation, and known postmaturity. Proteinuria (protein in the urine excreted at a rate of 500 milligrams a day on two successive occasions) is another such cause, as is severe anemia not responding to therapy. Women developing toxemia must be put under a doctor's care and cannot continue in an ABC.

Since a pregnancy can change from low-risk to high-risk at any point in the nine-month term, a couple should always be prepared for the possible switch out of the program to obstetrician and hospital care. For this reason, it's very important to identify a backup osetrician early in pregnancy, who will take care of you in the event you must leave the ABC. If you don't have an obstetrician of your own, you can almost certainly arrange to have the ABC's own backup physician. He or she will offer you the added plus of understanding the care you've received to date, and is probably sympathetic with your philosophy and reasons for choosing an ABC.

You should be further aware that transfer out of the birth center program can also occur "at the last minute."

About 15 percent of the women who arrive at their birth center *in labor* for the big event end up transferring to the hospital. However, only on rare occasion is this an *emergency* transfer. Most often, transfer takes place because of "failure to progress"—a woman's labor is considered too prolonged (as a rule of thumb, more than eighteen hours). The centers strongly prefer to err on the side of medical conservatism and send these women to the hospital. Hence, if you're prepared for and counting on an ABC birth, there's about a 15 percent statistical chance of disappointment even once you go into labor. Other causes for in-labor transfer include prolapsed cord, prolonged ruptured membranes and fetal distress. You might also be transferred *after* delivery if you have excessive bleeding, significant temperature elevation, large vaginal or perineal laceration or drug reaction.

It's for these reasons you should know your backup hospital's physical layout and admitting procedures, and have a specific physician, familiar with the birth center and the care provided there, to bring in.

Availability

There are presently more than one hundred ABCs in the United States handling an estimated 10,000 births a year. While the majority of these centers are on the East and West coasts, there are ABCs in thirty-one states, and as many as 300 others are being established or explored as an option in all but three states. (For some reason, Florida seems to be the state with the largest number of birth centers.) Thus, those of you who want to investigate the birth center alternative have an increasingly good chance of finding one near your home—particularly if you live in or near a populous area. If you should have difficulty locating an ABC, write or call:

> Cooperative Birth Center Network
> Box 1, Route 1
> Perkiomenville, PA 18074
> (215) 234-8068

The Network was founded in 1981 in order to promote a wider public understanding of the birth center concept. You'll find the people there friendly and happy to advise you about birth centers in your locale.

What to Look For

Make sure that the birth center you're considering is staffed by *certified nurse midwives* (CNMs). A CNM is a registered nurse who has completed *at least* one year of formal postgraduate academic study and training in midwifery, accredited by the American College of Nurse-Midwives. In recent years, ten states have adopted birth center licensing regulations and/or legislation establishing standards for ABCs; another thirteen states are considering such regulations. If the birth center you're considering is licensed by the state, you've added assurance about the quality of care. However, don't dismiss an ABC that is not licensed—chances are, the state just doesn't have licensing requirements! National standards have been established by the Cooperative Birth Center Network (CBCN), so ask whether the particular ABC has "affiliate" status with the CBCN.

Make absolutely sure that your ABC has around-the-clock backup by both obstetricians and pediatricians. The doctors should be able to be on the scene in the event of a medical emergency on very short notice. You should also insist on at least one examination by an obstetrician, at the beginning of your pregnancy, but a second is preferable, at about the thirty-sixth week. Furthermore, you should dismiss an ABC that does not have a formal and tested arrangement with a nearby hospital for transfer and admissions for medical emergencies. Make sure you fully understand your birth center's emergency transfer procedures, including available equipment for a mother and a newborn, transfer mode, telephone "hot line" to the hospital, etc.

Naturally, you'll also want to be satisfied that the ABC is a clean and cheerful place. The facility should be homelike, but professional in terms of staff and equipment that enables emergencies to be handled expeditiously. This would include oxygen, blood volume expanders, resuscitation equipment, maternal and neonatal emergency drugs, a neonatal transport Isolette, as well as a system for ambulance transfer to a nearby backup hospital.

Ask about the birth center's practice regarding (nonemergency) medication. While many couples hope and plan for a medication-free birth, they'd still like to know the woman could ask for and get pain-relief medication if she really felt the need. Some centers are strict in their no-medication policy (except for a "local" during sutures if you've had an episiotomy), and you may feel that's not right for you.

It should be mentioned that many, if not most, obstetricians are *opposed* to the concept of a freestanding birth center. So, if you broach the idea to a doctor, don't expect much enthusiasm, although there are naturally exceptions. Despite the fact of twenty-four-hour medical backup, and transfer and admission arrangements with nearby hospitals, most obstetricians maintain that out-of-hospital births are just too risky. The American College of Obstetricians and Gynecologists (ACOG) has on more than one occasion formally expressed its opposition to ABCs, emphasizing that ABCs can't respond in the event of emergency in the same way as a hospital. This—coupled with the fact that a significant percentage (some doctors say as high as 20 percent) of so-called low-risk women in fact develop problems during labor and delivery—makes ABCs an unacceptable risk to most obstetricians.

This isn't intended to scare you off from the alternative birth center but rather to fully inform you. Most obstetricians do believe that out-of-hospital births hold unacceptable risks for mother and baby, and you should consider this carefully in making your choice of maternity care.

Cost

Maternity care at an ABC is much less expensive than traditional prenatal care and delivery of your baby by a physician in hospital. *How* much less expensive obviously depends on the going rates for physicians and for hospital maternity care in your area. On average, according to a 1982 study reported in *Business Insurance magazine, birth centers cut childbirth medical expenses by at least half.* This estimate is confirmed in a later study by Blue Cross/ Blue Shield of Greater New York. In major metropolitan areas where doctor and hospital charges are substantially above the national average, birth center maternity care can be up to 75 *percent* less expensive!

I contacted several representative birth centers around the country in 1984, and found that the average fee was in the $1,500 range, although a few centers charge as much as $2,200, and some as little as $1,000. The fee is usually a single, comprehensive one which includes complete pre- natal care and counseling, birth at the ABC facility, newborn and postpartum services—including a home visit or two by a public health nurse. (Sometimes there's an extra charge for the pediatrician examination.) In a few instances there is one fee for all the medical care, and a separate fee for use of the birth center facility at delivery.

Your orientation visit to a birth center is free, and places you under no obligation to enroll in the center's maternity program. Most centers do, however, require that you pay for your initial medical screening (physical and lab work) at the time of that screening. In the event that the center cannot enroll you, or you change your mind and do not want to enroll, the fee will not be refunded. Charges for this work range from $40 to $130, with $75 to $80 being about average. Less routine medical procedures or lab tests—such as sonograms, amniocentesis, genetic screening, for example—are not performed at birth centers. The center professionals, however, will help you make arrangements for such tests, which also will be a cost in addition to your birth center fee. Also, if you're Rh negative and will need the Rhogam serum following birth, there will be an extra charge; for example, at Southwest Maternity Center in Albuquerque it's $150. (ABCs will not take Rh- *sensitized* women.)

Remember that in addition to the medical component of prenatal care, birth centers provide childbirth education and baby-care classes for expectant parents. These typically (but not always) include Lamaze or similar psychoprophylaxis training—hence, you will not need to incur an additional charge for these elsewhere. Nutrition and breastfeeding counseling are usually provided, too, as is family planning at the second postpartum checkup.

Payment *schedules* vary, but in general *you must pay in full before the thirty-fourth week of pregnancy.* Many centers offer a payment schedule of three equal installments—but again, you must be paid in full by the thirty-fourth week. You may find there is a discount for payment in full within the first month of enrollment; or there may be an extra charge for billing and administrative costs for the installment method of payment. At the Manhattan Childbearing Center, for example, that latter charge is $50.

Families who have paid the entire birth center fee but leave the program for any reason in advance of childbirth can nearly always receive a refund based on the amount of care actually provided. It's a good idea to check a center's refund policy during your initial orientation visit. Remember that in the event of transfer of mother and/or baby to a hospital, a birth center is not responsible for the hospital fees. If your baby is delivered in hospital by either your birth center's staff physician or by another physician of your choice, there will also be an additional charge for the doctor's services.

Health Insurance Coverage

Today, birth center services are reimbursed by many health insurance companies, and the situation is getting better all the time. A 1982 study by the Cooperative Birth Center Network of fifty-six affiliates showed about half of them covered by Blue Cross/Blue Shield contracts, 70 percent recognized by commercial insurance companies and 20 percent eligible for Medicaid reimbursement. All of those statistics have since climbed. Remember, however, in your own case that it is *your* insurance, and your responsibility to be sure in advance that your birth center program is reimbursable under your particular policy! As emphasized in Chapter 1, not all insurance contracts provide full or even substantial maternity coverage—whether you have your baby in a hospital or at a childbearing center. It's up to you to check. The point I'm making here is that in general the birth center alternative is increasingly well accepted by health insurers and hence is reimbursable, either in full or part, *according to the particular policy you have*. (For example, if your birth center charges one fee for professional services and an additional one for use of the facility at delivery, ask specifically if your insurer will reimburse for *both*. Some will reimburse only the professional fee.)

And why shouldn't insurers and employers be willing to reimburse a family who chooses the birth center alternative, when the costs are so much lower? Take, for example, two women I know, both of whom work at the headquarters of a Fortune 500 company in midtown Manhattan, and who are covered by the same health insurance policy. Kathy M. chose to have her baby at Manhattan's Childbearing Center. Linda S., in contrast, delivered her baby with an obstetrician at a Manhattan hospital. Both had routine, uncomplicated deliveries. A comparison of the costs appears on page 80.

Look at the difference in total costs and total benefits paid. Is it any surprise, then, that insurers and employers across the country are more and more willing to provide coverage for birth center maternity care? In fact, in some states (like New Mexico), if you have health insurance that includes maternity coverage, state law *requires* your insurer to cover the certified nurse midwifery services offered at an ABC. Your ABC will be able to tell you if such a law exists in your state.

So you can be optimistic about insurance coverage. In many instances, employers or insurers even dismiss the deductible and co-insurance if you choose an ABC, paying 100 percent of the fees! They do this because they save money if you opt for an ABC. Moreover, as you can also see from the case study, an ABC nearly always saves *you* money, too. In this example, Linda's out-of-pocket expenses

	KATHY/ABC		LINDA/TRADITIONAL
ABC fee	$1,325	Obstetrician	$1,800
	– 150 deductible	fee	– 150 deductible
	1,175		1,650
	× 90%* co-insurance		× 80% co-insurance
	$1,057 benefit paid		$1,320 benefit paid
Lab work	$ 100	Lab work	$ 150
	× 80% co-insurance		× 80% co-insurance
	$ 80 benefit paid		$ 120 benefit paid
Vitamins	$ 36 not covered	Vitamins	$ 54 not covered
		Lamaze	
		classes	$ 45 not covered
		Hospital bill	$2,210
			$2,200 benefit paid

Total expense	$1,461	$4,259	Total expense
Total benefits	$1,137	$3,640	Total benefits
Out-of-pocket			Out-of-pocket
expenses	$ 324	$ 619	expenses

* This health insurance plan, like many others, covers at a higher rate for *outpatient* care than for in-hospital services. ABCs qualify as outpatient.

were nearly twice as high as Kathy's. Frequently the difference is much more.

And a final word about birth centers and cost. A not uncommon perception is that ABCs primarily serve low-income families. This is not the case. While there is a laudable move under way to develop birth centers in areas of large migrant populations and in some low-income, rural areas, it's *not* true that most urban and suburban ABCs attract a predominantly low-income clientele. At the Manhattan Childbearing Center, director of public information Martin Kelly remarked to me that while the center was proud of the *spectrum* of families it serves—by no means were most of its users low-income. In fact, only a small minority are. While about 5 percent of the center's users qualify for Medicaid, the majority of the clientele is middle- and upper-middle-income, and weighted toward the educated—professionals or future professionals (such as graduate students). Mr. Kelly described the "typical" Manhattan Birth Center user as having three, four or more years of college, and as being more widely read on pregnancy and childbirth than the average expectant couple. In any case, Mr. Kelly added, "Most of our users—about three out of four—have insurance . . . they do *not* come to the Childbearing Center because of cost." My own view is that cost savings would be one of several perfectly valid reasons that a couple might consider the birth center alternative.

Is It for You?

It's clear, then, that ABC care can dramatically cut the medical expenses associated with normal pregnancy and birth. If the birth center movement gains the momentum and acceptance that so many of its proponents think it will, it might eventually become an important health care cost-containment measure. Already the birth center movement (and in particular, the "pioneer" Childbearing Center in Manhattan) has been credited, in a 1982 study released by the Federal Trade Commission, with having a "profound" and "positive" impact on obstetric care nationally. More specifically, the FTC report credits the Childbearing Center with providing an impetus for hospitals to "humanize the delivery of obstetric care" and with encouraging a nationwide trend for hospitals to include birthing rooms in their maternity departments and to expand the role of nurse-midwives.

In the meantime—is the birth center alternative for you? It may be, *if:*

• You meet the basic medical requirements, and medical screenings indicate you can anticipate a normal pregnancy and birth.
• The philosophy of the "naturalness," the "wellness" of pregnancy and childbirth strongly appeals to you and you are willing to assume certain responsibilities for your own care.
• You want a minimum of "obstetrical intervention"

(fetal monitors, IVs, medications, "prepping," episiotomies).
• You are made especially anxious or are intimidated by
hospitals and hospital procedures.
• You would like to have your baby in a homelike
setting, where (within the limits of safety) you and your
partner are free to "do it your way."
• You feel strongly about not being separated from your
baby following birth and want to bring your baby home
within twelve to twenty-four hours of birth.
• You have access to a licensed birth center staffed by
certified nurse midwives for which your insurer will
provide coverage and/or if you do *not* have medical
insurance, and cost is a significant concern.

and finally,

• You fully understand and are willing to accept the
limitations of birth centers as to their ability to internally
handle medical emergencies for mother and fetus or
newborn.

❖ 6

PEDIATRIC CARE

Your baby's pediatrician is about to become an important person in your lives. You'll want to select that doctor carefully and then use him or her in an effective, efficient and economical manner. After all, it's to no one's advantage to go to the pediatrician unnecessarily. It wastes time, and often money, as office visits to a pediatrician are frequently not reimbursable under otherwise even fairly comprehensive health insurance plans. On the other hand, a schedule of routine "well-baby" visits to the doctor is a vitally important investment in preventive medicine, and is not to be short-changed. Curious as it may sound, it's the "sick-baby" visits that are often unnecessary. Do you dash to the doctor every time you have a cold? Surely not—but that's what many new parents with a sick baby do. In fact, as will be discussed later in this chapter, with help from some good reference material, simple equipment and maybe a telephone consultation with the doctor, many—if not most—minor baby illnesses can be safely and inexpensively managed by you at home.

Selecting a Pediatrician

The last trimester of pregnancy is the right time to locate a pediatrician. That way, if your pregnancy should become complicated in the final months your obstetrician can discuss the situation with the pediatrician in the best interest of the baby. Or if delivery itself becomes difficult, your own pediatrician can be called in to attend and be immediately available to the newborn. Even in the more likely situation of a smooth pregnancy and delivery, your newborn will be promptly examined by a pediatrician. In the interest of continuity of care, many couples prefer that the examination be done by the pediatrician who will be the baby's primary medical caretaker, rather than by a pediatrician assigned by the hospital.

Begin the selection process by asking people whose judgment you trust for recommendations—your obstetrician, the obstetrician's nurse, friends. Try to get specific information from these referrals. A question to ask parents that usually elicits useful information about pediatricians is, "If you were transferred out of town tomorrow, what would you look for in choosing a new pediatrician for your baby, knowing what you now know from experience?" This usually makes people come up with specifics. For example, one professional woman replied, "Saturday office hours! And that usually means a group rather than a solo practice." Another said, "Coming from a family of allergy sufferers, I'd want a pediatrician with a subspecialty as an allergist." A California friend said, "I'd look for a small group practice. My pediatrician now is one of a six-doctor practice. That's too large to get a feeling of real personal attention."

After winnowing the recommendations you've received to two or three, arrange a *prenatal consultation.* A preliminary visit to a pediatrician for the purpose of determining whether you wish to engage his or her services is increasingly common, particularly in larger cities and communities characterized by high demographic mobility, where there are many pediatricians to choose from. While some pediatricians don't like these "interviews," disparaging them as "shopping around" for pediatric care, others actively encourage them—which I think in itself is a good sign about a doctor.

When you make the appointment, be clear that its purpose is a preliminary discussion without any commitments, and *ask if the doctor charges a fee for such visits.* In some communities it isn't customary to do so, in others it is, and in still others the practice among doctors is mixed. On occasion, a pediatrician *will* bill you for a preliminary consultation if you do *not* choose his or her services, but will not if you do, so clarify this. If there is a fee, it won't be reimbursable under your health insurance plan, which is one reason it's important to narrow your list of candidates to just a few doctors.

There are several things to consider and topics to discuss at this consultation. Obviously, the doctor's *medical qualifications* are a high priority. You probably won't have to ask which medical school was attended, since most doctors place their diplomas on the office walls. You might ask if the practice is limited *exclusively* to pediatrics, and if the doctor is *board-certified.* This means that the doctor has completed at least three additional years of hospital training in pediatrics following medical school and has passed a comprehensive exam given by the American Board of Pediatrics, which makes him or her a Fellow of the American Academy of Pediatrics (F.A.A.P.). Although there are many fine physicians qualified to care for your baby who are not board-certified, you have the extra assurance with an F.A.A.P. of specialized training.

Hospital affiliation is also important. Obviously, you want your pediatrician to have admitting privileges at a hospital convenient to you, which also has good emergency care facilities. Association with a good accredited public hospital can be a plus, because these are often less expensive than a for-profit hospital.

A pediatrician's *subspecialty* may be relevant, too. If, for example, you have reason to expect a complicated birth, a pediatrician-perinatologist would be a good choice; if you come from a family with allergies, a pediatrician-allergist is appropriate, and so on.

Is the pediatrician in *solo or group practice?* With a solo practitioner (and they're getting harder to find) you have the assurance of continuity of care, which can be reassuring to both mother and baby, and frequently results in a more personal and satisfying relationship. It may be a coincidence, but each time I've heard from a mother that she and her baby "love" their pediatrician, that pediatrician has been a solo practitioner. However, difficulties can arise regarding *coverage* in a solo practice, so satisfy yourself that adequate coverage procedures are in place. You don't want to end up in a hospital emergency room every time your doctor is unavailable. Emergency rooms are anonymous and expensive, as well as an unnecessary recourse for most minor childhood illnesses, and some insurance policies won't reimburse for care provided in them.

Group practices may be better for coverage and also offer a wider range of specialties "in-house." Group practices may also offer expanded or more flexible office hours, with partners rotating Saturdays or office hours one or two evenings a week. For a two-career family, this can be especially important. However, a group practice has possible drawbacks, too. A large one can have a hectic, impersonal air. In some group practices, the baby does not have a primary physician but is considered a patient of the practice. In this case, you may be shunted back and forth between doctors, and you and the baby will have to deal with "strangers" at each visit. In other group practices, the baby has a primary physician—but as a new patient is automatically assigned to the junior or the least busy associate. Be cautious about committing to a pediatric practice larger than four physicians, and insist on being able to personally select a primary doctor, who under normal circumstances will be the one to provide your baby's care. Another point about large practices: a 1984 study in a prestigious medical journal says that they may cost you more, because they tend to order as many as twice the lab tests as small practices.

Telephone availability of the pediatrician is very important. Many pediatricians set aside a specific hour in the morning or afternoon for *telephone consultation*, during which parents are encouraged to call with nonemergency concerns. *A telephone consultation hour is highly desirable and, properly used, represents one of the best bargains in medical care.*

If you're a *woman who works outside the home* and plan to continue doing so after the baby is born, you'd better discuss this with a prospective pediatrician. Although they may not say so openly, some pediatricians will disapprove, in the belief that it is not in the best interest of the child. (I've found that baby books written by pediatricians are more likely to disapprove of working mothers than are other baby books.) It doesn't seem to have sunk in yet with some people that most women working outside the home do so not "merely" for personal satisfaction, but primarily out of economic need. In any case, for whatever reason you work outside the home, if you detect even a hint of disapproval, continue your search for a pediatrician. It's difficult enough to manage both family and career—you don't need any background disapproval from the baby's doctor. In fact, you could use a little support and understanding—like an effort to accommodate you with appointment scheduling, and a welcoming attitude for the father who takes his turn in bringing the baby to appointments.

It's out of hope for such understanding that some couples go out of their way to find a pediatrician who is herself a young mother. One working woman I know said of her baby's pediatrician: "She has a two-year-old at home. She knows just what my husband and I are going through— how hard it is to leave the baby every morning, how tired we are, how we never seem to have any time, but how satisfying it can be, too." And pediatrics is a field of medicine where there *are* a significant number of (mostly young) women practitioners.

Finally, the thoughts of many parents about choosing a pediatrician are summed up by this statement from a New York mother of two: "In my opinion you have to *like* your pediatrician. Personal warmth is more important from a pediatrician than any other doctor—including an obstetrician . . . because a good pediatrician is not just a doctor, but a well-baby counselor, an adviser on the child's development. No sacrifice of 'bedside manner' in a pediatrician would be acceptable to me."

Fees

Don't conclude a prenatal consultation with a pediatrician without talking about fees. If the doctor prefers or you feel more comfortable, you can talk about fees with the office staff. You'll want to learn what the doctor charges for:

- Attendance at the delivery, should that be warranted
- The initial and subsequent in-hospital examination of the newborn
- Circumcision
- The first in-office examination/major physical
- Subsequent office visits (whether well-baby or sick-baby visits)
- Immunizations
- Emergency room care
- House calls, if offered

You should already know from discussions with your health insurer (see Chapter 1) what coverage you have for pediatric services. *Remember that many policies provide only limited coverage for justborn hospitalization and pediatric care.* Your policy may have a stipulation that a baby can't be enrolled until thirty days after birth. Or it may state that only a sick baby is covered for in-hospital pediatric care—not a well one. Moreover, you generally must have the kind of health insurance called medical services or physician expense benefits (the *least* commonly held insurance) to have coverage for pediatrician fees. You'll also recall that you must satisfy an annual deductible on the baby, before *allowable* expenses become reimbursable. *It's important that you understand that routine well-baby visits to the doctor are not "allowable" or covered expenses under your health insurance. You'll not be reimbursed for them. They don't even count toward the satis-*

faction of the deductible on your baby! The same is true
of immunizations under most policies. As a general rule,
only sick-baby visits to the doctor are "covered expenses"—
and, to repeat, only if you have physician expense benefits.
Of course, if you carry no health insurance, all sick-baby
bills will be yours, too.

Because of the limitations on insurance coverage for
pediatric care, a pediatrician's fees are directly important
to you. Fees range fairly considerably, even within the
same area or city. For *in-hospital pediatric care* of the
newborn, expect to pay $75 to $150, and more in the larger
cities. (Average fees across the country are $45 for the first
visit, $27 for subsequent ones.) Your in-hospital pediatrician
fees may also be higher—up to $250—if you deliver by
Cesarean and you and your baby stay in the hospital longer,
because your pediatrician will usually visit every day the
baby is in the hospital. Of course, if the baby suffers any
complications and requires intensive care, the pediatrician
bills will be very substantially more. If for some reason
your regular pediatrician is not called in to the hospital to
do this initial examination or subsequent in-hospital checkups, you should expect to receive a bill from the hospital-
assigned pediatrician for these services. Occasionally, however, no bills are forthcoming in this situation. In some
teaching hospitals it is not the practice for the pediatric
residents to bill for these services.

Circumcision will cost anywhere from $40 to $125,
with $50 to $65 the most common range. It's an expense
that is frequently not reimbursed by medical insurance.

"Well-baby" visits start promptly. Your pediatrician will
do a special, thorough, "get acquainted" examination on
the baby's first office visit at two to four weeks. This will
be a relatively long appointment and the pediatrician may
charge up to *twice* the fee for it as for subsequent well-
baby visits. For regular well-baby visits, expect to pay
between $20 and $35, although it is not uncommon in
more rural areas to find a pediatrician whose fees are still
under $20, which should be regarded as a bargain. In larger
cities in affluent neighborhoods, well-baby visits may cost

$35 to $45, and sometimes up to $50. I've also heard of some pediatricians who charge one fee for office visits up to the age of one, and a higher fee thereafter.

In the first year, your pediatrician will probably request that you bring baby in for five to seven well-baby visits (although some old-fashioned doctors still ask for monthly visits the first six months). After age one, well-baby visits are less frequent. Well-baby visits are usually linked with an immunization schedule. Babies are immunized against seven diseases—diphtheria, pertussis, tetanus, polio, measles, mumps and rubella. Babies are immunized against the first three diseases by a single vaccine, identified by the acronym DPT, and against the last three by the vaccine known as MMR (given at about sixteen months). The oral polio vaccine (OPV) is separate.

IMMUNIZATION SCHEDULE

DPT	OPV*	MMR
2 months	2 months	
4 months	4 months	
6 months	6 months	
18 months	18 months	15 months
Between 4 and 6 years	Between 4 and 6 years	

* Currently, the American Academy of Pediatrics is recommending two *first-year* OPVs rather than the three listed here. However, many pediatricians continue to give the three.

As you can see from the chart, babies require five DPT injections, one MMR, and four or five oral polio vaccines. The fees doctors charge for these immunizations vary. As a rule of thumb, expect to pay $10 for a single DPT—although some pediatricians charge as much as $22 and others as little as $5. For an MMR expect to pay $20 to $25, and for the oral polio vaccine about $6 to $10. Thus, baby's *immunization program* alone may cost more than $100—and to repeat, it is not reimbursable under most health insurance policies.

If you find that your pediatrician's office fee is somewhat on the high side, it may be because the immunizations are *included.* So when the doctor's well-baby fee is quoted to you, it's appropriate to ask if it includes immunizations, or if they are additional.

The federal government has stipulated that every child in the United States receive immunizations against the seven serious diseases mentioned above. The U.S. Public Health Service stewards this mandate through local health departments, which commonly offer *free* immunization clinics for babies and children. (Some of these clinics charge nominal fees ranging from 50 cents to $3.) Therefore, if you feel you absolutely cannot afford to pay for your baby's needed immunizations, contact the local health department to learn where to go for this free program. The immunization program may even be part of a free (or nominal-charge) well-baby clinic—that is, a clinic providing not just the vaccines but overall well-baby care. Some public hospitals also run well-baby clinics.

Another well-baby expense—special vitamins. The pediatrician will tell you which ones to buy; some come with iron and some with fluoride supplements. Vitamins cost about $5.50 for a two-month supply at a discount pharmacy—$1 or so a bottle less if bought at Toys-R-Us.

It's easy to see that the first year of nursery and subsequent well-baby care, immunizations and vitamins can result in pediatrician's bills of $250 to $300 or more, with little, if any, of that eligible for reimbursement by your health insurance policy. *(Note, however, that some pediatricians will write up a well-baby visit in a way that reads like treatment for a minor ailment, which makes the visit eligible for insurance coverage.)*

Handling Minor Baby Illnesses at Home

Well-baby visits are preventive or "maintenance" medicine—a solid investment in your baby's good health. Don't be tempted to skimp on them because they entail out-of-pocket expense. If anything, it may be the sick-baby visits to the doctor that are sometimes unnecessary. Many minor baby illnesses can be safely, effectively and economically managed by you at home, perhaps with a backup telephone consultation with the pediatrician. To help, you should have on hand a few simple pieces of equipment and certain standard medications. These include:

- A *humidifier* or *vaporizor.* A virtual "must." Adequate humidity in the home, especially a baby's room, "feeds" the respiratory system its needed moisture. It soothes the mucus membranes, makes breathing easier, helps prevent nosebleeds and sore throats (those of nonviral origin), helps postnasal drip and can help prevent dehydration. Especially useful to the family with a history of allergies, for whom an *air cleaner* may also be helpful. Humidifiers and vaporizers are available in various sizes. One with a 2-gallon capacity will provide twenty-four continuous hours of use. Look for a machine with a warranty, and with a good cover lock to prevent spills and an automatic shutoff when empty. Vaporizers are available in cool mist or hot steam, for as little as $15 to $20 from Sears. Humidifiers cost up to $150 for the fanciest models but perfectly good ones are available in the $30 to $40 range. Air cleaners or deodorizers can be found for as little as $15 at Sears.
- A *baby thermometer.* Another must. Most pediatricians suggest a rectal one, as young babies tend not to cooperate with oral thermometers, including the new, expensive digital ones. Alternatively, buy a digital thermometer and take the temperature under the baby's armpit, adding one degree for a true reading. A rectal thermometer can be purchased for less than $2.
- A *nasal aspirator.* A device for suctioning mucus from the baby's nose. Available for less than $2 at a store like Sears or at most pharmacies.
- A *medication dropper, syringe or special teaspoon.* These hold an exact *medical* teaspoon—5 cc of liquid. *Never* use a common household teaspoon, because such spoons actually vary from ½ to 1½ medically defined teaspoons, which means you'll probably give the child the wrong amount of medication. You can buy a "medical" teaspoon in a pharmacy for about $1—so there's

no excuse to stick with what you have in a kitchen drawer. For newborns and young babies, a plastic medicine dropper or syringe, available for about $1.50, is the easiest and most reliable way to administer medication.

• *Baby aspirin, or aspirin substitute.* A large bottle of baby aspirin costs about $3. Aspirin substitutes are useful for children intolerant of aspirin. They are also suggested by some pediatricians for use when a child has chicken pox, and perhaps flu, due to a *possible* connection between aspirin ingestion during those illnesses and the development of a very dangerous condition known as Reye's syndrome. Aspirin substitutes like Tylenol (acetaminophen) have the advantage of being available in liquid form, which is easier to administer to a baby than a tablet. A 4-ounce bottle of children's liquid Tylenol costs about $4. Check dosage, especially for a baby under age one, with the pediatrician.

• An *emetic.* This is a drug that causes vomiting and is the first defense against most kinds of poisoning. Syrup of Ipecac is an inexpensive (about $1.50 for a small bottle), nonprescription drug that is a must in your medicine cabinet. However, it should only be used on advice from your physician or a poison control center.

• *A kaolin-pectate solution.* Kaopectate is used against diarrhea but consult your pediatrician first, and follow the doctor's instructions about the amount to give. (Parents commonly give too little for it to be effective.) Kaopectate is available over the counter for about $3 for an 8-ounce bottle.

• *Desitin, petroleum jelly or A and D ointment.* These are used to soothe and protect against diaper rash. An economy-size jar of Desitin costs about $5. Petroleum jelly is cheaper.

• *A first-aid chart.* A must. It should cover choking, poisoning, burns, bleeding, artificial respiration, bites, stings and sprains and should be hung in a central place in your home. Available from your local Red Cross, or you can send $1 to the Publications Department, The

American Academy of Pediatrics, Evanston, Illinois 60204, for one. If you can also take a *first-aid course*, so very much the better. Definitely choose one that includes training in cardiopulmonary resuscitation (CPR). First-aid classes through the Red Cross cost about $15. CPR courses are about $7.

• *A reference book on childhood illnesses.* An absolute must! There are several excellent paperbacks available. A good choice is pediatrician Jack G. Shiller's *Childhood Illnesses: A Common Sense Approach*, a Day book available for $3.95. Shiller's book teaches you to distinguish between your baby's minor illnesses, which can safely be managed by you at home, and those more serious illnesses when a pediatrician's attention is needed. It will help you decide *when* you need to call the doctor in for help. This "team approach" to tending your baby's health will assure efficient, quality care for your baby and will help avoid unnecessary medical bills.

All together, then, your medicine chest and basic baby health care equipment (including humidifiers and first-aid course) will cost about $75. It's a small investment if it helps you safely treat many minor ailments at home, rather than incur the cost of a visit to the doctor—who would then tell you to go home and do what you could have done in the first place! Although it takes a while to gain the confidence to handle these minor baby illnesses yourself, the sooner you learn, the better—because you can expect your baby and growing child to have about one hundred such illnesses in his first ten years!

Even if you handle minor baby illnesses at home, however, the American Academy of Pediatrics estimates you should plan on about $415 per year for the medical needs of your child to age eighteen. In fact, the first two to three years will probably be more, especially if you live in a large city, and perhaps more again if the baby is in a group care or group play situation where minor infections are passed back and forth. A good health insurance policy will help defray some of these expenses but—remember—not well-baby visits or immunizations, and you first must satisfy a deductible on the baby.

❖ 7

THE HMO OPTION

In Minneapolis, a woman I know recently had a baby. Nothing unusual about that—except that she didn't pay one dollar in medical bills, despite a complicated pregnancy that required many extra tests, a Cesarean delivery and a short stay in the intensive care nursery for her newborn. Moreover, this new mother looks forward to complete coverage for all her baby's pediatric services—even dentistry—all without bills or insurance forms to fill out. What's more, her experience is being duplicated across the country by members of Health Maintenance Organizations (HMOs).

What Is an HMO?

An HMO is an alternative to traditional medical insurance and the usual fee-for-service ("pay as you go") health care. It's an organization of health care professionals and facilities that provides comprehensive services to members for a fixed, prepaid, monthly fee—in other words, it's *both their medical insurance and their health care delivery system.* The monthly fee is paid directly to the HMO, and is the same no matter how much (or how little) medical treatment one receives during the period. When a member *does* receive treatment at an HMO facility, she gets no doctor, hospital, laboratory or other medical bills (virtually no matter how complex or lengthy the treatment); there are no deductibles and no co-payments to speak of. While not new, HMOs are growing rapidly today, because they offer comprehensive, quality medical care to their members at significant cost savings.

HMOs can be either profit or nonprofit, and they have been founded by many groups: communities, doctors, hospitals, employers, unions, universities and insurance companies. Even Blue Cross/Blue Shield has started HMOs—a lot, in fact. HMOs differ dramatically in size—in numbers of enrollees, participating physicians, clinical facilities and affiliated hospitals. Some large HMOs even have their own hospitals. HMOs also differ in geographic scope. Many are strictly local, but many today are chains or networks that cross state lines. The largest and one of the oldest HMOs, the Kaiser Foundation Health Plan, has about 4,250,000 members and operates in ten states and the District of Columbia! Others serve 30,000 or less in their local communities. Today there are about 270 HMOs in the United States serving 12 million Americans. This is still a relatively small number, but by 1990, as many as 40 million Americans are expected to receive their health care through HMOs.

Kinds of HMOs

There are basically two: prepaid *Group Practice* (GP) or *Individual Practice Association* (IPA). The former is by far the more common, enrolling 90 percent of the nation's HMO members. In the GP model, care is primarily provided by physicians who are on staff as salaried employees of the HMO, or who are members of an independent medical group on contract to the HMO. Ambulatory care is provided in a centrally located, well-equipped facility (or facilities) belonging to and used exclusively by the HMO. Certain local hospitals are affiliated with the HMO and are used for treatment requiring in-patient care. The IPA, in contrast, is one that contracts with physicians in individual practice to provide health services to HMO members. Care is provided in the individual doctors' offices rather than a central facility, with the HMO acting as the corporation or fiscal agent of the IPA. The physicians bill the HMO, on a previously agreed upon, usually modified fee-for-service basis. When hospital care is required, you go to one of the participating hospitals, where your bills are paid by the HMO.

What Health Services Are Provided by HMOs?

For the set monthly fee, you are eligible for *comprehensive health care* from the HMO personnel and facilities. Basic benefits, which are both 100 percent covered (in the insurance sense) and directly provided by all HMOs, include:

- Physicians services, including consultant and referral services
- In-patient and out-patient hospital services
- Medically necessary emergency health services
- Diagnostic, laboratory and therapeutic radiology services
- Home health services
- Preventive health services
- Short-term out-patient mental health services
- Medical treatment and referral service for alcohol or drug abuse

These basic benefits are more comprehensive than those covered by traditional health insurance. A key difference is the HMO's emphasis on—and provision of services for—*preventive care.* Just as its name indicates, the emphasis at HMOs is on *maintaining* your health. This is obviously in the HMO's interest (not to mention your own!), because it gets paid the exact same amount of money each month whether you're well or ill. Illness exacts a financial toll on the HMO. So it provides and pays for preventive care—periodic physicals and checkups, Pap tests, eye and ear examinations, infant and child care, immunizations, preventive dentistry for children and (in many HMOs) such counseling services as weight control, family planning and hypertension screening. Because there's no charge for these preventive services, there's no temptation to skimp on them. And in addition to the basic benefits, many HMOs provide a range of *supplemental* benefits, like prescription drugs and facilities for intermediate or long-term care.

Maternity and Pediatric Coverage at an HMO

Now let's get specific about the services most on your minds these days—obstetrical care, delivery and hospital maternity stay, pediatric care and immunizations.

At an HMO, a pregnant woman receives as many prenatal visits with an obstetrician as required, including lab work and the use of advanced obstetrical equipment like sonograms, etc., if necessary. She probably receives prenatal counseling in nutrition, and perhaps in prepared childbirth techniques. Her baby is delivered in an affiliated HMO hospital by the on-call obstetrician. If anesthesia is necessary, it's covered in full by the HMO. The HMO provides pediatric care from the moment of birth, including the use of neonatal intensive care, if required. The mother receives all postnatal care, perhaps including visits at home from an HMO nurse if she chooses the "early discharge" option from the hospital. As the months go by, routine well-baby visits to the pediatrician are provided by the HMO—including immunizations. So are pediatrician visits when the baby is sick. The mother is provided with family planning services, and her routine gynecological visits are free. As the years go by, her child's pediatric care continues to be provided by the HMO at no extra charge—including eye and ear examinations. If the child ever needs to be rushed to the emergency room, the fee will be covered by most HMOs. There's a good chance that if the child needs counseling, it too will be covered by the HMO. All this, most probably without a single bill, other than the regular monthly HMO fee. Contrast this with coverage provided by traditional insurance, with its deductions, co-insurance, reasonable and customary fee restrictions and excluded services (like well-baby care). Indeed, *studies show that many couples are attracted to HMOs specifically because of the liberal maternity and pediatric benefits.* HMOs are usually a very good deal for a young couple planning a family, or planning an addition to the family.

What Is It Like to Go to an HMO?

Maybe by now you're intrigued by the services and coverage offered by HMOs but wonder what it's like to go to one. Is it different from going to a "regular" doctor? Is it like a clinic? Do you make appointments or just walk in? Do you see a different doctor every time?

First of all, even HMOs with centralized facilities are not like clinics—at least they should not and need not be. Nearly all the people visiting HMOs do so by appointment. Moreover, contrary to a common suspicion, HMO members do *not* wait longer for appointments than patients going to a fee-for-service doctor—according to a five-year study conducted by a major research organization. Moreover, the same study showed that once patients were in the office, they waited about eighteen minutes to see HMO doctors— versus about twenty minutes for "regular" doctors.

More important, an HMO is not like a clinic because *members do select a personal physician from among the HMO staff.* So forget about the worry that you'll see a different doctor every time. Your personal physician is responsible for your total health care and is your primary adviser on all health matters. He or she will either treat you directly, or refer you to a staff (or if necessary, outside) specialist. Each member of your family can designate a different personal physician—the woman might choose an OB-GYN and the man an internist, and they would choose a pediatrician for the baby.

Do HMO doctors have too many patients, are they overbooked so that you feel pressured to get in and out of the office as fast as possible? While HMOs differ in physician-patient ratios, just as fee-for-service practices do, the ratio *is* slightly lower in HMOs than the national average of fee-for-service practices. Still, available studies indicate that the time HMO physicians spend with each patient is within national norms. However, one way in which HMOs try to maximize the efficiency of doctors' time is by using other health personnel like nurse practitioners for preliminary or routine exams or procedures. This may be particularly relevant to a pregnant woman, as a good deal of prenatal care consists of routine procedure: blood pressure, urinalysis, weight monitoring, measurement of fundal height. One study reported in the *New England Journal of Medicine* in 1981 concerning maternity care at a Boston-based HMO showed that pregnant women there received about half their prenatal care from a nurse practitioner.

In some ways, going to an HMO may be better than going to a regular fee-for-service practice. An HMO provides centralized medical care (at least the more common group model does), with all medical services in one place, providing "one-stop shopping" convenience. Many HMO facilities have on-site laboratories, diagnostic and radiology centers, other advanced equipment and even pharmacies. What's more, all your records are in one place, and any staff doctor you're referred to has immediate access to them. This saves time and helps minimize duplication of testing. Moreover, because the peer review system is built into the HMO system, you have an automatic second-opinion safeguard.

Quality of Care

All these points relate to quality of care provided by HMOs, but there are more basic questions. First and foremost, *how good are HMO doctors?* Are HMOs staffed by second best?

Hardly. A recent study showed that most HMO doctors are either board certified or board eligible in their fields. That means they meet high standards of training. And if you think about it, HMOs have a strong incentive to hire quality doctors, because if a doctor doesn't solve your health problem promptly and efficiently (if a misdiagnosis is made or treatment is delayed so that the condition worsens), you're just going to keep coming back until the problem *is* solved. You won't pay any more—but it certainly will cost the HMO more. For that reason, a second-rate physician is terribly expensive to an HMO.

What about the concern that an HMO might skimp on medical care, since to treat patients and especially to hospitalize them costs the HMO money without producing any additional income? This is a serious concern, and those who express it sometimes cite the fact that HMO members are hospitalized over a third less frequently than people with traditional health insurance. Critics of HMOs cite this as indication that HMOs yield to the financial temptation to "undertreat."

Given the seriousness of this concern, the quality of HMO care has been much studied. No research supports the concern that HMOs skimp on medical care or provide lower-quality care than traditional fee-for-service practices. In 1980, for example, researchers at Johns Hopkins University concluded after extensive study that "there is little question that HMO care is at least comparable to care in other health care facilities, if not superior." Perhaps even more interesting is the study published by an American Medical Association (AMA) group. As the AMA has never been particularly sympathetic to the HMO concept, their conclusion is all the more compelling: ". . . the medical care delivered by HMOs appears to be of a generally high quality. . . . The HMO approach, where viable, appears to have the potential to provide health care of acceptable quality at a lower total cost to enrollees than many other health care systems." And, the AMA study added, "nothing in the literature indicates that HMO savings result from enrollees receiving less care than they need."

Then why *do* HMO members get hospitalized less? Because HMOs frequently substitute outpatient care for hospitalization. Since traditional health insurance often covers more of the bill if work is done in the hospital rather than a doctor's office, fee-for-service doctors have a tendency to hospitalize patients for certain minor surgical procedures and tests. HMO doctors have the opposite incentive. The patient doesn't pay in either case, but it costs the HMO much more to hospitalize someone. Hence, there's a strong incentive to perform procedures that lend themselves to it on an outpatient basis. Since it's estimated that 20 to 40 percent of all surgery can be performed safely on an outpatient basis, it's easy to see why many health analysts think that HMOs have the potential to be a major cost-containment development in health care. The Department of Health and Human Services has estimated that by 1988, increasing use of HMOs may save $20 billion in hospital costs alone.

Quality of Maternity Care

Along with these studies about the quality of overall care at HMOs, the quality of HMO maternity care has been the subject of analysis. In 1981, an article entitled "A Comparison of the Quality of Maternity Care Between a Health Maintenance Organization and Fee-for-Service Practices" was published in the prestigious *New England Journal of Medicine.* The paper was based on a study of obstetrical patients at a Boston-based HMO and a demographically and socially comparable group of fee-for-service obstetrical cases in Boston. It found the following:

• A significantly greater proportion of HMO patients had eleven or more prenatal visits.
• The rate of inductions was significantly lower in the HMO patients (12.3 percent vs. 21.1 percent).
• The HMO patients had fewer Cesarean sections (11.4 percent vs. 14.3 percent).
• There was no difference between the two groups in short gestations, the number of stillbirths, neonatal deaths, low birth weights or low Apgar scores (a test performed immediately at birth that is a quick measure of the justborn's well-being). In other words, the two groups had comparable *outcomes* of pregnancy.
• HMO infants were admitted to the special-stay nursery at about the same rate as fee-for-service newborns.
• Average hospital stay for HMO patients was 4.4 days vs. 4.8 days for fee-for-service patients. (These numbers average vaginal and Cesarean deliveries in both groups.)

Of course, this is just one study. But its findings coincide with what you would expect, knowing what you now do about HMOs. An HMO's emphasis on preventive care translates to frequent prenatal visits. You'd expect HMO obstetricians to perform Cesareans less often, because they require more hospitalization, drugs and medication than vaginal deliveries, resulting in medical costs that are between 50 and 100 percent higher. Most important, since the Boston study showed no difference in pregnancy *outcomes* between the two groups, there's no reason to conclude that the HMO group's fewer Cesareans were examples of skimping on medical care. Nor should the fact that HMO mothers and babies went home earlier be interpreted as hustling them out of the hospital to save money at the expense of good health. It's true HMOs have a particular incentive to develop early discharge programs for noncomplicated maternity cases. But there's no evidence to suggest early discharge jeopardizes mother or baby. Moreover, HMOs usually provide follow-up home visits by pediatric nurse practitioners to those women who elect early discharge. Early discharge for noncomplicated maternity cases helps keep overall hospitalization down for HMOs, generating savings that can be passed on in the form of lower premiums.

Availability and Eligibility

Many of the country's 270 HMOs are rapidly adding staff, facilities and membership, and new HMOs are being started all the time. However, one estimate has it that as many as *half* of all Americans live in areas still not served by HMOs. In general, HMOs tend to be concentrated in and around major urban areas and/or in areas of rapid population growth and mobility. A main reason for this is that an HMO needs a fairly substantial number of members to be economically viable. HMOs also seem to do best in places where there are a lot of newcomers who don't have existing ties to specific doctors. These people can enroll in an HMO with confidence about the quality of care, and avoid having to shop around on their own for a good doctor. In contrast, in small, rural communities people are more likely to have a long-time family doctor from whom they don't want to break to try something new. Today, HMOs are strongest in California, Washington, Oregon, New York, Massachusetts, Hawaii, Florida, Minnesota and certain rapidly growing areas in the South. In some cities in these states, more than 20 percent of the people are HMO members. In Minneapolis–St. Paul, as many as 80 percent of physicians are affiliated with one of the area's HMOs!

Who is eligible to join? Requirements vary by HMO, although a few stipulations are held in common. First, you must live in an HMO's service area. *Second, the majority of HMO members enroll through their employers.* Today, under federal law, an employer *must* offer employees the option of enrolling in a qualified HMO *if* the employer has at least twenty-five full or part-time employees living within the HMO's service area; contributes to a current health benefit plan; pays the minimum wage; and receives a written request from an area HMO. *Moreover, your employer's contribution to HMO coverage must at least equal the amount contributed to your current health plan.* If your company pays only part of your premiums in an existing health plan, and you pay the rest by payroll deduction, your employer must make a similar payroll deduction available to you for your share of an HMO premium. Finally, if your employer offers certain separate, *supplemental* health benefits—like prescription drugs, optical benefits and group dental plans—and these services are not provided by the HMO open to you, then your employer must provide you with continued eligibility for those supplemental benefits.

What if you're not eligible to join an HMO through an employer (say you're self-employed, or your employer doesn't contribute to an existing health plan for you)? Do HMOs accept single applications? It varies. Many do, but some do not. Of those that do, it's usually only during a designated *open enrollment* period. In other words, you may not be able to join at just any time that suits you. The only way to learn if (and when) HMOs in your service area accept single applications is to telephone and ask them.

The open enrollment stipulation also sometimes applies to those people joining HMOs through their employers. Perhaps you presently have a traditional health insurance plan through your employer, but would like to switch to an HMO. You'll probably have to wait until its next open enrollment period to do so, which may come only once a year. It's different if you're a new employee or an employee just eligible for health coverage. In that situation, if your employer has an existing contract with an HMO, you're eligible to join immediately.

Finally, many HMOs have a "health qualifier" of one sort or another for enrollment. If you try to enroll in an HMO with certain preexisting conditions, you may not be eligible to join until that condition has passed. Or you may be allowed to join, but not provided with coverage for that particular condition. *Pregnancy is one of the preexisting conditions for which some HMOs will not provide coverage.* In this way, some HMOs are like traditional health insurance.

By no means, however, is it the rule that all HMOs will reject you if you're already pregnant. It depends on the HMO, and it depends on your situation vis-à-vis a prepaid group contract. For example, Blue Cross/Blue Shield, the largest purveyor of traditional health insurance, also sponsors fifty-four HMOs, with more on the way. If you're a pregnant woman now covered by a traditional Blue Cross/Blue Shield insurance package and want to switch to an HMO, you can usually do so without any exclusions for a preexisting condition or waiting period for benefits, *if* you choose a Blue Cross/Blue Shield HMO offered through a contract with your employer.

For *individual* applications, it's more difficult for a pregnant woman to enroll with full maternity coverage. The pregnancy must be disclosed on a health statement, and in an HMO where a clear-cut policy doesn't exist, it would be up to the HMO's medical control board to decide whether the woman could enroll with maternity coverage.

Some HMOs are more liberal about preexisting conditions than others. You probably have a better chance as a pregnant woman of being allowed to enroll with full coverage in a *nonprofit* versus profit HMO. You might also have a better chance in a newer HMO that's really trying to build up membership. And it's probably easier to try to get in before the end of the first trimester, because HMO obstetricians, like others, prefer to provide a continuity of prenatal care.

Costs

Yes, you're probably thinking, this all sounds pretty good—but how much does it cost?

HMOs vary in the monthly fees or premiums they charge. Key variables are where the HMO is located, and membership size. HMOs also charge different fees for someone enrolling through a prepaid group plan versus an individual or single contract. Finally, of course, rates vary according to the benefits provided. Everybody gets offered the basic benefits package, but supplemental benefits like dental coverage are separately negotiated and obviously cost more.

The fees HMOs charge must be compared to those of traditional health insurers. Throughout the 1970s, it was commonly thought that HMO premiums were higher than those of the major insurance companies. However, according to a 1983 survey published by the Group Health Association of America, average HMO premiums for major groups have now crossed under the premiums charged by traditional carriers. As a rule, *most HMOs today are cheaper than traditional health insurance.* Moreover, the benefits are broader.

In early 1984, HMO premiums averaged $154 per month for family coverage provided through major group accounts, as compared with $173 for traditional health insurance. What's more, the gap is widening. For traditional insurers, rate increases of 25 to 35 percent in 1983 alone were not uncommon. (In 1984 and 1985, the rate of increase slowed, as overall inflation in the medical industry declined.) While

HMOs are also subject to increasing costs, it's estimated that their fees are rising only one-third to half as fast as traditional insurance.

COMPARISON OF HMO AND TRADITIONAL INSURANCE PREMIUMS,* BY REGION

	HMO	Traditional Insurance
Northeast	$153.77	$169.95
South	130.90	NA
Midwest	159.89	179.36
West	151.29	156.11

AVERAGE HMO PREMIUMS* BY SIZE OF PLAN

Number of Enrollees	Average HMO Premiums
100,000	$145.33
30–100,000	155.76
10–30,000	154.15
<10,000	161.21

* For family coverage provided via major group accounts, as of early 1984.
SOURCE: Group Health Association of America.

Since employers pay the biggest part of the nation's health insurance bills, it's easy to see why they're more and more interested in the HMO option. Some employers are even promoting HMOs by paying a *bigger* part of HMO premiums than they pay for traditional insurance, because they save money when employees opt for HMOs. Employer interest will surely intensify as the gap between HMO premiums and those of traditional insurance widens.

So HMOs can save your employer money—what about you? *The answer for most people is that membership in an HMO will reduce their overall out-of-pocket medical expenditures.* The reduction can be substantial in some situations. One major study indicates that HMO members' health-care bills average 10 to 40 percent lower than those of people covered by traditional insurance. Another study puts the figures at 20 to 25 percent.

To see how much money you might save by enrolling in an HMO, figure out your current health-care costs, by adding any insurance premium payments you make, together with all your out-of-pocket costs resulting from deductibles, co-insurance, reasonable and customary fee limits and excluded services. With an HMO, in contrast, there are virtually no out-of-pocket expenses. So, even *if* your HMO charges a *higher* fee than the standard insurance premium, and even *if* you're required to pay a significant part or all of that HMO fee—your *overall* medical bill might still be lower in an HMO versus a traditional plan, because of no or lower out-of-pocket expenses. In the instance where you pay part of your premium for traditional insurance and then switch to an HMO where monthly fees are *lower*, your employer still must put into the HMO the same dollars that were put into traditional insurance. So in that situation, the amount you yourself pay in premiums would be reduced—perhaps even eliminated.

Remember the case study in Chapter 1 that calculated Susanna's out-of-pocket medical expenses for pregnancy, childbirth and her baby's first year under her traditional health insurance policy? Those expenses totaled $2,109, when Susanna's share of the insurance premium for family coverage was included. Only at the end of the year did Susanna investigate the HMO alternative. When she did, she learned she could have switched to an HMO with which her employer had a contract, and had *no* medical expenses over that same period. Because her employer pays into its traditional insurance plan an amount for family coverage that's greater than her local HMO fee for family coverage, Susanna would not even have had to pay any part of the HMO premium! She'd have saved the full $2,109! The family has now switched to an HMO, and Susanna is planning a second pregnancy without giving a thought to medical bills.

Preferred Provider Organizations

HMOs have introduced an important element of competition into the financing and delivery of the nation's health care. In fact, they've even helped spawn the Preferred Provider Organization (PPO), which also is adding to economic competition in medical care today. A PPO is somewhat like an HMO in that it allows those who finance health care, largely the insurance companies, to contract in advance and directly for services with those who provide care—namely, doctors and hospitals. The insurance company will go to hospitals or a group of doctors and solicit competitive bids for the business of the insurance company. The bid is a pledge to provide a wide range of services—from hospital beds to obstetrical care—at a fixed, modified price. The hospitals and the doctors form PPOs for the purpose of contracting. The insurance company directs its plan members to whichever PPO wins the bid, with winning bids often representing substantial discounts off regular prices. Blue Cross of California, for example, contracted in 1983 with PPOs covering 7,000 doctors and 110 hospitals at discounts of 10 to 25 percent. While patients can choose to use a physician or hospital which is *not* part of the winning PPO, there's a strong economic incentive built into their insurance policy to get them to choose the PPO. That incentive is often the promise of *almost 100 percent* reimbursement for services performed by the PPO, versus 80 percent for going non-PPO. So, even if you stick with a traditional insurance policy, new competitive programs like the PPO may soon be available to you. With PPOs and HMOs everyone saves money—the medical consumer, the employer who pays insurance premiums and the country as a whole.

Drawbacks of the HMO

Attractive as they are in many respects, HMOs are definitely not for everyone. First of all, as many as half of all Americans live in places not served by an HMO. If you can't find one, that settles that!

Assuming, however, you have an area HMO you're

eligible to join, you may still face a serious dilemma. *To put yourself in the care of an HMO, you'll have to sever relationships with your present physicians* (or pay them out of your own pocket). This can be especially difficult if one has a long-standing relationship with a family doctor, and perhaps even more so for a pregnant woman who knows and trusts her OB. Having a baby is such an extraordinary event, there are so many days of uncertainty and anxiety, so many questions to ask, so much concern that you're being properly cared for—well, it's just easier with a known and trusted doctor. To have to leave such a doctor at this critical point will be completely unacceptable to some of you. The fact is that with an HMO you cannot freely choose your own doctor—you have to choose from among the HMO physicians. You might reject the HMO alternative for this reason alone.

A related point is that while HMOs have far from stolen the show on impersonality in medical care, a 1980 survey by Louis Harris & Associates did reveal that 49 percent of the fee-for-service patients felt they know their doctor very well, while only 30 percent of HMO members had that feeling. *Less personal service* is the most common complaint about HMOs.

The *greater use of allied health professionals* like nurse-practitioners to provide patient care is another drawback of HMOs in the view of people who are accustomed to a doctor's attention for even the most routine medical procedures.

Some HMO members also complain that they get "second opinioned" to the point of exasperation, as HMO doctors try to make doubly and triply sure that they're prescribing the least costly but still effective treatment. It's been the experience of some HMO patients that their doctors hesitate to initiate treatment until it's crystal clear it's necessary for the patient and so an unavoidable expense to the HMO. HMO doctors may be more likely to say, "Let's watch and see what develops" or "Come back next week, and if the problem's still there, we'll take care of it then." They may be more likely to suggest "old-fashioned" remedies like steam inhalation for a head cold before going to antibiotics. Of course, such behavior has its plus side— it can save one from unnecessary or premature treatment— but it clearly causes concern among some HMO members.

How to Judge an HMO

Just like everything else, there are good, less good and bad HMOs. Here's how to proceed in your HMO investigation.

• First, *understand exactly what you're giving up* in your traditional insurance plan—benefits provided and costs, so that you can make a meaningful comparison with potential HMOs. *Investigate whether and how you can get back into the traditional plan if you find the HMO isn't right for you.* You can usually switch back, but only during an open enrollment period, probably with exclusions for preexisting conditions like pregnancy.

• Locate HMOs open to you—you must live in their service area. Are they profit or nonprofit? A nonprofit may have more liberal enrollment procedures, but it's not necessarily cheaper.

• Ask about the HMO's hospitalization rate. If hospital days per 1,000 members are between 350 and 525, you can be reasonably sure the HMO has a commitment to efficiency and economy, which will work over time to keep premiums down.

• Check what benefits are offered in addition to the set Basic Benefits. Ask particularly about dental care, prescription drugs, physical therapy, extended medical health care. Make sure you understand any restrictions or limitations on these supplemental benefits (i.e., preventive dentistry for children *up to age six*).

• Thoroughly check out the cost of the HMO, even if your employer will be picking up all or much of the monthly fee. At what rate has the HMO fee been increasing in recent years? Are there any out-of-pocket expenses?

• Remember that enrollment size has a major bearing on cost—the biggest HMOs tend to be less expensive, with economies of scale providing the main explanation. Big HMOs are usually more established, stable and financially secure. They have more facilities and more doctors, including specialists. On the other hand, smaller HMOs may provide more personal service. With an HMO of 30,000 members and less, however, be sure to check that the full range of facilities and specialists is offered.

• What hospitals are the HMOs associated with? Do they have a good reputation in the community?

• Ask about the qualifications of the HMO's doctors. Hope to learn that all or most of the HMO's physicians are board-certified or at least board-eligible.

• Check out the overall fiscal health of the HMO. Sixteen have failed in recent years, commonly because of inadequate membership growth, overstaffing or understaffing of physicians, pricing their fees too low, and poor location. Ask if the HMO is a member of the Group Health Association of America, as that will give you some indication of financial soundness. Be sure the HMO you're considering carries insolvency insurance, which would provide you with coverage should the HMO fail. Look for a clause in the HMO contract that holds individuals "harmless" for medical bills in the event of HMO failure.

• Go to one of the HMO's "open houses." Listen to the pitch, collect the literature, ask your questions, tour the facilities. There's nothing like a firsthand view.

❖ II ◆◆◆◆◆◆◆◆◆◆◆◆◆◆◆◆◆◆◆◆◆◆◆◆

A Quality,
Cost and Comfort
Guide to . . .

❖ 8

MATERNITY CLOTHING

Determining Your Needs

It's a good idea to think about your maternity clothing needs early in pregnancy, before you even go to the stores. This is especially true if you tend to be an impulse buyer. While maternity wear usually costs less than "regular" clothes, it's not cheap, and unless you have a wardrobe plan in mind, you can easily overspend.

What you need and want in maternity wear depends on several factors. A key one is where you live. Those women living in big cities may feel they need a wider variety or more sophisticated clothing than those living in smaller towns. Are you willing to borrow? Do you have family or friends your size with maternity clothes to lend? What about sewing some of your maternity wear? What's your attitude toward clothes in general? If you're a "clothes horse" in your nonpregnant state, chances are you'll want more maternity wear than your counterpart who isn't especially interested in clothes.

Perhaps most important, do you work outside the home? What sort of clothes are appropriate for you to wear in the workplace? It's not a good idea to change your dressing style or "look" for work dramatically when you're pregnant. It just attracts all that much more attention to your pregnant state, which some of your colleagues may find distracting and which can bring out some old-fashioned prejudices. So if you usually wear conservative suits to work, you probably shouldn't start turning up in sweet little maternity dresses, or in trousers and overblouses. Aim for a consistency of image.

And finally, how much can you afford to spend? Read this chapter, set a maternity clothing budget, and stick to it. Be realistic, by figuring the kinds and number of clothes you'll need and then the probable cost, using estimates provided here. The plan should have some "give" for unexpected needs—including some self-pampering. Remember too that what you can afford and are willing to spend on regular clothing is probably not the same for maternity apparel. After all, these days you have many new and substantial bills. Moreover, you get such relatively limited use, in terms of time, out of maternity clothes.

Features to Look For in Maternity Clothes

In terms of *cut*, maternity dresses, jumpers and skirts are longer in the front, so that they'll hang evenly as your belly expands. (Remember this if you buy a jumper or dress that has to be shortened—follow the existing hemline carefully.) Maternity trousers and jeans have expandable front panels and stretch back waists. Today there are also new "no panel" maternity trousers, which feature either expandable tracks or rib-knit tops with drawstrings. Better maternity blouses have square-cut bottom seams and don't open all the way down, so they look neater when worn out over pants. For easier dressing in late pregnancy, you'll appreciate jumpers or dresses with extra long back zippers, or with a few buttons down the front, rather than a single button or short zipper at the back. The best maternity jackets are designed about three-quarters of an inch longer than regular jackets, to give them the correct proportion with maternity jumpers and dresses.

Although I've mentioned skirts, it's best to avoid the regular-style skirt suit when pregnant, even if you're a pregnant executive. This is because a skirt suit cuts your figure in two in a way that draws attention to your growing belly. Moreover, the skirt's elastic front panel must be covered by wearing a blouse on the outside, which may not be appropriate in more conservative offices. In contrast, suits composed of jumpers or dresses and jackets create a neat flowing vertical line, minimizing your (non!) waistline, and are also more comfortable.

In terms of *quality*, you'll probably find maternity clothes are a notch or two down from what you usually buy. (However, this chapter will direct you to some sources that are exceptions.) Maternity clothes are usually unlined, and made of lesser-quality fabrics. In fact, maternity clothing on the market seems to cluster at the lower and upper ends of the market, with relatively little representation in the middle. Perhaps this is because many middle-income women have resisted paying "normal" prices for maternity clothes, because of the short time they're worn. In any case, some firms have recognized a marketing opportunity in this situation and are now scrambling to fill the gap. The latest company to introduce a line of decent quality, moderately priced casual maternity wear is Levi's. Moreover, "off-price" maternity shops are opening around the country. These shops frequently sell the better maternity designers at discounts of 30 to 60 percent, putting them well within the range of middle-income women.

In your search for quality, give the item you're thinking of buying the "once over." Check hems and seams for straightness and firm stitching. Zip zippers up and down several times, fast. Make sure button holes aren't unraveling and that bust darts are correctly positioned. Look for durability. Remember, you may wear maternity clothes for a short time, but you wear them "hard."

It's important to choose *practical* as well as comfortable maternity clothes. Since you're unlikely to have nearly as many maternity clothes as you do regular ones, you'll be wearing what you do have often. This translates into frequent cleaning, especially because pregnancy raises your body temperature and increases perspiration. *So make sure most of your maternity wear can be machine washed and dried* (especially blouses and shirts). Otherwise, your dry cleaning bills could get prohibitive.

This is the place to interject that if you don't already have a *washer-dryer*, you should seriously consider buying a set. You'll never appreciate them more than during pregnancy and with a new baby. Quality units cost between $450 and $600 at a national chain store like Sears. (If you have a nearby discount outlet specializing in appliances, you may be able to find the same item discounted for 25 percent or more.) In addition, you'll also need a plumber to install the washer and maybe an electrician for the dryer. Depending on the going rates for these services in your area, and how much of a job your particular installation is, these could add another $50 to $200 to your bill. Also invest in a service contract for the appliances, as "house calls" by washer repair workers are expensive. However, despite the initial investment, most households with a baby regard a washer-dryer as a *must*. If you're going to buy one anyway when the baby comes, why not get it earlier and enjoy the convenience during pregnancy?

Back to maternity clothes. Along with the machine wash-and-dry feature, look for maternity clothes that are *no-iron* or require only touch-up ironing. Otherwise, every time you wash, you'll iron. Good choices in terms of easy-care material are silky polyester, wool or rayon-polyester gabardine and cotton-polyester.

Another way to be practical in your selection of maternity wear is to choose items that *coordinate* or *mix and match*. This is where planning ahead and making a list is especially helpful. Buying maternity clothes, after all, is not like buying regular clothes. With maternity clothes, you're (probably) starting essentially from scratch, so you have an opportunity to coordinate everything. This can expand an otherwise limited number of clothes into a real wardrobe and a limited budget into a perfectly adequate one.

Start by choosing one basic outfit appropriate to your needs. It might be a jumper and jacket if you work outside the home, or a good pantsuit if you don't. Let this basic outfit be both your color key and the "center" of your maternity wardrobe, around which you'll coordinate other purchases. It's easiest to coordinate around a "classic" solid color (like navy, gray, wine, black or tan) rather than a pattern or a more unusual color.

Then, start to add blouses and shirts in complementary solids or small, subtle patterns. (Bold patterns accentuate your belly, which may be fine in casual or sportswear, but less appropriate for work.) Next, a jumper. If you've started off with a pantsuit, you'll want to be able to wear the jumper with the jacket and the blouses you've selected. If you started with the jumper suit, you'll obviously want to wear the second jumper with the suit jacket as well as the blouses. Then, depending on your needs, you might add a washable, silk-look polyester dress in a coordinated color and pretty pattern, or a second pair of trousers. Then a sweater or two, depending on the climate. Finally, a pair of jeans, a few T-shirts, and maybe a sweatshirt or jogging outfit (even if you don't jog, because they're so comfortable) in a wonderful color, a nightgown (make it the nursing kind, so it'll serve two purposes), and your basic maternity wardrobe is in place. (For a cost estimate of this wardrobe, see the final chart.) Add to or subtract from it according to your needs, wants and budget. If you can borrow any of these basics, wonderful!

A few miscellaneous points about comfort and practicality. Be careful to choose clothes that have enough *"give"* to last through your entire pregnancy. A nationwide marketing survey by a maternity wear manufacturer showed that women's number one complaint about maternity clothes was that most weren't designed with enough room to be worn in the last month. To help test for sufficient "give," some maternity shops will provide you with a pillow sized to simulate your nine months' state. Secondly, don't buy maternity clothes that are as *heavy* as your regular clothes, because pregnancy raises your body temperature so that you tend to feel warm all the time. If you find you're perspiring heavily, you might also consider underarm perspiration shields. Avoid itchy materials and tight collars. Many pregnant women also find they need shoes one half to one full size larger. Low-heeled shoes are better during pregnancy, because your balance keeps shifting as you grow, which may make you unsteady. Low heels may also help with back and leg aches, as can support hose. The latter are essential to the many women who develop varicose veins during pregnancy. Maternity panties are available that provide additional tummy and back support.

Sources of Maternity Clothing

Borrowing is a good idea, because, after all, maternity clothes are worn for a short time, and they're needed at a time when you have many other new expenses. Some women even feel that borrowing maternity clothes is another way to get into the "spirit" of pregnancy. A mother from Lewiston, Maine, wrote: "One of the wonderful things about being pregnant is the community spirit it engenders. All sorts of women, even simply acquaintances, offered to lend me maternity clothes. It not only provided me with a large wardrobe, but with a sense that people wanted to help, that mothers have a certain solidarity all their own, and that friends were pleased with my pregnancy. I try to carry on the tradition with other pregnant women." By borrowing so much, this woman managed to keep her maternity clothing expenditures down to an astonishing $40—even though she worked part-time as a college professor throughout her pregnancy!

Identify from whom and just what you'll be able to borrow *early* in your pregnancy, before you buy anything. Don't wait until you need it—borrow it before, get it home, clean it. That way, you'll know what you have and what you *lack*, and so what you will have to buy. Overlap will be avoided.

Another way to acquire quality maternity clothes at reasonable prices is to *sew* them. Many maternity styles are relatively simple to make, and all major pattern makers offer maternity patterns, ranging in price from $2.50 to $6. To start with something especially easy, look for a pattern designated as such—McCall's "Make it Tonight," "Very Easy Vogue," Simplicity's "Jiffy." Appropriate fabric suggestions and amount for the patterns you select are provided on the package. For a standard jumper, you might require 2 to 2½ yards of material. Fabric varies widely in price and is the key item in your final cost. (Zippers, buttons, thread, etc. will probably cost less than $5.) However, even if you buy a good quality wool or wool blend costing $20 per yard, you might save 50 percent from the cost of a comparable-quality store item. One Texas friend told me she outfitted herself in three jumpers, four pairs of slacks and four shirts—for $100! And even if you don't sew, you might find you can still save money by hiring someone to sew maternity clothes for you.

Another source of maternity wear is the *mail-order catalog*. Mail order has become a more sophisticated business in recent years. To address people's natural reluctance to buy what they haven't seen—and in the case of clothes, tried on—lavish, detailed catalogs are available, either free or for a small charge which is usually put toward any item you end up ordering. Some catalogs even include color and fabric swatches. Moreover, you usually have the right to return an item within a reasonable number of days, if you're not satisfied. (Avoid any mail-order house that doesn't allow this.) Mail order has the added advantage of being a big time-saver—which can be especially important to women working outside the home. Prices are usually quite competitive, because often these mail-order houses market *only* directly and manufacture much of what they sell. Another nice thing about mail order is that the items are as available to someone in Minneapolis as they are to someone in Manhattan. A few years ago, I would never have considered ordering any clothes by mail. Today, because of the wide variety and frequently high quality of clothes available by mail, and because mail-order prices are so competitive, I think it's a great option.

For example, you can order from the maternity and baby catalogs of national chain stores like Sears and J. C. Penney. Prices are low, with especially good buys in maternity underwear, T-shirts and classic button-down shirts, jeans and sometimes simple jumpers. However, the mail-order maternity houses that may be of special interest to some of you are the ones that specialize in dressing the professional woman. By providing an elegant, tailored look for the working woman who wants to maintain her professional image throughout pregnancy, these companies are filling a real void.

One such company is ReCreations Maternity. In business since 1969, it offers a complete range of good-looking office wear for the professional woman. The quality is excellent. The clothes are selected for easy coordination and designed to be flattering and practical for the pregnant woman, with classic cut and colors, slimming small prints, soft, easy-care fabrics. For example, ReCreations offers a simple V-neck jumper suit in charcoal gray, navy, black and wine—both jumper and jacket together for about $80. Other jumpers go for about $45 to $75, and jackets for about $50 to $75. Good-looking, easy-care dresses are also offered in flattering shirt-dress and A-line styles. Many have the button front placket feature, which makes dressing easier as your pregnancy advances. ReCreations also sells casual clothes, including "no-panel," inexpensive corduroy pants and jeans, as well as accessories and lingerie. Attention to detail is impressive compared to most maternity wear, including bound finished seams, properly cut jackets, extra matching buttons. To order a catalog, send $3, refundable with a purchase, to ReCreations Maternity, P.O. Box 09138, Dept. AB-1, Columbus, OH 43209.

Another mail-order company dedicated to dressing the professional woman is Mothers Work. It sells directly to individuals—no intermediaries—and manufactures much of what it sells. That's how prices are kept reasonable—reasonable, that is, considering the clothes' high quality and good looks. Mothers Work sells a full line of executive-style maternity dresses or jumpers and jackets (the company calls these maternity suits), blazers, blouses—right down to the bow ties—all in fine, coordinated fabrics like 100 percent worsted wools, silks, polyester/rayon blends. Jeans, other casual clothes, and lingerie are also available. For a handsome catalog, send $3, refundable with first purchase, to Mothers Work, P.O. Box 40121, Department C7, Philadelphia, PA 19106.

There are an increasing number of *off-price maternity shops* these days—with any luck, you'll find one in your area. Prices are as much as 30 to 60 percent off, and the selection and size range is large. Quality off-price maternity shops carry known designers like Jane Schaffhausen of Belle France, Regina Kravitz, Evelyn DeJorge and M. H. Fine—the same designers you find in upscale department stores.

Nor should you ignore the possibilities in the *discount stores* like K Mart, Zayres, and Caldors. You can pick up some real bargains on the occasional maternity item at such places—sweaters and blouses for less than $10, for example. In addition, if you're lucky enough to have any maternity *factory outlets* in your area, take advantage of them. One Oakland, California, woman who filled out my survey reported that she enjoyed a large maternity wardrobe—all the more so because she had spent less than $200 shopping for it at a local Motherhood factory outlet.

National chain stores like Sears, J. C. Penney and Montgomery Ward, as indicated earlier, have maternity clothing departments selling low to moderately priced apparel. Along with price, the convenience of these stores is a plus. Charge cards are accepted, which may help manage your monthly cash flow. Another convenience is that these stores also sell a wide variety of baby products. You can start comparison shopping for cribs and car seats when you're in the store to buy maternity clothes.

Casual wear like simple polo shirts, velour shirts, turtlenecks, plain button-down shirts and Levi and Wrangler maternity jeans impressed me as the best buys in terms of cost and quality at both Sears and J. C. Penney. Most of the shirts were in the $14 to $18 range, and the jeans were under $30. There were also some nice maternity nightgowns for $14 to $18, full slips for as little as $11 and bras for $5. What these stores lack is the more tailored and "formal" office wear and dresses.

Finally, there are the *upscale department stores* like Saks, Bloomingdale's, Filene's, Dayton's and Lord & Taylor. These and comparable stores across the country have small maternity departments, with a full range of good-quality clothes. They may have seasonal minicatalogs of maternity wear from which you can order, and charge cards are usually accepted. Sales tend to be held in October through Christmas, and around Easter. Selection is fairly limited by the time sales roll around, but when you can find your size in an item you want, the savings can be substantial. For example, at a year-end sale at a Saks maternity shop, I found brand-name jeans reduced from $37 to $22; fashionable maternity trousers marked down from $40 to $24; and two lovely office dresses reduced from about $88 to $50—prices comparable to those at off-price stores.

Suggested Wardrobes and Costs

On the following chart, I've priced the clothes sold by national chain stores (using Sears and J. C. Penney as the examples); at an upscale department store (using Saks); at an off-price maternity shop (using Reborn); and from a quality mail-order house (using ReCreations Maternity). Also on the chart you'll see suggested numbers for the various clothing items, both for the woman who works outside the home and the woman who does not. These numbers are naturally only suggestions, but you may find them useful in your planning. Moreover, the suggestions for the woman who works outside the home jibe with those resulting from many years of research at ReCreations Maternity into the professional woman's maternity wear needs.

GUIDELINES FOR YOUR MATERNITY WARDROBE

| SUGGESTED NUMBERS OF CLOTHING ITEMS | | | COST RANGE PER ITEM | | | |
For Women NOT WORKING Outside the Home	For Women WORKING Outside the Home	Type of Clothing	National Chain Store	Upscale Department Store	Off-Price Maternity Shop	Mail-Order House
0–2	1–3	Dresses		$65–135* (most $85–125)	$35–95* (most $45–75)	$35–60* (most $40–55)
1–3	2–3	Jumpers	$22–25	$60–85	$35–70 (Denim less)	$60–90 (Denim less)
0–1	0–2	Skirts			$30–60	
1–2	1–2	Slacks	$12–15	$45–65	$16–60	$30–50
1–2	1	Jeans	$17–25	$35–45	$26–36	$28–36
3–6	3–5	Blouses (Shirts, smocks)	$12–20	$35–55 (most $40–45)	$22–32	$26–30
2–4	2	T-Shirts	$10–15	$20–30	$10–25	$27–37
		Long sleeves	$15–18	Up to $55	Up to $38	$25–40
1–2	1–2	Sweaters	$20–25	$50–80	$22–42	$30–40
1–2	1–2	Nightgown	$14–20	$30–50	$20–40	$35–40
		Underwear				
6	6	Maternity panties	$3–6 pair			$8–9 pair
0–2	3–4	Maternity support hose	$12–14/ package of 4	$6–6.50 pair		$7.50–8 pair
2–3	2–3	Bras	$5–12			$7.50–10
1	1–2	Maternity slips	$10–12			
		Sportswear				
1	1	Bathing suit		$40–60	$30–40	$50
1	1	Warm-up outfit		$70–90	$65–85	
1–2	1–2	Sport shorts		$35–40		$30

* "Dressy" dresses are higher.

❖ 9

BABY CLOTHES AND DIAPERS

BABY'S LAYETTE

Sizes

What size to buy for the baby is confusing for new parents, because the clothes labels themselves are misleading. Infant sizes are by age—newborn, 3 months, 6, 9, 12, 18 and 24 months. A reasonable (but inexperienced) new mother can be forgiven for thinking that since she has a newborn, she should buy the "newborn" size.

In fact, what the designation "newborn" or "3 months" really means is that the clothing item will fit an average size baby *up to* that age. The size/age designates the *upper limit*. This is your first clue that you should never buy a "newborn" size of anything (unless you have a "preemie" or an otherwise very small baby). Why buy a clothing item that will fit *up to* a newborn? Your baby already *is* a newborn! For that matter, why buy an item that will fit the *average* baby *up to* three months? Think how quickly that time will pass, and how little use the baby will get from that item. What you want is clothes that won't be grossly big on the baby, but which will provide growing room and longer use. So *start with the 6-month size.* Then, your initial layette purchases may actually last six months.

This is a rule of thumb. Maybe it's more "scientific" to use a weight chart to determine the size to buy for your baby, who may, after all, be other than average size. Maybe—but not necessarily. Even a new mother armed with a chart matching baby's weight to a clothing size can be misled, because, in fact, *the most important measure for determining a baby's clothing size is height, not weight.* For this reason, the Commerce Department has developed size guidelines that reference both height and weight, as well as age. Use these to guide your baby clothing purchases:

INFANT SIZE	HEIGHT	WEIGHT
3 months	24 inches	13 pounds
6 months	26½	14–18
12 months	29	19–22
18 months	31½	23–26
24 months	34	27–29

To measure your baby's height, straighten one leg and measure from the top of the head to the heel. If the baby's height falls in one size category and weight in another, the height predominates. A family friend from Meriden, Connecticut, learned all this by experience, the way most mothers do. She said, "I did find that sizing of clothes is very misleading. If I had a second child, I would not buy anything marked newborn or 3 months—the child grows too fast. I would only buy items marked 6 months—they're big for only a couple of weeks. Also, as the baby gets older, you again have to be careful about sizing—you need to measure your baby, not rely on the age to get the right size."

What to Buy a Newborn

Forget a full, prepackaged, prepriced layette. It's a waste of money. These usually contain some items that you won't want, and some contain too many of certain items. Moreover, the items are usually in the newborn size. What and how many clothing items a newborn needs are determined mainly by the climate and season in which the baby is born and whether or not you have a washer-dryer. Late spring-summer newborns need fewer and lighter clothes than fall-winter newborns. All a summer baby usually needs for everyday indoor wear is a T-shirt and diapers, or if you want to be fancier, a diaper set. Sleepers, creepers and sacques may be too hot for the summer newborn, whereas they're just right for the winter arrival. How many of these items you need depends on how often you plan to do laundry. (It always astonishes new parents how much laundry a baby dirties.) The suggestions provided here assume you have a washer-dryer and will do laundry every two or three days. Those of you without these appliances may need up to twice the suggested numbers of baby wear "basics."

T-shirts, receiving blankets, nightgowns and footed sleepers, baby bath towels and wash cloths are the "basics" of a newborn's clothing layette. Some parents also find sacques and kimonos useful as well as a number of cloth diapers (even if you plan to use disposables) for burping pads and wipe-ups. Some leads on each of these items:

There are three kinds of baby *T-shirts* that differ by how you put them on—the over-the-head, the side-snap and the wraparound and tie. Everyone has a different opinion about which is best. Many babies don't like anything pulled over their heads, which would suggest the side-snap or wraparound styles. However, sometimes the gripper snaps on the side-snap style are uncomfortable for baby to lie on. Side snaps are also a little more expensive. The wraparound tie style may be the most comfortable for the baby, and also leaves the most growing room. However, it's somewhat more difficult to find (Spencers makes good ones). In over-the-head style look for ones with *lap shoulders*, or with shoulder snaps for roominess. These minimize the on and off problem. In the side-snap style, buy ones with *adjustable tapes* for growth. (Sears has these.)

Baby *nightgowns* bring up the important point of *fire retardancy*. By law, any fabric used in baby nightwear must meet certain standards of fire resistance. The phrase you'll frequently see is "Meets U.S. Standard FF3-71." There are two points you'll want to understand. First, fire retardant is not equal to fireproof. Sleepwear made from these fabrics *will* burn—but more slowly than a nonretardant fabric, and they'll extinguish if the source of the flame is removed. Second, there are two ways that fire retardancy can be attained. One is by a certain selection and composition of fibers to make up a fabric. These fabrics are called "naturally" or "inherently" flame-resistant. Certain all-cotton blends are "naturally" flame-resistant, but certain synthetic fabrics qualify as "inherently" flame-resistant, too. This designation has nothing to do with whether the fabric itself is natural or synthetic. Rather, it means that by virtue of *intrinsic fiber composition*, the fabric is flame-resistant.

In contrast, other fabrics are flame-resistant by virtue of *added chemicals*. This kind of flame-resistant sleepwear was given a bad name several years ago, with the discovery that a chemical flame retardant called Tris was a possible carcinogen. Tris has been banned as a sleepwear additive, and the chemicals now used to produce flame resistance in nightwear are not known to pose any health dangers. However, if you prefer not to put sleepwear with added chemicals on your baby, be sure to look for the designation "inherently flame-resistant." And in synthetic sleepwear, stick with trusted names like Carters, Sears, Spencers, Health-tex and Absorba.

Full-length, *drawstring nightgowns* provide the cool-weather baby with special warmth. A drawstring gown is a practical purchase because it can accommodate a lot of baby growth—remove the drawstring as baby gets longer. A summer baby, in contrast, may be more comfortable sleeping in just a T-shirt and diapers, or possibly a *kimono*. Kimonos are lighter than drawstring gowns, are full-length and open at the bottom. Kimonos are especially good for newborns because they allow the fastest access during the early period of very frequent diaper changes.

Footed sleepers or *stretchies* are one-piece, form-fitting pajamas that snap from neck to toe. They are absolute essentials. Better ones are made of a heavy stretch-knit terry, and sometimes have cuffs that convert to protective mitts. Stretchies are primarily for the cool-weather baby.

Receiving blankets are another "must." They're lightweight blankets about 36 inches by 36 inches with many uses—for swaddling, as a light sleeping cover or as a ground cover. Cotton ones are especially soft and absorbent.

In addition to these layette basics, if your baby is an autumn or early winter arrival, a zip-up *bunting* may be useful. It's basically a hooded, zip-up bag with arms, good for outdoor outings. However, buntings are expensive; baby blankets and dressing in layers are an alternative. Layering usually involves a *sweater set*—lightweight for summer and a heavier one or two for winter. The knit should be fairly tight, so baby can't entangle fingers between the weave. And it must be machine washable.

Babies also need *hats* or *bonnets.* In the winter, the ears and neck should be covered as well as the top of the head. In the summer, a bonnet is necessary, because of the susceptibility of baby skin to the sun. *Booties,* in contrast, are not especially useful, because most babies don't like them and kick them off. Moreover, babies don't need to have their feet covered while indoors. Their feet are naturally cooler than the rest of their bodies, and are quite sensitive to stimulation, which is good for developing body awareness. If you do want to cover baby's feet, fuzzy baby *socks* are a better choice.

BASIC NEWBORN CLOTHING LAYETTE

Clothing Item	Summer Baby	Winter Baby
T-shirts	6 short sleeve 2 long sleeve (opt.)	2 short sleeve 4 long sleeve
Nightgown	2–3 kimono (opt.) sacque (opt.)	3 drawstring 1 sacque
Footed sleepers	–	3 or more
Receiving blankets	3–4	5–6
Cloth diapers (for a baby using disposables)	12	12
Bath sets	3 or more	3 or more
Sweater set	1 (opt.)	1–2
Bunting	–	1 (opt.)
Hat/bonnet	1	1–2
Booties	opt.	opt.
Socks	opt.	3

Remember that these are bare basics, and just for newborns, by which is meant up to six months. If you do laundry only once a week, you'll definitely need more. The emphasis is on the functional, not the decorative. You'll obviously add to the basics, and so will grandparents and friends. Be careful, though. Baby clothes are adorable, so it's tempting to buy more than you actually need.

Looking ahead several months, let's consider the "best buys" for six-month- to one-year-olds. At this stage, the emphasis on the functional and the practical should be, if anything, more pronounced. Clothes must always be appropriate to the baby's stage of motor development and coordination. As the baby starts to crawl, it's imperative that the clothing doesn't interfere.

The best clothing choices for these ages are bright *T-shirts* that are easy to put on and launder. Pair them with straight-cut *overalls* with adjustable shoulder straps for growth and snaps up the leg to the crotch for easy diaper change as well as roominess. Denim, quilted or sweatshirt material overalls can help protect baby's knees from falls and carpet burns. Corduroy and velour are also good choices. One-piece stretch *creepers* are also a good choice, as is a two-piece *jogging suit* or playsuit, in a soft, colorful, washable fabric. Washable *sweaters*, either cardigans or with side buttons at the neck, are also useful. If your baby needs a *snowsuit*, the practical, longer wearing choice may be a two-piece one of overalls and jacket, so the jacket can be worn separately in less cold weather. It should be hooded, washable and water repellant, with full-length zippers to ease dressing, and not so bulky as to restrict the baby's movement.

For sleepwear, *nightgowns* continue to be practical, because they allow for growth and fast diaper changes. Drawstring gowns are also good, because this is baby's kicking stage. With the drawstring, baby will keep covered even if the bedclothes go flying. If you prefer footed sleepers (and most mothers seem to), make sure they're not too tight and have reinforced toes for durability, and that the baby isn't too hot in them.

Regarding *shoes,* the recommendation from pediatricians is to leave them off whenever possible. Baby's feet are not just naturally cool, they're naturally flat, too. As the baby learns to crawl, to stand up and then to toddle, bare feet help with balance and grip. The soles of the feet have natural nonskid surfaces. So shoes aren't needed indoors for warmth, to help develop the arches, or to help baby walk. When you put on shoes for going outdoors, the best bet for both baby's comfort and your budget is inexpensive tennis shoes. When buying baby shoes, look for proper fit, nonskid soles, and flexibility.

As for numbers of these items, you'll be the best judge by the time baby is six months old. By then you'll have a laundry routine, you'll know how many times a day or night your baby needs a clothes change (it's fewer as the baby gets older), what the baby seems happiest in, what's easiest for you. (One tip: If your baby is a drooler, use a bib at all times to save on laundry.) I would guess you'd want *at least* six T-shirts and panties, three to six nightgowns, two to three sleepers and three to four stretch creepers as six-month basics. Remember to buy a size or two ahead.

Features to Look For in Baby Clothing

What specific features make a baby clothing item practical, comfortable, durable and good value for money? Here's a useful checklist:

- Find *easy-to-care-for* clothes that can be washed and dried in a machine and need no ironing or only touch-up ironing. Make sure clear care instructions are provided on the label, and then follow those instructions. This is especially important with flame-resistant fabrics, which can lose their flame resistance if laundered incorrectly.
- Many *synthetic fabrics* are virtually "care free" today. Look for designations like "stain or soil release," "no fade," "wrinkle-release," "crease-retention," "treated for greater absorbency," "shrinkage controlled." In con-

trast, 100 percent cotton may be prone to shrinking, fading, shredding and graying after repeated washings. However, cotton's advantages are natural absorbency and softness. It "breathes," it's hypoallergenic and it has no chemical odor. A combination of 50 percent cotton with 50 percent polyester, especially in T-shirts, may give you the best of both fabrics.

• Look for clothes that are *easy to put on and take off the baby.* These will have such things as snap crotches, lap shoulders, full-length covered zippers, shoulder snaps and padded, elasticized back waists. Zippers are better than buttons. Choose clothes that allow access to the diaper without having to remove the whole outfit.

• *Insist on handling and examining any baby clothes item before buying it.* If it's in a sealed package, open it or have a salesperson open it for you. Feel for fabric softness and pliancy. Examine its thickness and "give." Check seams and stitching for finishing and ravel resistance. Baby clothes should not bind at the neck, wrists, ankles or waist. Knit baby garments are usually the most comfortable—they're light but warm and absorbent, and they allow maximum movement for arms and legs.

• Select clothes with *built-in growth features.* These include two-way stretch fabrics in sleepers and play suits, wraparound T's or snap T's with adjustable tapes, extra-long sleeves and legs with turn-back cuffs, adjustable shoulder straps on overalls, and drawstring gowns.

• *Baby clothes should not be so bulky* that they restrict arm and leg movements. This can interfere with motor development and coordination. Nor should they be so warm that the baby is constantly damp from perspiration. In general, babies don't need to be dressed any more warmly than adults. (In fact, overdressing can cause prickly heat and miliaria.)

• And finally, if you plan on a second baby, make an effort to select clothes that will last and work for two. An old friend of mine who is now the mother of two wrote, "For a first child, buy as many *all-season clothes* as possible, so you can use them for the next child. Also, *unisex* clothes. . . . It pays to put money in quality brand kids' clothes like Health-tex and Carters. They last a lot longer." Avoid buying clothes in a color or print for one child that you wouldn't put on a baby of the opposite sex.

Sources of Affordable, Quality Baby Clothes

Many parents-to-be receive all of the clothes they need for their newborn—and more—from family and friends at *showers*. Sometimes, however, gift givers are not as practical as you might like. Chances are you'll get too many sweater sets, booties, footed sleepers and maybe frilly dresses. Many of the gift items may be in the newborn size, too. If possible, tactfully tell a family member or friend who's bound to be involved in your shower plans that you prefer practical basics, in the 6-month size. In addition, suggest that gift givers include a card from the store with their gift. That way, if you get five sweater sets, you can return or exchange a few. In any case, don't buy any layette items until after your baby showers. And don't buy many before you get home from the hospital, because some people will bring you baby presents at that time.

The next best way to acquire newborn clothes is to *borrow* them from parents with older babies. Many parents are delighted to see the clothes get additional use and will lend freely. An added plus is that secondhand baby clothes tend to be softer.

Next consider babywear *resale shops.* They've sprung up all over. (I can think of a half dozen or more in New York City.) Started mostly by mothers and grandmothers disgruntled over the high cost of quality baby clothes, the short use babies get from them, and thus the fact the clothes are "like new" after they're outgrown, these shops are definitely worth the visit. Good shops accept only quality, thoroughly cleaned items in perfect or near perfect condition. Prices are about one-third to half of the original— sometimes lower. Resale shops are especially good for expensive items like snowsuits, jackets, the occasional party dress, etc. (If you use these shops to *sell* clothes after your baby outgrows them, you'll get 40 to 50 percent of the shop's selling price.)

Nationally known chain stores that are great for baby clothes include J. C. Penney and Sears. Even if you wouldn't normally shop in these stores for your own clothes, you should seriously consider them for baby wear. They offer good quality, wide selection and reasonable prices. They also offer the convenience of catalog shopping, if you prefer. Be sure to check Sears' and J. C. Penney's own "store labels" of baby clothes, which compare pretty favorably in terms of quality and very well in terms of price with name brands like Carters.

Big *department stores* carry more expensive labels—both their own and name brands like Health-tex, Izod, Absorba, Osh Kosh, and Carters. These stores also carry a few specialty items like Calvin Klein diaper sets, Dior christening gowns and Pierre Cardin pram suits. *Children's specialty stores*—whether small neighborhood "baby boutiques," or chains like the Children's Place, with 102 stores around the country—usually emphasize better-quality labels, too. However, layette prices at these stores are substantially higher than at Sears or J. C. Penney. Still, good bargains on quality clothes *can* be found during seasonal sales—one-fifth to one-third off is common. Sales on winter clothes tend to be held in February and on summer clothes at the end of the summer. To exploit these sales, you have to be buying a year ahead for your baby.

"Off-price" retailing has hit the baby wear market, too, and is spreading fast. These stores offer most of the name-brand kids' clothing lines, and frequently all the accessories—from Buster Brown shoes to Carters crib sheets—too. All of these items are 30 to 60 percent discounted. Take the new Kids-R-Us, owned by the nation's number one toy chain, Toys-R-Us. Kids-R-Us opened its first two stores outside of New York City in the summer of 1983 but is adding stores across the nation at a rapid clip—twenty-five by the end of 1985. Kids-R-Us offers first-quality, in-season clothes, at 30 percent and more off

retail—for instance, I recently saw Osh Kosh overalls that retail elsewhere for $17 to $18, at Kids-R-Us for $11.97.

The good news for consumers is that retailers across the nation are trying to get in at the beginning of what's expected to be a booming off-price kids' wear market. The Children's Place, for example, has started its own off-price chain, The Children's Outlet, to which it's adding stores at a rate of fifteen a year. Kids Mart is another off-price chain. And where traditional babywear retailers are *not* getting into the off-price business, they're increasingly cutting prices to meet the competition from off-price stores.

Comparison Shopping

Babywear basics are available in a wide range of prices. The highest-priced designer labels can cost three to four times more for basic items as Sears and J. C. Penney private labels. While there are *many* babywear manufacturers, the following chart shows how some of the more popular lines relate to one another in terms of price.

High Price	Absorba/Izod/Health-tex/Osh Kosh
↓	Private Department Store Labels (Sakswear)
	Carters
	Spencers
Low Price	Sears/J. C. Penney labels

See the chart on the next page for specifics. Babywear sales are held three to four times a year—generally in January and March and at the end of the summer. Discounts of 25 to 30 percent are common.

THE DIAPER DECISION

There are three alternatives—disposables, cloth, or a diaper service. There are advantages and disadvantages to each. As it's estimated that you may change more than 6,600 diapers before your baby is toilet-trained, the diaper decision is definitely an important one!

BABY CLOTHES COST COMPARISON

	Sears/J. C. Penney	Carters/Spencers	Upscale Department Store	Absorba/Izod
T-shirt—plain				
Short-sleeve	$3.40–4.50 (pkg of 3)	$3–5 (pkg of 2)	$6.50–8 (each)	$10–13 (each)
Long-sleeve	$4.50–5 (pkg of 3)	$8–12 (each)	$7–8.50 (each)	$12–15 (each)
T-shirt—fancy	$4.50	$8–12	$9–12.50	up to $18.50
Diaper set	$4–6	$8–15	$6–12	$15–18.50
Terry sleeper	$4.50–11 (most $6–9)	$6.50–12.50	$12–28	$16–30 (velour more)
Overalls	$5–15 (most $8–10)	$12–18	$15–18	$16.50–30
Sweater	$6–10	$12–18	$19–60 (most $20–24)	$20–26
Jogging outfit	$9–18 (most $9–12)	$16–22	$21–27	$25–40
Dress	$7–15	$16–26	$25–100 (most $35–45)	$25–45
Receiving blanket	$3–5	$6	$10–15	$17.50
Snowsuit	$13–37		$28–40	$50–55

NOTE: Prices are approximate, as of early 1985.

Disposables Dominate the Nursery

Disposables are a $1.7 billion annual business in this country. As many as three-quarters of the diapers changed daily in the United States are disposables. The overwhelming reason for this is convenience. Disposables eliminate the need for rinsing, soaking, wringing, washing, drying, folding and stacking. With disposables, there is no diaper pail and no resulting bathroom odor and clutter. There are no potentially dangerous pins and no plastic pants. Disposables save time—a precious commodity for tired new parents.

Disadvantages of Disposables

With all these "plusses," why would any modern couple choose other than disposables? There are actually several reasons. Many people believe cotton, a natural product, is softer against the baby's sensitive skin. Some pediatricians say the chance of diaper rash is greater with disposables, because of the "hothouse effect." Some parents don't like the mark elasticized disposables leave around baby's legs, but some disposables without elasticized legs leak. Moreover, disposable diapers are not biodegradable. You don't have to be an ardent environmentalist to be concerned about the possible hazards of dumping 13 billion synthetic diapers—or 540,000 tons—into the environment each *year!* Disposables can also pose a public health hazard if discarded improperly—they shouldn't be just thrown in the trash. Instead, they should be sealed in a plastic bag so that garbage collectors and others (including animals) don't come in contact with human waste.

The biggest drawback of disposables, however, is expense. As usual, *convenience costs.* How much disposable diapers cost obviously depends on the brand you buy, and how many your baby uses a week. The biggest selling brands are Pampers, with 40 percent of the market, Luvs, with about 20 percent, and Huggies, with slightly more than 15 percent. The rest of the market is supplied by private brands—from Sears, J. C. Penney, and Toys-R-Us, to discount brands sold by supermarket and drugstore chains. Luvs and Huggies are the most expensive, Pampers are in the middle, usually followed by the Sears and similar brands. The least expensive are nearly always the super- market and drugstore brands, although most parents say that the quality of these is so low that they are poor value. Disposables come in different sizes—small (newborn, up to 12 to 14 pounds), medium (12 to 26 pounds), and large (toddler, over 23 to 26 pounds), and there's a big difference in price according to size. Luvs newborn size, for example, costs about 17 cents per diaper; its medium size costs about 22 cents per diaper; and its toddler-size diapers are about 32 cents each! There's also a difference in price depending on how *large* a box you buy—the larger the box, the lower the per diaper price. For example, a box of thirty newborn size Pampers costs about $3.80; a box of ninety costs about $10.60—you save about 80 cents buying the large box. Savings like this add up fast, considering the number of diapers a newborn goes through.

Another key factor in the cost of disposables is where you live. Some states tax diapers—New York is an exam- ple—others, like Massachusetts, do not. Disposables are also usually much more expensive in big cities, probably because of the amount of shelf space they take up. The prices I've quoted here are big-city, nondiscount prices— they're the most you could be faced with.

Let's estimate what you might pay *per week* for various brands of disposables, assuming a newborn needs 13 or 14 changes a day, or 90 to 100 diapers a week, at least for the first month; and that 12- to 26-pound babies and toddlers need 6 to 8 changes a day, or 42 to 56 diapers a week. (These numbers are purposely on the high side—they'll be the *most* diapers your baby could go through.)

COST PER WEEK OF DISPOSABLE DIAPERS		
Newborn	*12–26 Pound Baby*	*Toddler*

	Newborn	*12–26 Pound Baby*	*Toddler*
Premium brands	Up to $16	$10.50–12.50	$15–18+
Pampers	$10.50–13+	$7+–9.50+	$10–11.50
Sears	$9–10	$7–8	$7+–10
Supermarket brand	$7–8	$6–7.50	$8–9.50

How to Save Money on Disposables

Obviously, if your baby needs fewer changes, you won't have to spend this much. After the first month or so, babies differ significantly in frequency of bowel movements. It's perfectly normal for some babies to have five or six bowel movements a day—and equally normal for other babies to have one every three or four days! Still, you can see that disposable diapers will make a difference in your weekly supermarket bill. There are, however, ways you can save money on disposables. First, comparison-shop. Find the area supermarket, discount store or department store that has the best prices on disposables. (Toys-R-Us is often the cheapest.) Buy by the case. Watch for sales. Definitely try one of the less expensive brands. If they should work satisfactorily for your baby, you'll save considerable money over the course of two and a half years of diapering. Also try disposable liners inside the diapers. Although most think of using them with cloth, they can work just as well with disposables. Liners cost less than 2 cents apiece at places like Sears, so you might find them worthwhile, particularly on a 32-cent toddler-size Luvs!

Most important, *watch for coupons* on disposables. Even people who have never redeemed a coupon in their lives find it worth doing on diapers. Coupons are often enclosed in *large* boxes of disposables. You'll also find them in newspapers, and sometimes they're mailed to your home as promotions. You should also collect the *proof-of-purchase symbols* from Pampers and send them into the company in exchange for coupons (or for a savings bond offered by the company). One Missouri mother wrote that she even started collecting proofs of purchase from the Pampers boxes in the hospital nursery! Many mothers report that they "always have a coupon for diapers" and by using them, by buying on sale, by the case, and at a discount place like Toys-R-Us, they manage to spend as little as $1 a day on name-brand disposables like Pampers.

Why Some Parents Choose Cloth Diapers

This recitation on the cost of disposables is the main reason why one in four couples still decide to go with cloth diapers. In comparison with the 6,600 disposable diapers your baby might go through, you'd need only 48 cloth ones (and they may even be around for baby number two). So they're worth at least considering for many parents.

How to Care For Cloth Diapers

This section could equally be titled "disadvantages of cloth diapers." Yes, cloth diapers will save you money— some estimates are savings of $800 or more over two and a half years of diapering—but they cost time and effort. If you're considering cloth, be sure you know what's involved in caring for them.

Diaper stains are difficult to remove, so to help prevent permanent staining, soiled diapers must be rinsed in the toilet as soon as they're taken off. Then they must be wrung out and put in a pail containing water with a teaspoonful of Borax to deodorize and kill ammonia-producing bacteria. Before laundering, the water must be wrung out. Diapers must be washed within a day or two of being soiled and they must be washed separately from the rest of the laundry. Wash them in a good-quality detergent, using the hottest cycle on your washing machine. As detergent residue can cause diaper rash, it's best to put diapers through *two* rinse cycles. Diapers must be thoroughly dried—in the sun is best. Then they must be folded and stored.

Cost

There are several brands of cloth diapers, in gauze or birds-eye weave. Curity, Sears and Montgomery Ward are all good quality. Four dozen Sears prefolded gauze diapers cost about $50. Curity gauze are $40 to $45 for forty-eight. The same number of unfolded birds-eye cost about $30, and some people think birds-eye are more absorbent.

You'll also need *diaper pins*. Choose rustless, stainless steel ones with a safety-lock feature. Pins need periodic replacement when they get dull, so you'll probably spend $5 to $10 on them over the course of diapering. An alternative: Denbi sells an adjustable *snap-on* cloth diaper that eliminates pins, at about $70 for forty-eight. Available at Sears, these are faster, safer, and definitely worth considering.

Cloth diapers require *waterproof pants.* Pull-on style in nylon is usually the most comfortable. Buy at least six pairs at $1.50 to $3 each. Next buy a medium-size (thirty-to-forty-diaper) pail, because a big one full of soggy diapers is too heavy to carry to the washing machine, and the diapers shouldn't sit too long in the pail anyway. Choose one with a lock top, a carrying handle, and maybe a deodorizing compartment. Kiddie Products makes a good one for about $12. Pails without lock tops are less, but toddlers and pets have a way of getting into them.

There's also a useful device called a Diaper Duck that hooks onto the back of the toilet seat. You clip the diaper to it, flush and then use it to wring the water out of the diaper before dropping it into the pail. You don't get your hands wet, and it makes the whole thing much less messy; it costs about $5. Look for mail order ads in baby magazines. Finally, disposable *diaper liners* help prevent soiling and staining of cloth diapers, and save time and messy rinsing. They also keep your baby drier. Johnson & Johnson makes them and so does Sears, at less than 2 cents apiece.

Hidden Costs of Cloth

All in all, your initial investment for cloth diapers and related paraphernalia could approach $100. In addition, you'll have the ongoing costs of laundering them. These include the cost of presoaks, detergent, bleach, electricity for the washer and dryer, heat for the water, washer-dryer wear and repair, and even septic tank wear. And if you live in a community which bills you for water, your water bills will probably jump, as your washer can use up to 28 gallons a load.

To minimize the laundering costs, don't use special diaper or baby detergents—they're more expensive and unnecessary. Don't use fabric softeners, as they too are expensive and can leave a chemical residue on the diaper that may irritate baby's skin. The same is true of special enzyme presoaks. Cheaper borax is fine. When possible, let diapers dry in the sun—it saves on electricity and can help prevent diaper rash.

Nevertheless, you still have the costs of electricity, water, heat, detergents, depreciation and repairs. These vary across the country. All sorts of figures for the cost per load of laundering diapers are bandied about—depending on whether the figure is cited by a disposables proponent, a cloth proponent or a diaper service proponent. However, even manufacturers of cloth diapers acknowledge it might cost up to $500 over thirty months of diapering for the initial purchases *plus care.* So it's important to factor in the hidden costs. Nonetheless, the very rough estimate of $500 for the cost of diapering your baby in cloth must be compared to the rough $1,000 to $1,300 estimate for diapering your baby in quality disposables over the same two and a half years. It's up to you to decide between cost and convenience.

The Diaper Service Alternative

A diaper service is the in-between option. It's more convenient than doing your own—no lugging wet diapers to the washer, no double rinsing, drying, folding and putting away. You still have the diaper pail, but you don't have the disposal problems of disposables. The dirty diapers are picked up and clean diapers are delivered to your door. Service diapers are softer than disposables, and are *sterilized,* so that diaper service babies tend to have less diaper rash.

A diaper service is usually less expensive than disposables. They cost about $8 to $10 per week, depending on the number of diapers used. A service can be particularly good in the first few months, when new parents are especially tired and frazzled and the baby may be going through 100 diapers a week. But many parents find a diaper service a good value at other times, too. A Maine mother wrote, "A diaper service is cheaper than plastic diapers and more ecological. The former is especially evident when you compare the cost of plastic diapers for *older* babies. These are significantly more expensive than for newborns." And from a Los Angeles couple: "A diaper service really makes money sense. Shop around for the best in your area. They are offering great service in response to competition with disposables. Some provide liners. No washing or rinsing. Unless one is watching every penny, even *with* a washer-dryer, the service is not much more money and saves *time*. Also, if one tries to conserve the number of diapers used, as with disposables because of their expense, one may compromise the infant's skin by changing less often."

If you're interested, give a diaper service a call and ask about prices, delivery times, whether liners are provided, and what's required of you. (If they don't provide liners, you should buy them to save yourself the toilet rinsing stage.) Arrange for the service before the baby is born and make sure someone telephones to "activate" it before you leave the hospital. Possible problems: because disposables rule the market, in most areas there are fewer services than there used to be, so it may not be so easy to locate one; also, some services require you to take a set minimum number of diapers a week. If your baby needs less frequent changes, you might not go through the minimum, and a service would be wasteful.

Other Diapering Equipment and Products

No matter which diapering method you rely on, there are a few pieces of diapering equipment and products you'll probably need. For example, you'll want a changing table in place when you come home from the hospital. Choose a table with sturdy guard rails, a restraining belt that's easy to use, easy-to-reach storage and overall sturdiness.

There are many models to choose from, in a price range from $40 to $500 or more. Most, however, are in the $75 to $300 range. You can buy changing tables in wood that look just like a chest of drawers with a pad and rail on top, open wooden models with shelves rather than drawers, wicker or wickerlike ones with clothes or diaper bins, ones with removable bath tubs in the top compartment and models that fold for storage. As you'd expect, the wooden chest of drawers models are the most expensive. Child Craft makes several handsome styles that coordinate with their cribs and bureaus, in the $170 to $300 price range. Century Products makes less expensive "dresserettes," as they call them. They are the wickerlike-vinyl kind, with staggered bins rather than drawers or open shelves. They range in price from over $50 to $90 or more. Sears sells changing tables from about $40 to $80. An inexpensive alternative is to cover a regular bureau with a vinyl-topped pad with a safety strap. However, with no guard rail, you'll have to be *especially* attentive. *Never* leave the baby unattended, even for a second, on a changing table! Other options: just plunk a vinyl changing pad on a bed, or make a changing area in a baby closet by constructing a waist-high, wall-to-wall shelf. Cover it with a vinyl pad, a safety strap and preferably a guard rail.

Another product you'll want is a *diaper bag.* It should have its own changing pad, and lots of pockets and zippers for stuffing baby items into. The interior should be wipable and the whole bag machine-washable. There are Snugli, Gerry and Sandbox diaper bags, among many others ranging in price from $10 to $50. Or, you can get a $7 diaper bag at Toys-R-Us and a separate rubberized flannel pad for changing for a few dollars.

Baby wipes are important at changing time and you'll go through a quantity of them over the course of diapering. Available at supermarkets and pharmacies, there are many brands to choose from. Some brands, however, have alcohol, which can dry out baby's skin, so read the labels. Unit pricing will show that buying the large size saves money. Desitin's Dabaways are without alcohol, are flushable and seem to be among the least expensive—seventy for about $1.30. Even if you use only one per diaper change, you'll see that wipes will be in your shopping cart every week. So clip coupons for them from *American Baby,* other magazines and newspapers. A less expensive alternative which some hospitals recommend—reusable Handi Wipes, cut to size, and water.

About baby powders, lotions and oils. Manufacturers won't like me for this, but I'm far from alone in saying that these are by and large unnecessary—and they're expensive. Instead of talcum powder (which has an ingredient that can actually *irritate* baby's skin), buy much cheaper cornstarch. You don't even need to buy special cornstarch baby powder—just plain cornstarch will do. However, if your baby develops diaper rash, there's an ointment called Desitin that most mother's describe as a "must." It's fast, effective and the ointment most frequently recommended by pediatricians. An economy-size jar costs about $5 for a pound. Petroleum jelly is a cheaper alternative when there's no rash, and it gives protection against wetness.

Whichever diapering method you choose, it's clear that you're making a real investment in your baby's comfort, and in your time and money—anybody for toilet training?!

❖ 10

FEEDING YOUR BABY

One of the early and most important decisions you'll make is how to nourish your newborn. Will it be breast or bottle? Later when you introduce solid foods, will you make your own or rely on commercial products? And what's needed in the way of feeding equipment and furniture?

BREASTFEEDING

Advantages

Years ago, of course, nearly all mothers breastfed their babies. However, with the development of infant formula and aggressive marketing efforts by its manufacturers, middle-class American women in the postwar years abandoned the breast in favor of the bottle. But today, similar women are leading the rush back to the breast. According to a report in the medical journal *Pediatrics*, the incidence of breastfeeding has more than *doubled* in the United States in the last decade—to more than 55 percent of mothers. Women are not only breastfeeding *again*, but they're breastfeeding *longer*. In the early 1970s, only 5.5 percent were still nursing after six months. Today, that figure has increased fivefold. This change results from the fact that the many benefits of breastfeeding for both baby and mother have become increasingly well understood by health professionals and mothers alike.

The most important of these benefits: breast milk is better suited to providing nutrients and calories to a growing baby than any available alternative. The American Academy of Pediatricians has summed it up: "The best food for every newborn infant is breast milk."

Other advantages: *faster maternal weight loss.* Studies show that generally women who breastfeed lose most of their stored pregnancy fat faster and get back to their normal weight sooner than women who do not nurse.

Breastfeeding may also protect a child from obesity in adolescence and later life. This is thought to be because the fat content of breast milk is greater toward the end of the feeding, making it more filling. This signals the baby to stop nursing, preventing overeating. Babies who consume more calories than necessary for normal growth and development will develop an excessive number of fat cells. The problem is that once one has fat cells, one *always* has them—they can be shrunk, but not eliminated from the system. Hence, breastfeeding, which discourages overeating naturally, can play a role in preventing later obesity.

While breast milk has higher levels of *cholesterol* than formula or cow's milk, interestingly, nutritionists regard this as good. They believe high cholesterol intake in very early life triggers the enzymatic system to better metabolize cholesterol throughout life, so that breastfed babies may have lower cholesterol levels as adults. The body seems to work in reverse with regard to sodium, however. Breast milk is quite low in *sodium*, which is good, as high salt intake even in infancy may be related to hypertension—high blood pressure—in later life.

Another key benefit of breast milk is that it's full of *antibodies* and *immunologic factors* that are transferred to and protect the newborn from many different kinds of infections, harmful bacteria and disease. This is important, because during the first weeks of life, the baby is most vulnerable to infection, and cannot manufacture his or her own immunoglobulins until about three months. Moreover, breast milk contains living white cells called macrophages, which kill harmful bacteria and viruses in the stomach and intestines. Breast milk is also more easily digested than formula or cow's milk. The protein in breast milk, unlike that in cow's milk, will not form large curds in the baby's stomach, which can cause stomach distress and spitting up. So the breastfed baby spits up less than the bottle-fed one. Moreover, breastfed babies are rarely constipated. Because breast milk is so easily digested, the baby feeds more frequently and has a loose, watery bowel movement with each feeding. Breastfed babies also develop diaper rash less often than do bottle-fed babies.

It's small surprise, then, that scientific studies show breastfed babies have a significantly lower incidence of both serious illnesses and common disorders, such as skin rashes; colic; gastrointestinal, respiratory and ear infections; severe diarrhea and vomiting. Indeed, one study indicated that *hospital admissions and total illness incidents were three times more likely for bottle-fed versus breastfed babies.* Further studies show a positive correlation between the *length* of time a baby is breastfed and good health.

Finally, many couples find breastfeeding simpler and more convenient than its alternative. Assuming the nursing mother is in good health and eating a well-balanced diet, the baby's food supply is always ready when the baby is, and it's clean, fresh, and at the right temperature. There's no formula to fetch, no bottles to fill and warm and later scrub and sterilize, and no trips to the kitchen in the middle of the night. Instead, when baby is hungry, you settle yourself in a comfortable chair and, once having mastered the technique, enjoy a quiet half hour or so with your child.

This brings me to the important point of mother-baby bonding and attachment which breastfeeding so naturally promotes. To nurse you obviously must hold your baby; you can also make eye contact, talk and fondle the infant in the process. As you hold the baby at your breast, the distance between your faces is precisely the distance over which a newborn can focus best, and babies love to look at human faces and eyes. Breastfeeding has a soothing, calming effect on most babies. They feel secure and content during nursing, so it's no surprise that many mothers find the experience enormously satisfying.

Is Breastfeeding "for Free"?

No, not quite, but it *is* highly economical compared with formula feeding. Indeed, many women consider the cost advantages of nursing third only to the health benefits to baby and psychological satisfaction, as the foremost motivations for breastfeeding.

What are the costs associated with breastfeeding? First, you must maintain a high-quality, protein-rich, well-balanced diet during lactation, and consume about 500 extra calories a day above and beyond your normal intake. If you ordinarily eat well, your diet need not change much— just add some protein and healthful carbohydrates, drink extra (but not excessive) healthful liquids—and you may not even notice an addition to your food expenditures. You should also continue to take *vitamin, calcium and iron supplements* at least until weaning. These will cost $12 to $15 per 100-pill bottle—about a three-month supply. In addition, many pediatricians will recommend nutritional supplements for nursing *babies,* as they think that breast milk is possibly deficient in vitamins D and K and possibly in iron, calcium, phosphorus and fluoride. If your pediatrician recommends them, expect to pay about $5 for a three-month supply.

Other costs incurred by many breastfeeding women are for certain nursing paraphernalia. *Nursing bras,* for example. Although some women find ordinary stretch bras, lifted up for nursing, to be fine, most women buy special nursing bras with pull-down flaps. Choose a comfortable one easily unclasped with one hand. There are also soft, Velcro-fastened nursing bras, nothing to unclasp. Sears, Montgomery Ward and J. C. Penney sell nursing bras from about $5 to $15. Three should do.

Many women also purchase *nursing pads or shields* to tuck into the bra to absorb milk leakage between feedings. These pads protect your outer clothing and so save on laundry bills. They also protect the nipple and areola from any residue of detergent which may be on the bra and can irritate the sensitive breast. Evenflo and Johnson & Johnson make good pads, and Sears sells a box of forty-eight for $5. Cheaper ways yet to deal with milk leakage—cut a disposable diaper or a minipad to the right size, or fold a men's cotton handkerchief and tuck it into your nursing bra.

For women who want to "express" milk, store and refrigerate it for later use, or who simply need to express milk because they've become engorged, a *breast pump* is the answer. One friend pointed out, "You can't know ahead of time if you'll need a breast pump for engorgement, but when you *do* need it, you need it right away. You can't wait. I was in such discomfort, I sent my husband out in the middle of the night, looking for all-night pharmacies to find one. Much smarter to plan ahead and have one on hand." All women who are planning to breastfeed should consider that advice. While some women find the idea of a breast pump unappealing, if you need it, you need it. Even if you never experience engorgement, as a nursing mother you'll find a new definition of security in having several bottles of breast milk in the freezer! And for women who remain committed to continued breastfeeding after returning to work, a breast pump is a virtual must.

Essentially a breast pump consists of a suction cup or cone placed over the nipple and areola and attached to a sterile container, and a pump activated by a small motor or by hand. The suction cup should be comfortable—no sharp rim; the collection bottle should convert to a feeding bottle, by adding a standard nipple; the whole thing should be sterilizable.

Breast pumps come in a range of prices. *Don't buy the cheapest.* They can be had for as little as $3, but these are ineffective and don't hold up. Recommended hand breast pumps include the Loyd-B-Pump, with a ninety-day warranty at about $35, and the Kaneson hand pump, available in maternity stores and good pharmacies for about $20. Sears sells a hand pump for $15.

Some women prefer *electric* breast pumps for their

greater efficiency. You nearly always *rent* rather than buy these. Check with your nearest good pharmacy to see if they make such rentals. You may have to check several pharmacies, as electric pumps are popular items and are often all already out on rental. Expect to pay $1 to $2 a day—yes, they are expensive for a woman who plans to nurse for several months. If you are having trouble finding a rental, one brand, Medela, has a toll-free number (800-435-8316) to call and learn of your nearest rental station.

(Before you purchase or rent any breast pump, however, you might check with your local chapter of La Leche League—"leche" is pronounced "lay chay," the Spanish word for milk—to see if they can *lend* you one. This is a national organization devoted to the active promotion of breastfeeding. Check in your phone book—there's a league chapter in most cities—or call the league's national number in Illinois, 312-455-7730. The league is an excellent source of information on all aspects of breastfeeding.)

The least expensive way to extract your milk is, of course, to *hand express* it, but it's more time-consuming and less efficient.

Nursing nightgowns are another purchase made by many breastfeeding mothers. These nightgowns have a pleat- or fold-concealed front opening on either side for nursing. Good buys can be had at Mothercare stores for $10 to $15, Sears for somewhat more. Another possible purchase— *breast cream* to help prevent, or if it's too late, to soothe dry, cracked or sore nipples. If you develop these, the best thing to do is go braless for part of the day and let your breasts air dry after nursing. If you want to use a cream, use only Vitamin A or D cream, or (better and cheaper) pure lanolin, available in pharmacies for a few dollars.

About the advantages of breastfeeding, a friend and mother of four of Southington, Connecticut, wrote: "Nursing a baby can save a lot of money; not only can you save the obvious (and considerable!) cost of formula and paraphernalia, but the 'hidden' savings include: the cost of visits to the doctor for formula intolerance (allergies, constipation) and many common infections; the cost of parents' and infant's clothing ruined by baby's spitting up of formula (breast milk doesn't stain); the cost of babysitters, since the breastfed baby is so portable; possible future savings in dentist bills (putting baby to bed with a bottle of formula can really rot teeth); the cost of baby food (babies can be totally breastfed for six months before advancing to 'people' food). The costs include: a normal, balanced diet for the mother; continued use of prenatal capsules while nursing; a few nursing bras and nursing pads; an imported beer now and then (which stimulates milk production and adds nutrients to the milk); perhaps a book on nursing or at least a few phone calls to a friend. I also joined La Leche League, with optional dues of $12 at that time."

Disadvantages

Clearly, breastfeeding gets high marks from the increasing numbers of women who choose to do it. However, it's not for everyone. There are certain possible drawbacks. For example, some mothers feel breastfeeding is *too time-consuming* compared to bottle feeding, even after you factor in the time required to shop for formula, heat bottles, then sterilize and put them away. Because breast milk is so easily digested, babies tend to feed more frequently. In fact, some women report their babies want to nurse as often as every two or two and a half hours— despite what their pediatricians tell them in advance! A woman whose baby is feeding six to nine times a day in the early months can be forgiven for feeling that all she does all day and night is nurse.

Another drawback of nursing is that the *mother's freedom of movement is curtailed.* The short time between feedings makes it difficult for the mother to be away from the baby—to get out of the house alone whether to do errands, or to pamper herself in some way. A nursing mother and baby are pretty tightly tied, unless the mother has a good stock of frozen breast milk. But it takes time to pump breast milk, too! Moreover, a woman breastfeeding her baby can't turn the midnight (or other) feeding over to her husband, as can be done with bottle feeding. She's always the one on-call, because she's the food source.

This brings us to the point that *breastfeeding and working outside the home is difficult.* It's certainly possible—many mothers have done it successfully—but let's face it, it usually isn't easy. You may have to pump once or more during the day to prevent engorgement. Even if you're lucky, and you and baby can get together for a midday feeding, the running around it may entail makes for a hectic day. The point is, you may feel that even at work, a good part of your life still revolves around nursing requirements. Then again, it's only temporary and the difficulty depends in part on how soon you go back to work. A three-month-old feeds less frequently than a four-week-old. If you can take three or more months off, the baby will have more of a feeding routine and will "demand" fewer nursing sessions. If you're going to continue to nurse your baby after returning to work, women who've done it successfully suggest you accept the fact of a midday supplemental formula bottle.

Breastfeeding also becomes problematic if a new mother must be on *medication.* Almost any medication a nursing mother takes passes into her breast milk. Although many medications have been proven safe for use during nursing, the most conservative advice is to avoid all medications during this time, unless one is absolutely necessary according to your physician. A nursing mother should never self-medicate—even with over-the-counter items like aspirin, laxatives, or nasal decongestants! If your doctor tells you that a certain medication *is* safe during lactation, you should still try to take it just *after* a nursing session, so that it will be fully metabolized by your system prior to the next feeding.

Another drawback is that *breast and nipple complications sometimes arise from breastfeeding.* Between 2 and 5 percent of nursing mothers develop a painful infection called *mastitis,* which requires one or more doctor's visits and is usually treated with an antibiotic.

Some women, through no fault of their own, do not produce sufficient milk to satisfy their babies. These women may try formula supplements, or may find it easier and more satisfying to their babies to switch to bottle feeding entirely.

A final problem is that *some women are simply "put off" by the idea of breastfeeding.* Some say it makes them feel like a "cow" or "old-fashioned." They may find it messy and embarrassing. Some find it slightly painful, at least in the early days. For whatever reason, if a woman continues to be "put off" by nursing after reading about it, talking to breastfeeding mothers and perhaps (preferably) trying it, it may well be best to forgo it. Many experts feel that a positive maternal attitude is essential to successful breastfeeding, so it may even be that the woman who finds it distasteful proves *unable* to nurse. In any case, if it makes you tense or unhappy, don't do it. Feeding your baby should be a happy, warm, loving experience—by all means go by the bottle versus the breast if you have substantial reasons for preferring not to nurse.

BOTTLE FEEDING

Advantages and Disadvantages

By and large, the advantages of bottle feeding are the flip side of the perceived drawbacks of breastfeeding. For example, bottle feeding can be less time-consuming. This is especially true if you use ready-to-eat formula and disposable nurser kits, thus eliminating time required to mix formula and sterilize bottles. Most babies will drink a bottle in about ten minutes. Moreover, bottle-fed babies tend to go longer between feedings. Related to this, the mother has more freedom of movement and feeding the baby can be a shared responsibility among family members or other caregivers. The woman who plans to continue to work outside the home after her baby is born may be able to do so more quickly and easily if baby is bottle-fed.

And, of course, bottle feeding can be just as gratifying an experience as breastfeeding for all concerned, as long as the mother understands the many needs of the baby that should be satisfied by the feeding session. The baby should always be held (semiupright) and cuddled during feeding, eye contact should be made, and "sides" switched (it helps develop eye coordination and focus). A baby needs more sucking when bottle feeding, so a pacifier should be considered.

The key drawbacks of bottle feeding include the loss of the benefits of breastfeeding, described earlier. Other drawbacks: *Bottle-feeding equipment must be properly handled and maintained.* Time-consuming! Nondisposable nursers must be thoroughly scrubbed, then sterilized before each use. The problem with all of this scrubbing and sterilizing is the seemingly endless repetition of it.

Possible health-related drawbacks of bottle feeding include "nursing bottle syndrome" or *"baby bottle mouth,"* a serious condition of tooth decay which can result when certain rules about bottle feeding are not practiced. "Baby bottle mouth" is caused by acid and bacteria buildup on the teeth when the baby is given a bottle of formula or fruit juice at bed or nap time. When the baby is awake and eating, the saliva washes the sugar and acid away, but if the baby falls asleep with a bottle, the formula or juice pools around the teeth, setting up a perfect medium for decay. To avoid this, the American Dental Association recommends babies be given only a water bottle at bedtime, or that a pacifier be used.

Evidence also suggests that babies allowed to bottle-feed lying on their backs may suffer increased incidence of *inner-ear infections,* caused by the dripping of milk into the inner ear canal. Once again, correct bottle-feeding technique—baby held semiupright—can avoid this.

Cost of Formula Feeding by the Bottle

This is one of the biggest drawbacks. There are several pieces of equipment you'll need, and formula itself is costly. Although there *are* ways to cut costs here, they entail considerable loss of convenience.

Starting with the *bottles,* there are the traditional non-disposable and the newer disposable systems. In nondisposables, the rigid clear plastic version is probably best—

unbreakable, easily cleaned. *You'll need at least eight bottles, with extra nipples, snap-on caps or hoods, filter funnel, and nipple and bottle brush.* Buy them all together in convenient nurser sets. Sears Super Nurser is a good buy at about $16 for six 8-ounce and two 6-ounce boilable plastic bottles, twelve quality Nuk orthodontic nipples, eight plastic hoods and collars, plastic filter funnel, and bottle/nipple brushes. (These items separately would cost up to $25.) Gerber and Evenflo also make good nursers.

Nipples are the most important part of the nurser, and finding the right one for your baby may come down to trial and error. (Small babies usually prefer shorter nipples and older babies, longer ones.) You'll hear a lot about Nuk and other orthodontic nipples, which are designed to conform with the baby's palate, to encourage nasal breathing and closed lips. They also make the baby's tongue move more as it would in breastfeeding and require harder sucking action. Some babies take to these orthodontic nipples, but others do not, so you might try one before buying a full set. The Nuk nipple will fit all standard bottles. A package of two costs about $1.60. Standard nipples are cheaper.

The disadvantage of these traditional nurser sets is, of course, that they must be scrubbed using *nipple/bottle brushes* (up to $2 a pair) and then sterilized. Today most sets are adequately sterilized by a hot-water cycle in your dishwasher. However, if you don't have a dishwasher, or if your pediatrician says that dishwasher sterilization isn't enough, you have two choices. One is a *stove-top sterilizer.* If you have a big enough pot with a cover, you can use that. Or you can buy a stove-top sterilizer that holds eight bottles. Look for one with a lift-out rack. Sears' model costs about $10. Alternatively, there's the *electric sterilizer.* Choose one that's "thermostatically controlled" (which means it has an automatic cut-off system to prevent accidental overheating) and has at least a one-year warranty. Sears sells one for about $22.

Disposable nursing systems eliminate much of the scrubbing and sterilizing and so are increasingly popular. While they are more convenient than traditional screw-top bottles, the convenience is costly.

Disposable nursers consist of a plastic bottlelike holder supporting an inner plastic sac, and of course a nipple. Only the inner sac is in fact disposable. The bottlelike support frame and nipples are reusable, and so they *do* have to be thoroughly washed. The inner sacs are presterilized, so your baby gets a fresh, sanitary "bottle" every time. A disposable nurser which comes with six 8-ounce holders, six nipples and plastic caps, and forty inner sacs, costs about $10. The forty disposable sacs, however, may last only a week for a "frequent feeder." Refills in boxes of eighty cost about $2.25, which means they could amount to more than $50 in the baby's first year. Moreover, the holders and especially the nipples may need periodic replacement. Look for coupons and refund certificates for disposable nursers and refill sacs in your baby magazines.

You can see that the cost of this equipment can add up—and I'm just getting to what you actually *feed* baby!

As for that, the emphatic answer is *baby formula, not cow's milk!* The American Academy of Pediatricians has plainly stated that the best alternative to breast milk during the first year is infant formula. Cow's milk can stress the baby's immature digestive system. It contains too much protein for the developing kidneys, and a kind of protein that's difficult for an infant to digest. It also contains too little fat and too much salt and is low in vitamins C and E, copper and iron. And it's by far the food that most often causes an allergic reaction in babies. All in all, cow's milk does *not* meet the special nutritional needs of a baby.

Formula, in contrast, has been developed to be as similar to breast milk as possible. Most formulas are derived from cow's milk, but their caloric distribution and nutrients are altered by processing to simulate breast milk. In addition to *milk-derived* formula, there is *soy-derived* for the milk-sensitive baby; and even a *meat-base formula* (MBF). The soy and MBF formulas require nutritional supplementation, so should not be given without a doctor's instruction. All formulas are available either *nonfortified* or *iron-fortified*. Finally, there's the "form" the formulas come in—*pow-*

dered, concentrated liquid and *ready-to-eat liquid!* How to choose?

Your pediatrician is your best adviser. If you and the doctor have no reason to suppose your baby is milk-sensitive, start off with a milk-derived formula. If baby spits up excessively and doesn't seem to be thriving, the pediatrician will suggest switching to one of the hypoallergenic formulas. Doctors have different opinions about whether an iron-fortified formula is necessary from day one.

As to which "form" of formula to use, it's more your choice than the pediatrician's and depends on your preferred trade-off between cost and convenience. *Prepare yourself for the cost of formula!* Ready-to-feed formula in disposable bottles is obviously the most convenient and the most expensive. Plan on the baby eating about 32 ounces per day, although this naturally varies. Older babies will eat more.

Ready-to-feed formula comes in various size cans—like most supermarket items, the bigger sizes are cheaper on a *unit basis*. Similac and Enfamil ready-to-feed in a 32-ounce (one-quart) can cost up to $2. Shop around for the store with the best formula prices. The difference can be up to 30 cents a quart. To use this preprepared formula, pour about 8 ounces into a sterilized nurser, warm to body temperature and feed. The opened can goes in the refrigerator and must be used within forty-eight hours.

An equivalent amount of iron-fortified milk-based *powder* costs 10 cents to 30 cents less than ready-to-feed. To prepare powdered formula, boil water for five minutes, cool, add 7 ounces to the sterilized bottle, mix in a package of the powder, put on the sterile nipple and feed. You can prepare several sterilized bottles of boiled water ahead of time and add powder just before using each one.

Concentrated liquid formula is usually somewhat less than powdered formula. To prepare it, you add equal amounts of water to the concentrate. Again, sterilization of all equipment is recommended unless your pediatrician says it's unnecessary. Boil the water, too, for five minutes.

Measure out 4 ounces, add the water, cap the bottle, shake and feed. Cover the opened can, refrigerate, and use within forty-eight hours.

This detail about preparation is given so you can better consider how much you're willing to do to save formula money: Converted to approximate weekly and monthly totals, based on consumption of 32 ounces per day, ready-to-feed formula will cost about $14 to $15 per week; powder about $12 to $13 a week; and concentrated liquid about $11 to $12. In other words, plan very roughly on almost $2 a day for formula. Of course, when your baby is a few months older, it will cost more. Several women told me they spend $16 to $18 per week on formula for their four-to-six-month-old babies.

It's clear then, that if you've made the *basic* decision to bottle-feed your baby, your decisions are just beginning! Essentially, however, it comes down to your preferred trade-off between cost and convenience. You have to look at this trade-off, moreover, in an *overall* context. For example, maybe you're willing to use nondisposable nursers and prepare formula from concentrated liquid to save money—but are not willing to use cloth diapers to do so. Fine! You can think of it as putting money saved in the former toward the latter.

Here's what some mothers say about bottle feeding. From St. Louis, Missouri: "Formula feeding *is* expensive. I've bought a dozen bottles, extra nipples and caps, an electric sterilizer and an unbelievable quantity of formula. But for us it was the only practical choice, as I returned to work six weeks after our daughter was born. To save money, I buy concentrated formula by the case." Waukegan, Illinois, parents of a one-year-old: "We definitely feel the *convenience* of ready-to-feed formula and disposable Playtex bottles is worth the extra money!" But an Oakland, California, couple disagreed: "Our pediatrician says dishwasher sterilization is fine, so I think disposable nursing bottles are a waste of money. They really don't save so much time anyway. You have to put the sacs in the holder, fill them, remove and discard them, wash the holder and nipple. Clear plastic bottles with formula made from concentrated liquid are just about as easy, and much cheaper."

INTRODUCING SOLID FOODS

Most pediatricians today advise that a baby be fed *exclusively* breast milk or formula for the first four to six months. Then, the gradual, paced introduction of solid foods should begin. While your baby will continue to get many of the necessary calories from breast milk or formula, these will be supplemented by calories and nutrients received from the first solid food—iron-fortified cereal. After it is clear that the baby tolerates cereal well, you can introduce pureed fruits, then a month or so later, vegetables, and by the seventh and eighth months, pureed meats. By ten months, your baby can eat most table foods—properly prepared, of course.

Why Make Your Own Baby Food?

Many parents in recent years have decided it's worth the extra effort to make baby food at home, rather than rely on commercial preparations. There are two basic reasons.

First, *you have greater knowledge of and control over what goes into the food.* You can see to it that the food has no added salt or sugar, chemical additives or modified food starches (used to make a watery preparation more solid)— all virtually "empty" calories in terms of nutrition, and which may cause or contribute to later health problems like obesity and hypertension. While baby food manufacturers in recent years have eliminated additives like MSG, sodium nitrite and BHT, and have lowered or removed salt and, in some instances, sugar from many kinds of baby food, much of this food is still less nutritious than its freshly prepared counterpart because the high-heat processing used to make it destroys many nutrients. Thus to better assure freshness and quality calories, many parents are preparing baby food at home.

A second reason for doing so is comparative cost. Commercially prepared baby food is generally two to three or more times expensive than home-prepared baby food. On some items, the difference is greater. Once again, of course, it's the trade-off between cost and convenience. It *is* easier to just open a jar. And, if you're an educated consumer, you *can* select baby foods without added sugar, salt, starches and excess water.

But is making your own baby food really so difficult? The answer is no. You probably already have most of the kitchen equipment you need. Key items are a steamer (because many vitamins and minerals are water-soluble, steaming best preserves nutrients) and an electric blender, food processor or grinder. To save time and money, make baby's food out of the same food you're preparing for yourselves. Extra attention to cleanliness in food handling and equipment is important in making baby food, as is food freshness. Chop the food, steam it or bake it in aluminum foil, then cool and puree. Make extra quantities to freeze in labeled serving-size portions—about the size of an ice cube (3 tablespoons or 1½ ounces). Then, when it's nearing time for baby to eat, pull a balanced meal out of the freezer, thaw to room temperature (baby food doesn't *have* to be heated—that's an adult preference) and feed.

Becoming an Educated Buyer of Commercial Baby Food

If you're willing to pay the added cost for the convenience of commercially prepared baby food, there's little need to worry that baby is getting second best—as long as you're an educated buyer. That means being a *label reader*.

Many stores stock only two brands of baby food because it takes up so much shelf space. Usually those are Gerber (with 70 percent of the market), and Beechnut or Heinz. While all baby food makers have removed *much* of the salt, sugar and preservatives they used to add, *Beechnut brand* has removed *all* added sugar, salt, preservatives, artificial flavor and color enhancers. (Beechnut also has a toll-free hotline—800-523-6633—which you can ring with any questions about infant nutrition.) Along with sugar, salt and preservatives, look out for food starches like cornstarch, rice starch or tapioca (which some Beechnut foods *do* have). These starches are used to thicken a preparation, which tells you that water is a main (perhaps even the largest) component of the food. Why pay for a too watery preparation that has to be thickened with an agent that is almost 100 percent carbohydrate, with no "redeeming" nutrients? Modified food starch doesn't even have usable calories (so that saliva won't start digesting the starch in an opened jar).

The best advice is to *generally avoid any baby food that has added sugar, including corn syrup or dextrose, salt, preservatives, flavor or color enhancers, hydrogenated oils and food starches, including tapioca, cornstarch or rice starch.* Of course, an occasional dish containing sugar or tapioca will not hurt the baby—it's just not a good idea in terms of nutrition and calories to be fed such things regularly.

By law, *all* ingredients in the food must be listed on baby food labels. What's more, *the ingredients must be listed in order of relative quantities in the food.* In other words, if the food contains more water than anything else, water is listed first. *Knowing what you don't want to see on a baby food label, and knowing the ingredient order rule, you can make nutritionally wise selections of commercial baby food.* For example, I picked up a fruit dessert (fruit is healthful, right?) in the supermarket the other day. It looked delicious—and then I read the label: "Water, fruit from concentrate, sugar, modified cornstarch, tapioca." Hardly a good buy, in terms of either nutrition or calories. Expensive, but virtually empty calories.

Some foods are labeled "enriched"—which means niacin, riboflavin, thiamine and/or iron have been added, sometimes to replace vitamins and minerals lost in processing. You'll also see "fortified" foods. This means nutrients have been added that are not normally present in the food. Foods labeled "natural" or "organic" are usually more expensive and you should know that manufacturers often use the terms in ways most of us would call "loosely"—perhaps even misleadingly. So don't necessarily believe "natural" when you see it blazoned across, say, a fruit drink. I found a fruit juice labeled "natural" that did indeed have some natural fruit flavor in it—but also had several additives and sugar.

Also read the labels to buy food of the right consistency for your baby: the finest strained consistency for four- to six-month-olds; more textured foods for babies who have begun teething; chunky foods for toddlers who have started to self-feed. Finally, check expiration dates on the label.

Jar sizes and costs are consistent across brands. There are small jars of 3½ ounces of meat products, and 4½ ounces of fruits, vegetables, cereals and desserts. Larger jars of the latter foods are 7½ ounces. In 1985 the smaller jars usually cost just under 60 cents, 30 cents, and 40 cents, respectively in large cities. (Heinz is usually a little cheaper.) At these prices, it's not hard to spend $2 or even $3 a day on commercial baby food. To cut costs, look for coupons in magazines and newspapers—they're in every issue—and for in-store promotions. Use unit pricing to compare costs of various size containers of fruit juices and cereals. And don't feed your baby right out of the jar. Because if you do, you should discard what's left because it's subject to rapid spoilage once saliva has touched it—not very economical.

FEEDING EQUIPMENT

A *baby spoon* should have a small, shallow bowl that's easily emptied by your baby. A small plastic picnic spoon is all right; so is a small relish or demitasse spoon. The baby's *bowl* should have steep sides for scooping and a suction base to resist tipping, and should be unbreakable and dishwasher safe. Tommee Tippee makes such a bowl, available at Sears, $2. Bowls with two or three compartments go for $6 and up. A *baby cup* should be unbreakable and

dishwasher safe and have a weighted bottom to help keep
it upright. Some training cups have removable, tightly
fitting lids, and a raised lip for sucking liquids out. Others
have no lids, but do have a curved lip and two handles for
easy grip and cost between $1 and $2.50.

Warming dishes—either hot water or electric. The hot-
water version should have firmly lockable spout caps, so
the baby can't pull them off and ingest them, or get burned
from spilling hot water. Electric models should have a
temperature regulator to prevent overheating. Both versions
should have two or three compartments, and a suction
base. It's good if one compartment is unheated. They
should be break-resistant, immersible and preferably dishwasher safe. You can buy a hot-water warming dish for $4
at Sears or from Kiddie Products. Electric warming dishes
are more—good ones by Evenflo are $10 to $14. Warming
dishes are useful because you get the warmer and feeding
dish in one—so there's nothing extra to wash. Remember,
however, that there's no medical or nutritional reason for
heating the baby's food. Moreover, food should not sit
around in a warming dish, because it provides the ideal
temperature for bacteria growth.

Bibs—check out the wipable plastic, snap-on kind with
a bottom "pouch" or pocket to catch spilled food; cloth
bibs have to be laundered. Tommee Tippee and Mothercare
make good plastic bibs; with cloth bibs, you need at least
a half dozen. These can cost as little as $5 for six, or as
much as $7.50 or more apiece, depending on how fancy
you want to be. Cloth bibs can be used to wipe up after
the baby at the end of a meal.

Infant seats, also called infant carriers or rockers, have
many uses, but they can be especially helpful in the early
days of solid foods if your baby isn't yet sitting upright
unassisted. These seats are adjustable to several positions;
the nearly erect position is good for babies with digestive
problems, frequent vomiting and nasal congestion. Infant
seats can be had for $20 to $30. See Chapter 11 for more
detailed information.

High chairs are for the baby who can sit up on his own

for feeding. Choose a high chair carefully, as it's a potentially dangerous piece of equipment—the U.S. Product Safety Commission estimates there are as many as 7,000 high-chair-related accidents a year.

To address this safety concern, the Juvenile Product Manufacturers Association in 1976 accepted a set of standards for high chair safety developed by the American Society for Testing and Materials. A chair meeting these standards carries a certification label stating that it is an "Approved High Chair," in "compliance to A.S.T.M. F-404 Safety Standards." Understand that these standards are *voluntary*—a chair need not meet them to be legally on the market. Hence, it's up to you to look for the special seal. Even if you find the seal, check the chair—the seal shouldn't give you total, uncritical assurance. Look for:

- A chair wider at the legs/base than the seat for stability. Legs should have *at least* one cross brace for the same purpose. A collapse-prevention lock. Avoid chairs on roll-around casters—they tip over.
- A tray that locks firmly in place, but also one that is easily removed.
- No sharp edges, scissor joints or pinching latches.
- A sturdy restraining system, with both crotch and waist belts, attached to the chair, not the tray.

In addition to these safety features, look for a large, plastic tray with a wraparound lip to catch spillage. The tray should be removable, break-resistant, wipable, immersible and preferably dishwasher safe (although it would take a lot of room in a dishwasher). The upholstery should be easy to clean—vinyl is a good choice. The footrest should be adjustable to accommodate a six-month-old as well as a two-year-old. A chair that folds compactly is nice, especially if space is at a premium for you.

The Classic High Chair by Strolee is an excellent model, selling for about $45 to $60. Cosco's top-of-the-line Folding High Chair is a good one, at about $50 to $55. So is the Hedstrom Folding High Chair, which sells for a little less.

At about $95, the Brevi high chair (which was designed by a pediatrician) is excellent. Sears sell high chairs in the $30 to $50 range, but the less expensive ones lack certain features like cross braces. A word about wooden high chairs—handsome, but often expensive and lacking adequate restraining belts.

A newly popular item is the *feeding chair*, which hooks on to a table. They're small, portable, easy to store, and inexpensive. This makes them great for small apartments, travel, restaurants and visits to grandparents. Another plus is that you have baby right with you at the table. Hook-on seats are for infants that can sit up on their own—but the good ones will hold toddlers weighing up to 40 pounds, too, so you can enjoy long use from them. Many of them rest on table-top suction cups, and are supported by brackets underneath the table. The chair is actually held in place by the baby's own weight, although at least one brand (Bilt-Rite) has spring-activated arms that automatically lock under the table for added grip. The seat part is made of either plastic or vinyl for easy cleanup, or of machine-washable canvas or nylon. One disadvantage of these feeding seats is that they can be awkward to get a baby in and out of—sometimes they even pull off the table as you pull baby out, so be careful.

There are several brands to choose from. I've seen an ad in *American Baby* for a carry chair for as little as $10, but most brands are in the $20 range.

❖ 11

THE NURSERY

There are so many baby products on the market, it's easy to get overwhelmed. (One father-to-be wailed to me, "Just tell me what to buy!") However, if you learn to distinguish between the necessary and the optional, how to pace your purchases, and the features to look for in each item, your shopping will be simplified. Just remember *not* to rely totally on what you read—or what a salesperson tells you. Insist on setting up, handling and checking any and all products before you buy. Always know the return policy of the store from which you buy (and think twice before buying from a store without a liberal policy). Save all sales slips, and note on them model number and date of purchase.

Decorating the Nursery

Before getting to baby equipment and furniture, what about the nursery itself? Some of us living in small apartments don't have a separate room for the baby, who may share the parents' room or even take over a corner of the living room. If so, a partial room divider allows some privacy and separation of room functions. It could be a large, sturdy bookcase, a folding screen, or even a cloth or bamboo curtain—all relatively inexpensive solutions to making a "room" for baby.

Strictly speaking, decorating (versus equipping) a nursery is not a necessity, although many parents-to-be do want new carpeting, wallpaper or paint, and heavy drapes or blinds for it. To figure your *carpeting* needs, multiply the room's length times width for total square footage. Carpeting is sold by the square yard rather than foot, so divide total square feet by 9 and round up. Carpet comes in a wide range of quality and price ($6 to $35 per square yard), but it is an item you can usually find heavily discounted if you comparison-shop. Some discount stores also run special sales and reduce their already discounted prices further, offering saving up to 60 percent. Prices often *don't* include *installation* and *underpad*, which may run another $7 a square yard. Carpeting has the advantage in a nursery of being a good sound and heat insulator and a "cushion" against a wobbly toddler's spills.

To figure *wallpaper* needs, measure your room, noting window and doorway dimensions. Then call a reputable store and they'll calculate the number of rolls required. Wallpaper, too, comes in a range of quality and price—as little as $3 a roll up to $30, and even much higher for very fine versions. You can definitely find good-quality wallpaper for $9 to $10 a roll, however. (Make it one you can clean with a damp sponge.) Then, decide about installation. I've never done it, but my husband has, and he tells me it isn't difficult. Wallpaper store staff will give you instructions. You may have to pay $8 to $20 or more a roll to someone else for installation, although some paper hangers will give you a flat room rate rather than a per-roll one.

Alternatively, you could paint the room. (And if you live in an older home and don't know when the nursery was last painted, definitely cover the existing paint, on the chance it might be lead-based. Lead ingested by baby from old, peeling paint can cause severe intellectual impairment.) Two gallons and a few hours' effort would finish the room, and cost about $25 to $40. Don't buy the cheapest paint, as it doesn't adhere well, clean or last.

Levolor or similar style *window blinds* can always be found 40 percent discounted off list price—so don't pay full price. For a large window, 3½ by 5 feet, Levolors list for about $100 but can be had for $50 to $60. Drapes are more expensive, unless you make them yourself. Drapes are, however, an excellent light block, and if thermally lined, good against drafts, heat loss and sound. If they help baby sleep longer, drapes can be a good investment for tired new parents.

So, even with middle-priced materials, a typical 10-foot by 12-foot nursery could easily cost $300 to $600 or more for the basics. If you get into structural work—like built-in closets—the nursery will cost substantially more. And that's before you put anything into it! Let's turn, then, to baby equipment, furniture and toys.

Necessary versus Optional Baby Equipment and Furniture Purchases

This breakdown between necessary and optional baby equipment is one that most parents would agree to:

NECESSITIES

Sleeping and storage:
  Crib
  Crib mattress, bumpers and
    bedding
  Chest of drawers

Diapering:
  Dresser/changing table
  Diaper bag

Traveling:
  Car seat
  Stroller
  Infant Carrier

Miscellaneous:
  Camera
  Toilet trainer

Feeding:
  Bottles and paraphernalia
  High chair
  Warmer dish and training
    cup

Health and safety:
  Humidifier or vaporizor
  Smoke detector
  Fire extinguisher
  Cabinet locks or latches
  "Stop shocks"
  Safety caps

Play:
  Simple, safe toys
  Toy chest

OPTIONAL

Sleeping:
Bassinet
Cradle, mattress, bumpers
Portable crib
Crib canopy

Traveling:
Carriage and bedding
Car seat covers
Back pack

Bathing:
Baby bath

Play/exercise:
Walker
Swing
Jumper
Playpen

Health and safety:
Baby scale
Bed guards

Pacing Your Purchases

Here the optional equipment is mixed back in with the necessary, and the focus is on the *pacing* of purchases. There's little point in buying an item way ahead of when baby will use it—unless you find an excellent and not-likely-to-be-repeated sale on the item.

INITIAL EQUIPMENT PURCHASES

Sleeping and storage:
Cradle and accessories
Crib, mattress and
    accessories
Chest of drawers

Traveling:
Car seat and cover
Carriage and accessories
Infant carriers

Diapering:
Dresser changing table
Diaper bag

Feeding:
Bottles and paraphernalia

Bathing:
Baby bath

Health and safety:
Smoke detector
Fire extinguisher
Humidifier/vaporizor
Baby scale

Miscellaneous:
Crib mobile
Camera

SIX- TO TWELVE-MONTH PURCHASES

Sleeping:
  Portable crib

Traveling:
  Stroller
  Back pack

Feeding:
  Warmer dish and training
    cup
  High chair
  Feeding table

Play/exercise:
  Swing
  Jumper
  Walker
  Safe simple toys
  Playpen

Safety:
  Cabinet latches/locks
  Stop shocks
  Safety gates

SLEEPING EQUIPMENT

Cradle

Definitely *not* a necessity, in view of the short time it's used. If you do decide to buy one, look for:

• *Deep, solid sides,* which are safer than slatted sides. If the sides do have slats, be sure they're no wider apart than 2⅜ inches, the federally approved safety distance. A *locking mechanism,* so that the cradle can be locked in a nonrocking position for sleep.
• *Tip resistance.* Proper balance and weight, so that the rocking motion is gentle and presents no danger of tipover.
• *Avoid cradles suspended by protruding hooks* or resting on long rockers. The former can hurt a baby who's bumped against them when being put back in a cradle in the dark. Long rockers are easily tripped over in the middle of the night by sleepy adults. Cradles suspended from a frame that allow for a locked position are better, followed by low cradles on short rockers.

Cradles are available in a range of style and price. At Sears, for example, they range from about $80 to $140.

The $80 Sears cradle, however, is suspended from hooks and has slatted sides. Still, many of the more expensive cradles ($120 to $140) made by nationally known juvenile furniture manufacturers like Hedstrom and Williamsburg are also hook suspended and most seem to have slatted sides. Cradle accessories—bumpers, sheets and quilts—can add $20 to $65 to the cost, for an overall outlay of $100 to $200.

Cribs and Accessories

Although there are people who maintain that a baby can sleep in a well-padded bureau drawer, a big basket or the parents' bed, or on a pad on the floor, most couples take a crib as a necessity. It's perhaps the most important piece of baby equipment you'll buy, as it's where baby will spend the most time for the first few years. A crib and mattress are where you should put your money—economize elsewhere (although I'm not suggesting you need to buy the most expensive crib or even that these are the best).

Because many baby accidents and even fatalities have occurred in cribs, the Consumer Product Safety Commission in 1974 established regulations that all cribs manufactured and sold after that year in the United States must meet. This is why it's generally safer to buy a new crib than one made before 1975. Look for these features in a crib:

• *Standard size.* The interior dimensions of the crib should be 28 inches wide and 52⅜ inches long. This is so a standard crib mattress will fit snugly. A space of two adult fingers or more between crib and mattress can invite head entrapment. *If your older crib is not of this dimension, you will have to have a mattress specially made for a close, safe fit.*
• *Deep sides.* Multiposition, *adjustable spring* heights, so that the mattress can be raised and lowered according to the baby's size and climbing ability. *Narrow width between slats*—no more than 2⅜ inches—three adult fingers wide. Otherwise, there's an unacceptable risk of head entrapment.

• *Sturdy double lock.* The locking or latching mechanism that holds the drop sides up should require at least ten pounds of force to release and two coordinated movements—usually a simultaneous pulling up on the side and a push on the release. At least one, preferably two, *steel stabilizing bars* running the length of the crib under the springs, to enhance *overall sturdiness.*

• *Smooth* wood surfaces and hardware. Quality *teething rails* that are firmly attached and continue around the head and panels as well as the side rails. These attachments prevent baby from getting splinters in the mouth when chewing on the crib rails.

• *Hardwood* composition, at least for the structural parts of the crib. Better-quality cribs are put together with screws, not nails. *Nontoxic* finishes and *oversize casters,* for easy movement for cleaning.

• Cribs shipped unassembled must have *detailed, clear instructions,* a warning about keeping the bolts safely fastened upon assembly, and one saying the *crib should not be used by children over 35 inches tall.*

You can find a crib in any style, ranging from Early American to slick Contemporary. Leading manufacturers include Simmons, Hedstrom, Childcraft, Williamsburg, Bassett, Medallion and Sears. Sears sells cribs from about $80 to $400—the latter including a mattress and with two drawers underneath. There are good, safe cribs at Sears in the $140 to $160 range. Simmons cribs are mostly in the $210 to $250 range. Childcraft and Bassett offer cribs in that range, and also some that are less. (Prices are generally for the crib alone—mattresses and bedding not included.) While there are certainly cribs that cost more, there are numerous quality ones available in the $150 to $250 range.

Crib *mattresses* may seem an uninspiring topic, but they're actually important purchases. There are three kinds: inner-spring, all foam and hair block. *Inner-spring* mattresses, which are widely used, are made up of spring steel wire coils, sandwiched between layers of padding and insulating materials, plus the outside covering. *Foam* mattresses are either polyether or polyester, and rely on "bubbles" in the foam for firmness and resiliency. *Hair block* mattresses aren't sold in all parts of the country. They're usually made of sanitized and curled hog hair, bonded together in a block and sandwiched between layers of foam or felt. While these mattresses are very firm, they're generally less resilient and don't maintain their uniformity as well as quality versions of the first two kinds. Moreover, many pediatricians advise against hair block because of their allergy potential. Features to look for in quality *mattresses* include:

- *Super firmness and resiliency.* With inner-spring mattresses, firmness and resiliency come mainly from the number of coils and the quality of wire used in them. Don't buy an inner-spring mattress with fewer than eighty-eight coils. In foam mattresses, these features come from density. Buy only a high-density one in polyether. Don't confuse thickness of a foam mattress with density.
- *Good venting.* A mattress must breathe to prevent mold, mildew and odor. It does so by multiple side vents.
- A mattress cover that's *fire-retardant, heavy-duty, tear-* and *stain-resistant* and *moisture-repellant* and can be cleaned with a damp cloth. Triple-laminate vinyl is a good cover; cloth binding around the edges makes for added tear resistance.

It's safest to buy a crib mattress from a nationally known manufacturer like Sealy, Simmons, Kolcraft, Colgate, Questor, Gerico, Century or Sears. Inner-spring mattresses with 500 to 600 coils, vented borders and heavy-duty covers are available from J. C. Penney and Sears for $60— more elsewhere. Foam mattresses can be had for as little as $25, but superior quality ones go for $50 to $100, with $75 about average. The advantage of foam is that it's lightweight and has no inner breakable parts.

Crib bumpers are a necessary comfort and safety purchase. They help protect a baby from getting wedged in the crib bars, from bar bruising and from drafts. Crib bumpers should be firmly padded and 8 inches or more high, with at least six ties to secure them. They should go around the ends as well as the sides, and be flame-retardant, tear-resistant and machine-washable. Washable cloth bumpers are preferable to vinyl, as the ties on vinyl snap off and seams tear. So, while vinyl bumpers are cheap—$8 to $15 at Sears and discount stores—they're a poor value. At the same stores, cloth bumpers cost $15 to $20. Designer bumpers cost $30 to $50 from the likes of Red Calliope, Lambs & Ivy, and NoJo.

Crib *bedding* needs frequent changing, so stock up on the necessities—at least four fitted sheets, two waterproof mattress pads and two blankets or quilts. (No pillows— they can pose a suffocation threat.) The bedding should obviously be moisture-, stain- and shrink-resistant; machine-washable and -dryable; no-iron and nonallergenic. Corner seams should be reinforced. You can buy fitted crib sheets at stores like J. C. Penney and Sears for $5 to $7. Red Calliope, NoJo and similar makers sell crib sheets for $10 to $15. Lightweight blankets start at $5 and go up to $20 at Sears and similar stores, where crib quilts are in the $10 to $15 range and comforters a little more. Red Calliope, for example, offers blankets in the $20 to $30 range, and many beautiful quilts and comforters for $35 to $50.

Diapering and changing equipment is discussed in Chapter 9.

TRAVELING

More than one thousand children under the age of four are killed in car accidents annually and another seventy thousand are injured. What makes this shocking as well as sad is that experts estimate that 80 to 90 percent of the deaths and 65 percent of the injuries could be prevented by the use of a quality car safety seat. More than forty states have laws *requiring* use of such seats. But more important than any law government can pass is your vital responsibility to see that your baby has a quality car seat—properly installed and always used—from the very first ride home from the hospital. Don't be one of the ignorant ones who think that holding the baby tightly in your arms will be enough protection. Studies show that even in only a 20 mph crash, a baby held in a parent's arms will in fact be thrown forward, with a force of up to 300 pounds. That's equal to falling from a three-story building.

It's safest to buy a *new* car seat because by law these must meet the more stringent requirements of the revised Federal Motor Vehicle Safety Standard No. 213. FMVSS 213 requires that the seat be dynamically crash tested and sets standards for durability of the restraint materials used, the amount of force required before the belts will release, and the availability of clear instructions for installation and use. *Car seats made before 1981 did not have to meet FMVSS 213*—so a seat doesn't have to be very old to be potentially obsolete. Better buy new, and from a brand-name manufacturer like Collier-Keyworth, Cosco-Peterson, Questor, Century, Kolcraft, Strolee, Pride-Trimble, International or General Motors.

Car seats are available for infants up to 17 to 20 pounds, toddlers up to 40 pounds, and children up to 65 pounds. There are also seats designed to accommodate infants when used one way, and toddlers when used another. *For economy, these latter are the seats to buy.*

Car seats differ in how they're anchored to the car. Many have long tether straps that come out of the upper back of the seat and are bolted to the car frame. Some seats require tethering when used in the infant position—in the front seat, facing rearward—but not in the toddler position—in the middle of the back seat facing forward. Other seats rely on the car's safety belts for anchoring. The seat belts buckle through the back of some car seats, like the Cosco-Peterson Safe-T-Shield; or across the front, preferably over a padded safety shield (seat belts should not touch the baby) like Kolcraft's Quik Step.

The problem with the tether system is installation. Studies show as many as half the buyers of this kind of seat bolt them into the car incorrectly, negating much of the safety value. Anchoring the car seat in via the safety belt is easier and faster and makes the seat more readily adaptable to other cars—although with some cars the seat belt is too short. So be sure to tell the car seat salesperson the model car in which you plan to use a seat to find out if it will fit. Also ask for a precise description of how the seat gets installed. On the chance you're given the wrong advice and sold a seat that won't fit your car, make sure you buy from a reputable merchandiser with a liberal return policy.

Car seats further differ in how they "restrain" the child in them. Some have three- or five-point harnesses; others have safety shields; many have both. The advantage of some of the newest designs relying exclusively on a safety shield is the ease with which you can get the baby in and out; harnesses are more cumbersome. (Note that harnesses are nearly always required when a seat is used in the *infant* position.) If a car seat has *both* harness and safety shield, you must secure *both* for adequate security.

While knowing that a car seat "meets or exceeds all Federal Motor Vehicle Safety standards including Standard 213" or is "dynamically crash tested" is assuring, you should also look for:

- Seats constructed out of a *single high-impact molded plastic shell on a steel frame.*
- A *high head rest,* which helps prevent whiplash, and *large, flared head sides,* to absorb energy from a side crash.
- The shell of *the seat should be large enough* to comfortably accommodate the growing child, or a child in heavy clothing. Straps and harnesses should be easily adjustable for the same reasons. A harness lock or buckle should be "child-proof."
- *The seat should sit up high* enough for a toddler to see out.
- Seats upholstered in soft material rather than vinyl are less hot and sticky in summer months. If you buy a

vinyl car seat, you'll want a fabric cover; they cost $10 to $20.

Retail prices for most car seats are $50 to $90. However, car seats are often discounted off the list price, so it really pays to shop around. Seats are cheaper at a reputable lower-cost chain store, like J. C. Penney or Sears, than at most baby stores. Remember that the best buys are the seats that can accommodate both infants *and* toddlers by setting them up in different ways. To cite specific examples, you can find infant-toddler seats like the Collier-Keyworth Safe & Sound for about $50 at J. C. Penney and the popular Bobby Mac at Sears for about the same. The Century 100, 200 and 300 models retail for $65 to $80 but can be found discounted. Seats relying on safety shields are usually more expensive than harness restraint ones.

Another option is to rent your baby's car seat. Hospitals increasingly offer a rental program for car seats, at reasonable monthly cost. Some police departments have similar programs.

Carriages

A carriage is not practical for the way many of us live today. If you're a city dweller, it's a nuisance with elevators, traffic, road curbs, buses, taxis, and small apartments. If you live in the suburbs and are in and out of the car all the time, a carriage is too cumbersome to collapse, hoist into the trunk, open up again, etc. every time you go to the market. Moreover, carriages are expensive and babies over six months old are not usually willing to recline in them. If you should decide to buy a carriage anyway, make sure:

- It's *tip-resistant* and *not too heavy* to negotiate over curbs and steps. It has a good, preferably *four-wheel, braking system.*
- It's as *easy as possible to collapse* and open, but has a good safety latch system to prevent accidental collapse. It has *no dangerous scissor joints.*

Silver Cross of England is the "Cadillac" of carriage makers—with prices to match at about $200 to $600! Perego carriages from Italy can be found in the $100 to $200 range. (However, before you buy an English or Italian carriage, make sure the store carries parts. Otherwise, should you need them, you'll have to wait for them to come from Europe.) You'll also need a carriage pad and two or three sheets, which will cost about $15.

Strollers

A quality, lightweight stroller is good value. It gets *extended* use—starting at three to six months (sooner if it has a full recline position) to three years or so. And because it weighs only about 15 pounds, its maneuverability and mobility result in *extensive* use during that period. Note that the quality range of strollers is wide. Particularly if you plan to use the stroller through a second child, it definitely pays to buy a better model. Cheap ones are notably nondurable. In any case, you don't want to skimp on basic safety and comfort features, including:

• *A sturdy, steel frame, tip resistance and balance*—test by placing the baby (or heavy package or whatever) as far back in the stroller as possible. Loop a full diaper bag across the handle bars or back basket. Press downward on the handles. The base of the stroller should be wide enough and the wheels large enough for stability.
• *A secure, adjustable restraining system*, for both waist and crotch. This should be attached to the frame, not just looped around the seat, and should actually make contact with the baby.
• *Positive locking-action brakes.* A better braking system involves *both* back wheels and presses tabs between spokes on these wheels (positive action), rather than just pinching against the rubber. Also a *safety lock* to prevent accidental collapse.
• *Good steering*, aided by swiveling, double wheels. Try to steer the stroller with one hand—with the better models, it's easy to do. Cheaper ones tend to veer off.

- *Very firm, adjustable back.* Essential for baby's comfort—sling-type fabric models provide inadequate support.
- *Handle bars at a comfortable height.* Cheaper strollers often require an adult to bend down uncomfortably.
- *Easy to open and collapse.* A main point of these lightweight strollers is their ease of use. Look for a model that lets you open and close using one hand and foot. (However, don't accept a loss of stability for this convenience—there are plenty of strollers available that offer both one-hand collapsibility and stability.)
- *No sharp, protruding hardware*—scissor or cross joints.

Some of the best strollers are made by Silver Cross, Perego, Aprica, and MacLaren. As usual, quality costs. While each of these manufacturers offers several models, all in all, they're the most expensive strollers on the market—mostly $100 and up. Sears offers a steel-frame Perego model, with swivel front wheels, dual positive-action brakes, firm, adjustable back and restraint system for about $100. I priced the full line of Aprica strollers at a discount baby store for about $90 to $180. MacLaren strollers are about $70 to $220. Good strollers for under $100 include Questor's Maxi-Taxi, with a steel frame, swivel front wheels, firm, adjustable back, restraining strap and an easy-fold feature, sold for $65 to $70 at J. C. Penney and Sears. Strolee's the No Stoop Coupe is sturdy, although only one rear wheel locks. It sells for about $70. Delta's Luv Buggy, which does have a double wheel brake and also reclines for use as a quasi carriage, is another popular model—about $70.

Infant Carriers

Soft carriers are made of cloth and a harness and are worn by a parent with the baby seated inside, parent and baby snuggled up against one another. *Hard carriers,* also called infant seats, are rigid, molded plastic and have carrying handles. Both hard and soft carriers get most of their use with newborns. Then there are *backpacks* for the time the baby begins to sit up erectly—usually at about six or seven months.

The advantages of a soft carrier include the special feeling of closeness between parent and infant it promotes. It's also lightweight, leaves parent with both hands free, and is easy to store. Most parents find soft carriers are better than hard for actually carrying the baby, and certainly for outings involving shopping. A hard carrier or infant seat, on the other hand, can be used for sleeping, playing, and feeding before a baby is ready for a high chair. Many parents buy both hard and soft carriers.

In choosing a *hard carrier* or infant seat, look for:

- A *wide base* with a *nonskid bottom* for stability. A base with sturdy rockers is fine. A sturdy *restraining system*, including crotch strap.
- A *wide bottom* so that baby can be in the spread-leg, froglike position that is most natural. *Adjustability* to several degrees of recline.
- *Avoid* hard carriers that rest on thin wire supports rather than a tubular steel frame or molded plastic bar.

Hard carriers/infant seats are available in the $20 to $30 range. Century, Kolcraft, Cosco-Peterson, Questor and Welsh are among those making good ones.

Features to look for in a *soft carrier* include:

- *Easy on, easy off.* Choose one that you can get in and out of without assistance. A carrier that can be worn on your *front or back.*
- *Adjustability,* to accommodate a growing baby. Roomy, *expandable leg holes.*
- *Sturdy construction* of durable, washable fabric. *Padded shoulder straps* for parental comfort.

Along with Snugli, the originator of the soft carrier, you now have models from Century, Cosco-Peterson, Questor, Welsh, Strolee, Gerico and many small "cottage industries" to choose from. Price depends on whether the carrier is hand- or machine-made, and on the fabric. The usual range is $30 to $45, although a top-of-the-line Snugli can go for $60. Choose a fabric right for the season the carrier will get the most use—lightweight for summer, perhaps corduroy for winter.

For the baby six months and up, you might want to switch to a *tubular-framed backpack,* which helps distribute the weight of a heavier baby better than a soft carrier. The baby can also see the world better in these. Check carefully for the following safety and comfort features, however, because many backpacks have proved to be poor products— some even subject to recall and issuance of warnings by the Consumer Protection Agency. Look for:

• *Overall sturdy aluminum frame,* durable fabric, and construction. Reinforcement at stress points. *Proper weight distribution,* centered on the parent's shoulder blades and lower back, versus neck and shoulder muscles alone. Good weight distribution will have the baby seated deeply—not up high.

• *Roomy leg holes* that are *not* above the level of the seat (which can cause dangerous leg constriction). *Good padding* on the shoulder straps and on the frame in front of the baby's face.

• A good *restraining strap* to keep the baby from trying to stand in the seat. *Secure, sturdy rings and latches.*

• No scissor or cross joints, which have caused the recall of some older packs.

Most backpacks range in price from $20 to $40.

Feeding equipment is covered in Chapter 10.

PLAY/EXERCISE EQUIPMENT

Walkers

An optional purchase, but a popular one. Contrary to what you might assume, a walker does *not* help baby walk earlier. In fact, if it's used for extended periods during the day, when the baby might instead be creeping or crawling, it may actually inhibit the baby's natural progression to walking. Walkers shouldn't be used *before* the baby can sit up in an erect position—six to seven months—and they shouldn't be used *after* thirteen months or more than 25 pounds, because the baby's weight makes it too easy to tip over. On the other hand, a walker does give the baby an early opportunity for a little independent mobility and exploration and the parents a little time with hands free, which can seem pretty precious. If you decide to buy a *walker* look for:

- A *base much wider than the seat,* for greater stability. The base should be a full "surround" of high-impact plastic, with heavy-duty casters, not just wheels.
- A *seat that's securely attached to the frame,* not a suspended sling. The seat should be comfortably padded; a high back provides additional support.
- *Adjustable height* with a mechanism to prevent accidental collapse. *Covered joints* and hardware.
- A *wide surrounding tray* with a deep lip for use as a feeder. *Easy to fold* flat for storage.
- Don't use a walker as a babysitter—keep the baby in sight. Don't use near the top of any stairs, around loose throw rugs, door ledges, extension cords or other items that can impede its motion. Fifteen minutes at a time is long enough.

Graco, Century and Aprica make some of the best walkers, in the $25 to $40 range.

Jumpers

A jumper is a cloth or plastic sling suspended from the top of a doorway by rubber or spring straps, so that the baby can just touch toes to the floor and thus can jump up and down. A highly optional purchase. For one thing, many accidents have occurred in them. Moreover, they can be used for a relatively short time (basically the crawling period, although manufacturers will tell you four months at the earliest, and to a maximum of 25 pounds). Moreover, babies seem to either love or hate jumpers, so be sure to test yours out in one before buying. If you find your baby likes a jumper, make sure:

• The *baby fits in it snugly but comfortably.* Watch out for jumpers that leave a red welt on the baby's inner thigh.
• It's *easy to install.* Some are so much bother that they're not worth it. It should also, obviously, install securely, with a mechanism that prevents accidental release.
• The *height is adjustable,* the seat is washable. *No exposed hardware* or coils.
• *Use it only in a wide door,* with nothing nearby baby might bounce into.

Some of the big baby companies making jumpers include Strolee, Reliance Products, Questor, Graco, Hedstrom, and Pride-Trimble. Expect to pay $15 to $30.

Swings
A baby swing is another funny product. Like jumpers, babies either love swings or hate them, and correspondingly, parents will tell you a swing is one of the best purchases to make or a real waste of money. It's helpful to try your baby out in a swing a few times before buying one. In any case, a swing is certainly an optional purchase. It's used for a relatively short time—until a baby weighs 22 pounds and/or is aggressively crawling, pulling and grabbing. Another drawback of a baby swing is that it takes up a lot of space—something those of you with small city apartments probably can't afford. On the plus side, a swing can sometimes soothe a colicky baby, and it does give a parent a little time with hands free. Never, however, use one as a baby sitter. If you buy a *baby swing,* look for:

• Overall sturdiness, which means a *wide base stance,* a *tubular steel frame,* and *locking cross bars* between the legs to prevent accidental collapse. The bottom of the legs should have a *nonslip* rubber surface.

• A *seat of rigid molded plastic*, the whole length of which is attached to the swinging bars, so it can't flop forward. The *bars* should be sturdy *metal* or *plastic*— not wires or fabric.

• The seat should have a good *restraining strap*, an *adjustment* to several angles, and *easy-in*, *easy-out* access.

• All of the seat, including the *front bar*, should be well *padded*. The leg holes shouldn't be higher than seat level, or leg constriction may result. *No-wind/no-crank* swings are more convenient, less noisy.

Graco, Century, Aprica, Strolee and Gerico are among the manufacturers of baby swings. (However, not all of their models have all of the desired safety and comfort features.) Expect to pay $30 to $50.

Playpens

Also highly optional. I don't know if recent statistics on playpen sales would verify this, but more and more parents seem to be against putting baby in a "pen"—a closely confined environment offering little stimulation or opportunity for movement. (It's because of such new attitudes that manufacturers have euphemistically renamed playpens "play yards.") In any case, playpens take up a lot of space, and they're expensive for the relatively short time they can be used—by babies less than 34 inches tall and/ or weighing less than 30 pounds. Moreover, many playpens have proved unsafe. There are more than 2,000 playpen-related accidents each year serious enough to require emergency room treatment, with several deaths reported. For this reason, Safety Standard F406-83 has been established. F406-83, however, is a *voluntary* standard—*a playpen does not have to meet it to be legally on the market*. Testing for this standard is supervised by the Juvenile Products Manufacturers Association (JPMA), which awards a safety-approved label to playpens meeting the requirements. *Don't buy a playpen without this label!* Features to look for in a playpen include:

- *No sharp edges*, protrusions or points. Covered hinges. In mesh pens, firm, secure vinyl upholstery that can't be pulled off and aspirated.
- A pen at least *20 inches high*, measured from the pad to the railing top. A *secure locking device* to prevent accidental collapse.
- A specification stating that the floor of the pen can withstand 80 pounds of static weight and 50 pounds of bouncing weight without giving way. (Still, don't use a playpen for a baby weighing more than 30 pounds.) Railing that can support 50 pounds.
- On a wooden playpen, the *bars* must be smooth and *no more than 2⅜ inches apart*, with teething rails all around. On a mesh playpen, the *mesh should be so small or tight* that its openings can't trap babies' fingers, toes, or clothes buttons.
- *Easy to fold and store.*
- *Never leave an infant in a mesh pen (or portable crib) with one side left down.* When one side is left down, the mesh forms a pocket that a young infant can fall or roll into and suffocate. Several deaths have been reported, most of them involving babies younger than six weeks.

Good wooden playpens are usually sturdier than mesh. The baby can see out better, the bars can be used as "pull-me-ups" and there's no vinyl that could be aspirated. Several models of both wood and mesh playpens by Bilt-Rite, Century, Cosco-Peterson, Collier-Keyworth, Graco, Pride-Trimble, Questor, Nu-Line and Welsh, two models by Hedstrom and one by Strolee have the JPMA safety label. (However, this doesn't mean that *every* model made by each of these companies has been awarded the safety label.) Wooden models cost about $75; mesh pens with the label cost about $45 to $65.

TOYS

There are more than 150,000 toys on the U.S. market, and sales exceed $5 billion a year. Faced with such an overwhelming array, how do parents make an intelligent choice? Here's help in selecting toys that are fun, safe and good value.

• *Choose toys appropriate to baby's age and skills.* Better toys provide guidelines as to the appropriate age range. However, these are guidelines—not gospel. (Indeed, one of the leading authorities on baby development, Burton L. White, has emphasized that manufacturers often get the age guidelines for toys all wrong.) You know your child's interests and abilities the best. If you have reason to believe your one-year-old would enjoy and benefit from a toy labeled twenty-four months, trust your judgment.

• *Don't buy a newborn many toys.* An infant's abilities are too limited to appreciate much more than a crib mobile and crib toy with safety mirror.

• As the baby gets older, present *a well-balanced variety of toys.* Some should be "realistic," others "symbolic"— toys like blocks and art materials, which can be anything the child wants them to be, encouraging imagination and creativity. Choose some multipurpose playthings that can be used in different ways and teach different things.

• Toys that require *active participation or interaction* will be more interesting than passive or decorative ones. A toy should be such that a child can learn how it works and what it does and have some degree of control over it.

• Toys should be *sturdily constructed,* and nonbreakable with normal use. You shouldn't be able to pull parts off or expose sharp pieces. No detachable small parts or small holes. Stuffed animals, for example, are better if they're constructed of a single piece.

• All fabrics should be *flame-resistant* with *nontoxic* finishes. Stuffed toys and dolls, etc., should be *hygienic and washable.*

• *No toys small enough to be crammed into baby's mouth.* In particular, look out for small squeeze toys that can be put in the mouth, and then inflate, causing suffocation.

• *No toys that make loud noises, or shoot objects.*

• Electrical toys should have *Underwriters Laboratories (UL) approval.* Electric toys are for older children and require adult supervision.

• *Examine secondhand toys and imported toys especially carefully.* The latter may not be subject to the safety standards that American-made toys are.

• Immediately remove and *carefully discard plastic wrappers* that toys come in.

• *Read all labels and instructions thoroughly. Maintain toys carefully to extend their life.*

• *Only buy a toy chest with either a removable lid or a spring-loaded support that will remain securely open via a safety mechanism.* Children have been severely hurt or killed when the lids of toy chests not meeting these requirements have slammed down on their heads. Wooden toy chests should also have ventilation holes and smooth edges. A good alternative to a toy chest is low, open shelving in the baby's room.

• You can make many fun, stimulating toys for your baby and you can pull others out of kitchen cabinets. While toys are important, that doesn't mean that they have to be expensive commercial ones.

• Set a toy budget and a buying plan before you go to shop. Avoid impulse buying. Comparison-shop and check newspaper ads for sales. Many stores will lower the prices of popular toys as "loss leaders" to attract customers.

• *Buy from a reputable store with a liberal return policy.* For wide variety plus discount prices, shop at a toy supermarket like Toys-R-Us. Purchase toys from known manufacturers, who mark their products with their address in case of questions or complaints. Give preferences to toys with a *warranty or guarantee.*

• To stretch your toy dollars, buy some "classics"— toys on the market a long time, and so usually lower-priced—balls, crayons, modeling clay, blocks, etc. Choose multipurpose toys that can be used in different ways through more than one age and skill level.

• Know if the toy you're buying requires accessories or batteries, etc., which can add substantially to the cost over its lifetime.

• Particularly if you're planning more than one child, *look for quality.* It will pay to spend a little more the first time around, as cheaper toys are notably nondurable.

• Start an informal "toy co-op" with a group of friends. Trading toys between children means more variety and novelty and less money spent. It also lets you try the toy out on your child, to see if it is of interest.

• Keep a list of toy manufacturers' addresses and write to the Customer Service Department for missing parts. They are amazingly cheap, and sometimes free. (Toys with missing parts can often be bought for a few cents at rummage sales.)

CHILD PROTECTION EQUIPMENT

Having discussed the safety and comfort features to look for in baby equipment, furniture and toys, let's conclude with the products you'll need to baby-proof the *house* itself. Baby-proofing your home is vital because, after the car, the home is the primary place child accidents occur— and accidents kill more small children than the five leading fatal diseases combined.

Smoke Detector and Fire Extinguisher

As new parents, there's no better time to buy these if your house doesn't already have them. Buy quality ones that are Underwriters Laboratories (UL) approved. *Detectors* come either battery-powered (which will run about a year before needing a battery change) or to run off house current. With the latter, installation is more complicated and expensive unless you already have the wiring and electricity in place. Battery-powered units are usually easily self-installed. Whichever kind you buy, check it every few months with smoke from a snuffed candle. Quality units are about $17 to $20.

Choose a UL-approved, multipurpose, dry chemical *fire extinguisher*, labeled ABC (which means it will put out all types of fires). Once you own it, be sure you know how to use it and keep it close to the cooking area. Cost: about $25 to $30. *Inform your home insurance agents that you have good fire detection and extinguishing equipment in place—you may get a break on your premiums.*

Intercom

Many new parents install an intercom in the nursery, so they can hear a baby cry throughout the house. Pick a simple model requiring no wiring or installation. Look for ads in baby magazines or go to a discount store, where you can find these "electronic babysitters" for $22 to $35.

Safety Latches

These prevent the baby from getting into cabinets, cupboards and closets containing potentially dangerous items. A must. Kinder Gard, Shur-lock and F&H Baby Products all make good ones. They're easy to install and not visible when engaged. An economy pack of seven from Kinder Gard costs less than $6. Sears sells cheaper ones.

Corner and Edge Guards

These are "cushions" designed to minimize injury from bumps against sharp tables and counters throughout the house. Kinder Gard cushions are clear plastic and easily installed. A package of ten corner cushions is about $4. The company's edge cushion comes in an 8-foot length that you can cut to any size, for $6.

Child Protection Plugs

For unused electrical outlets. An absolute must, these prevent a child from inserting fingers or objects into empty outlets and getting a nasty shock. Don't leave a single "unplugged" outlet in your house. Sears sells a package of twelve for $1.

Safety Gates

If you have stairs in the house, or sometimes want to keep your toddler confined in a room, these may be the answer. Choose carefully, however, because many accidents have been associated with safety gates. There are two kinds—the wooden, accordion style that latch-close, and pressure gates that depend on spring-loaded tubes and surface-contact pads to lock in. The "accordion" is less expensive, but be sure the slats, when extended in your particular doorway, will not be "open" enough to be climbable or a potential head trap. One nuisance—you have to install these to the doorway with screws. At discount stores, accordion gates cost from about $6 to $8, depending on length. Of the pressure gates, the Gerry 4 Sure Security Gate seems a good value. It's easy to install, with spring-loaded steel tubes and large surface-contact pads for four-point locking action. It also has a small mesh and telescope adjustment of 27 inches to 42 inches. Available at Sears and discount stores for about $15, but before you buy, insist on setting it up to test its "hold."

❖ 12

CHILDCARE

Can You Afford to Go Back to Work?

Rosalyn W., her husband and their newborn live in a suburb of Houston. Before Simon was born, Rosalyn commuted downtown to her job as an office manager for a word-processing firm, and earned $26,000. She planned a three-month maternity leave, during which she intended to make childcare arrangements. What Rosalyn had in mind was a woman coming to the house five days a week, for forty-five hours, to both care for Simon and do basic housekeeping. She wanted someone with references who could speak English, drive and occasionally stay late if Rosalyn got stuck at work. Rosalyn put ads in the local papers offering $100 a week.

"I was so naive!" she now says. "I didn't bother to calculate that my offer amounted to less than $2.25 an hour—way below minimum wage. When I got no interest and started to think it through, I was startled to realize I was paying my cleaning lady five dollars an hour—and there I was advertising for childcare plus housekeeping at not half that! After three months of solid looking and interviewing, the best I could do was $150 a week plus bus fare with overtime after 5:00 P.M. for a woman with a vague reference and little English."

So Rosalyn decided to do some cost-benefit analysis

about going back to work. She calculated her monthly work-related expenses: $77 for lunch ($3.50 a day times 22 days); $213 for commutation and parking (36 miles a day times 20 cents times 22 days plus $2.50 times 22); $60 for professional wardrobe additions and maintenance, and the whopper, an estimated $625 for childcare. Expenses totaled $975, as against her $1,340 take-home pay. So Rosalyn calculated her net gain from returning to work at $365 a month ("Way, way less than minimum wage!" she exclaimed), and that's *before* figuring the tax advantage of her staying home—a lower bracket because of lower family gross income. "It just isn't worth it financially for me to go back to the office now," Rosalyn concluded. "It's the cost of childcare that's keeping me home. I don't have any relatives to rely on. I could put Simon in family day care, which would be a lot cheaper than a housekeeper, but I just don't want to. I want him in his own home, with someone looking after him and him alone. I'll go back to work when he's in school. Meanwhile, I'm thinking of buying a word processor and free-lancing out of the house."

Can You Afford NOT to Go Back?

With her husband earning $36,000 a year, Rosalyn figured she could afford not to go back to work. However, her situation—while far from rare—puts her in the minority. Researchers estimate that nearly 75 percent of women who work outside the home do so because they must financially support or help support themselves and their families. (One in five mothers in the labor force is the sole support of her family.) More than half of all mothers today are employed, and of these, more than *40 percent* are mothers with children under the age of three! Indeed, mothers with babies are thought to be the fastest-growing group in the labor force.

"One reason I have to work," said Sylvie M., who lives outside Boston, "is precisely because I *am* a new mother. A baby is expensive! In our household, I'm the one with the steady pay—my husband is a writer—and the one whose job provides health insurance for the family. It would be irresponsible of me to stay home! I'm lucky, though. My mother watches the baby." And many middle-income women echo these words from an Oakland, California, mother, "My working makes the difference between our getting by and living a very comfortable life. To us, that means I 'have' to work."

And then there are the new mothers who technically could afford not to work but who regard career continuity as a must. "I have all those years and so much money invested in my education. Work is the payback on that investment," a young Manhattan pediatrician with a four-month-old told me. "I look at it as an investment in the future, too," she continued. "Sure, childcare is costing me a fortune—but it's worth it. Jessie won't need the care forever, and these are the years I have to be building my practice and reputation."

Research confirms this young doctor's thoughts. The decade between the ages of twenty-five and thirty-five—the period when women are most apt to leave the labor force or become part-time workers to have babies—is the most critical period for skill acquisition and promotion. Withdrawing from the work force during this time extracts a hefty *lifetime* economic cost. In fact, a recent study showed that women who take even just two years off for child rearing suffer a 10 percent *permanent* decline in pay.

In any case, for whatever reason a new mother may decide she can't afford *not* to work, one result is the same—childcare arrangements must be made. For many two-career couples, finding good, affordable full-time childcare is one of the toughest problems of new parenthood. What are the options?

CARE INSIDE YOUR HOME

If most new parents had their druthers, they'd have their babies cared for in their own homes. Home is the most "normal" setting for a baby's care, and the most convenient—no lugging the baby and equipment around town to a sitter or center. The caregiver is ministering to your child (or children) alone, which should mean more personal and extensive attention. A caregiver who comes to your home is more likely to have some flexibility, if you occasionally get stuck late at work, than is a group care situation. Moreover, many group caregivers—day-care centers particularly—will not take infants. And with in-home arrangements, if baby is sick, care is still available.

As usual, however, convenience and personal attention *cost.* How much depends on who you get—relative or friend, babysitter, au pair, housekeeper or nanny-governess. It also depends somewhat on whether the caretaker is live-in or live-out. It depends, too, on where you live—going rates differ across the country and are particularly higher in large cities. And to an important degree, it depends on whether you abide by the law.

Relative or Friend

Given the cost of childcare, plus parental concern about a loving quality of care, many couples jump at an offer to help from a relative or close friend. Count yourself lucky if you have a willing and able mother, aunt, or the like—according to a 1979 *Family Circle* magazine study, only one in five mothers today can count on a relative to provide childcare in her stead.

If you are so fortunate, recognize that this arrangement demands special tact and flexibility. After all, it's not a professional situation but a familial one. You cannot treat a relative or friend as an employee (no matter how well you might treat an employee). And don't expect such arrangements to be free. You might be surprised by a relative's expectation of or willingness to accept payment. Don't assume! (Your mother, after all, knows what she's getting into—she's done this before!) While there's every likelihood a relative will provide the care for below market rates, discuss money openly and up front. Even if she won't take any pay, you'll want to provide carfare if needed, occasionally a nice present, good lunches, etc.

An important financial point. If you *do* pay a relative for childcare, you're eligible to apply for the childcare tax credit discussed below. You must have good records, canceled checks or receipts for cash payment. Make sure you discuss your intention to file for the credit with your relative, who may have had an off-the-books arrangement in mind. Understand that you can file for the credit *even if* the relative you're paying for childcare lives in your home—*unless you claim the person as a dependent.* For most people, the childcare tax credit will make a bigger dent in their tax liability.

Babysitter

In this context, by a sitter I mean a nonrelative who comes to your home daily to look after the baby and to do that alone—no housework. Nor would you expect a babysitter to have professional childcare qualifications. Sitter care of this sort is often referred to as "custodial"—merely looking after baby's physical needs.

It's hard to find a full-time sitter these days, because while it's not cheap for you (given the number of hours for which you pay, and especially if you need cleaning help, too), it's nonetheless not likely to seem much for the sitter. Except in the largest cities, sitters are generally paid way less than minimum wage—commanding between $35 and $75 a week. Nor do they usually get fringe benefits like vacation or sick pay. So there are hardly hordes of people anxious to be full-time sitters. Be aware that these low "going rates" are despite the fact that in-home sitters *are* covered by federal and state minimum wage laws. Moreover, you as an employer also legally have certain tax obligations for an in-home employee. So if you pay a sitter below the $3.55 per hour minimum wage, and "off the books" as most people do, you are in violation of the law and could be subject to certain penalties if discovered. These penalties are noted below, after the obligations themselves are discussed.

Au Pair

Common in Europe and increasingly so in the United States, au pairs are generally seventeen- to twenty-two-year-old European women who live full-time in your home, providing childcare assistance and light housekeeping for modest pay. Often these young women are taking a year or two off between high school and university, or before settling down to start a family of their own. They usually don't have professional childcare qualifications, although often they come from large families where they had lots of practice caring for younger siblings. Being an au pair is a way to "see some of the world" and is quite socially acceptable in their home countries. An au pair doesn't expect to be and generally isn't treated exactly like an employee—more like a younger cousin that has come to stay and help out. Despite the turnover, generally every year or two, an au pair otherwise can be a good solution to your childcare needs.

That is, when the au pair works out well. There are plenty of potential pitfalls. One is that Americans often don't understand the au pair tradition and treat the young woman strictly like a servant. This can result in frustration for all and hasty departure of the au pair. Such departure exacts a financial toll, because *you generally pay her airfare from Europe.* (Indeed, some less than scrupulous au pairs will sign themselves up just to get the airfare and then deliberately not work out.) Another not uncommon problem is the au pair who has in mind not just "seeing the world" but also "sowing wild oats." If this happens, your confidence in the au pair is obviously undermined, and you'll probably fret over your responsibility to her parents and to the au pair herself as a visitor in this country. Another snag is that the au pair usually does not have a legal right to work in this country—she enters the United States on a visitor visa. Savvy immigration officials at major airports can often spot an arriving au pair, and after questioning, some get sent right back home. You're out the airfare and any advance, plus have to start the hunt for the help you need all over again.

On the other hand, when an au pair works out, parents are usually delighted with the solution. They get young, bright, energetic, live-in childcare plus light housekeeping, while the au pair gets $50 to $100 (generally $50 to $75) per week, plus full room and board, usually weekends off, frequently some car privileges and a chance to see some of the United States.

Housekeeper

A housekeeper is a very practical choice for the two-career couple with a new baby—for the couple, that is, who can afford one. A housekeeper both cares for the baby and does basic housekeeping, and often some cooking, too. A housekeeper usually offers flexibility in terms of hours, particularly if she is a *live-in*. (Live-ins are expected to work a forty-four-hour week.) A live-in housekeeper gets a private room and bath and telephone privileges and is occasionally offered use of a car for private activities. If you plan on a live-in housekeeper, you must also decide on whether you want the person there for five days or seven days. Five-day live-in arrangements are generally most desirable (unless both parents are subject to emergency weekend calls from home), because they afford the family some private time. However, a five-day live-in worker is often more expensive, since the housekeeper must maintain a separate residence for weekend use.

It may surprise you that live-in housekeepers are frequently *less* expensive than live-out—but it makes sense in that you're providing room and board for the former. A *live-out* housekeeper generally expects transportation in addition to salary, plus one or two meals a day.

In 1983, the American Council of Life Insurance (ACLI) conducted a study to determine the going rates for full-time live-in and live-out housekeepers across the country. The study relied on data supplied by fifty private employment agencies and state employment departments. Hold on to your hats. Here's what the study found.

WEEKLY HOUSEKEEPER SALARY, 1982		
Urban average	*Statewide average*	*U.S. average*
Live in	$201	$130	$164
Live out	$194	$152	$171

And these are 1982 numbers! But, I know some of you are thinking, "I don't believe those figures! So-and-so pays her housekeeper way less!" I, too, know people who pay less—even in New York, Los Angeles and Houston. However, in each instance I'm familiar with, the "underpaid" housekeeper has limited English, is *without* legal working papers and/or is being paid *off the tax books*. It's no surprise that such women command less—couldn't you afford a pay cut if you weren't paying taxes? In any case, we all know it's common to employ such individuals for household help. But I want to continue to emphasize that being common doesn't make it legal—and that the prudent person knows and assesses the risks before doing it.

Nanny/Governess

A nanny is a childcare specialist—usually meaning both that professional credentials of some sort have been obtained (like a certificate from a nanny school, a degree in child psychology or teaching, or perhaps experience in pediatric nursing) *and* that childcare is provided *only*—no housework to speak of. People who employ a nanny generally have cleaning help, too. While one woman I know described a nanny as opposed to a housekeeper as "doing less for more," most employers have a different set of expectations for a nanny, and are willing to pay for those expectations.

For example, they expect a nanny to have excellent references and a practical grounding in child psychology and child-rearing practices and to be willing and able to engage in creative, educational activities with the child. That is, a nanny is expected to provide *developmental*, not merely custodial, care. Even if foreign-born, a nanny is expected to be able to communicate well in English and to have legal working papers. Employers of a nanny usually hope and anticipate that she will be with them for a long time, for the continuity and consistency of childcare that's so desirable.

Nannies can either live out or live in (five or seven days). Either way, their going rates are steep—generally $200 to $250. In New York, I know couples paying up to

$350 to $400. Moreover, a nanny will generally expect correct, on-the-books payment (which will add significantly to your cost, as discussed just below) plus overtime, "appropriate" vacation, holidays and sick pay. "Appropriate" is considered to be two weeks vacation after one year of service, and at least six days each of paid legal holiday and sick days annually. Carfare for live-out nannies and occasional car use for live-in ones for private activities are also common. Less often, employers provide health insurance and uniforms.

Your Legal Obligations to Household Help

Household help—whether full-time sitter, housekeeper or nanny—are protected under the *federal minimum-wage law*. In 1985, hourly minimum wage was $3.55. Moreover, if *state or local law* provides a higher wage than federal law, a housekeeper is entitled to the more liberal rate. Live-out housekeepers are also covered by the *overtime provision* of federal wage law—1½ times the hourly rate for hours exceeding forty per week. (According to the Code of Standards of the National Committee on Household Employment, the National Urban League, live-in housekeepers should be paid overtime for more than forty-four hours per week; double time for excess of fifty-two hours.)

If you pay in-house help a minimum of $50 in a three-month period, you also owe *Social Security tax.* Quarterly filing is required on IRS Form 942, obtainable the first time from your local IRS office. In 1984, Social Security taxes were 13.4 percent of wages. You and the employee are supposed to contribute equally to them. *However, if your employee refuses to have half this amount deducted from her pay, you're responsible for the total payment.* Many employers willingly offer to pay the entire tax. *Note that no statute of limitations applies to this obligation. The government can charge an almost 50 percent penalty on back Social Security taxes, even years later.* Unfortunately, paid-in Social Security taxes on a household employee are not tax-deductible, because the government considers them a personal expense—not a business one. However, they do go toward the calculation of the childcare tax credit, explained below.

Another obligation—*federal unemployment tax (FUTA)*. If you pay $1,000 or more a calendar quarter to household help, you must pay this tax, which in 1984 was 3.5 percent on the first $7,000 of wages paid during the calendar year. The employee is *not* required to share in this. File Form 940. *State unemployment insurance* is also required of you as an employer of full-time household help. Finally, about half the states also require that employers pay into a state fund for *worker's compensation.*

If your employee asks you to withhold income tax, you may comply—although you don't have a legal obligation to do so. However, you do legally have to give the housekeeper a filled-in *W-2 Form* by January 31 of the next year, and file a copy with the Social Security Administration by the end of February of that year. Civil and criminal penalties can be imposed on an employer who willfully fails to furnish or furnishes a false W-2.

So you see, if you abide by the law, salary alone isn't your only expense in employing in-home childcare and housekeeping help. *Your legal obligations can add 20 percent or more to base salary.*

Other Costs

One significant expense of full-time in-home childcare that few people think to figure is the extra electricity, heat, air-conditioning, water and telephone use resulting from someone being in your home all day, every day when before it was empty while you were at work. Don't underestimate these. They definitely add up. For example, Joan V., who lives outside New York City, calculated it costs her about $1,200 a year more for these items now that she has a full-time housekeeper.

Tips on Finding and Keeping Good In-home Childcare

• Start early—definitely during pregnancy if you plan a maternity leave of three months or less. Decide on what kind of care you want—or more realistically, can afford—and tell everyone you're looking. Local newspaper ads are good. Mention hours, nature of duties (e.g., "childcare plus light housekeeping"), wages, any special needs or prohibitions.

• Consider use of an employment agency. Some specialize in childcare-housekeeping services, and a few in au pairs, providing applicant screening and reference checks. Cost: up to 25 to 50 percent of the first month's salary. (Check to see if you can get an agency refund if you hire a person who proves not to work out within a set, short time.) Or try the state employment agency, which is free.

• Learn to do "first-cut" interviews over the phone. Write out questions of importance to you in advance (e.g., "Do you smoke? Drive?"). If the interviewee passes first cut, arrange for a face-to-face meeting in your home. Both parents and child should be present.

• Ask for references and check them out. Don't accept vague responses from the references.

• Be realistic. If you're paying babysitter rates, don't expect nanny performance. In any case, no one's going to take care of your baby (or your home) just the way you would. Decide what's most important to you and is thus nonnegotiable. Be flexible about the rest.

• Make the employee's duties and your expectations clear up front. Ditto on salary, including your offer regarding overtime, vacations, holidays, sick pay, and raises. Discuss the "on-the-books" or "off-the-books" question immediately—don't assume that since you want to be legal, the employee does, or vice versa.

• Be fair and communicative. Stick to the ground rules originally set. No creeping addition of chores without a discussion and possibly a raise. Never view gifts of clothes or food as part of payment.

• If you decide you must fire the person, do it fast. Give one to two weeks' salary in lieu of notice.

CHILDCARE OUTSIDE YOUR HOME

Childcare outside your home has certain advantages. First, one kind of such care—family day care—is *relatively* easy to find and *relatively* inexpensive. Moreover, if your child is cared for outside your home, it's likely to be a group situation, and even young babies can enjoy and benefit from being with other children. And if you take the baby outside your home for care, you are *not* subject to pay Social Security, etc.

The downside is the transportation back and forth, the wide range of quality of caregivers and centers, the fact that you as an individual can exercise less "quality control" (after all, it's not your house, and the caregiver is probably responsible to several children and their parents), probably less personal attention and less flexibility regarding hours, and the probable need to make special arrangements when your baby is sick.

Family Day-Care Home

This is childcare provided by a woman in her own home for a small group (average is 3.5) children. Use of family day care for preschool children has almost doubled over the last twenty years—as many as 45 percent of preschoolers with full-time working mothers are being cared for in another home. Yet family day care is somewhat controversial, even (perhaps particularly) among parents who use it.

Many parents use family day care because they have no viable choice. According to the *Family Circle* study mentioned earlier, about half the parents who use family day care would change arrangements if they could. Why? Because the quality of care is often low—"merely custodial" wrote one St. Louis mother to me. She continued, "The sitter watches too many kids, including three infants. Even they are plunked down in front of the TV. She gives the older ones candy to keep them quiet. I'm trying to get my son out, but it's not easy to come up with something better that I can afford."

That's family day care at its worst. Happily, there's a much brighter side. Family day care at its best can be a practical, low-cost and caring solution to your childcare needs. First, family day-care providers generally *will* take infants—most day-care centers will not, and many housekeepers and nannies will decline charges under age two. Moreover, family day care can be the "closest thing to home." Because it is, after all, a home; it's a natural, spontaneous setting providing the wide range of stimuli a normal home provides, including the opportunity for your baby to interact with other children. Compared with a day-care center, it may provide more personal attention, more consistency of care because a single caregiver is usually all who is involved. If everyone is happy with the situation, so that your child stays in the same home, with the same provider for all the preschool years, family day care offers the continuity so helpful in fostering healthy attachments. This again is in contrast to center care, where the baby is cared for by several caregivers each day and where staff turnover is often high. While finding good family day care certainly requires effort and attention, it probably is more available than quality centers, or housekeepers or nannies for that matter. Available and accessible. Family day care generally costs $25 to $70 per week, depending mainly on the number of other children cared for. If your child is the only one cared for other than the woman's own, that's still considered family day care but will be more expensive.

Day-Care Center

So much is written and talked about day-care centers, you'd think they were available in every neighborhood and providing care for the majority of children of working parents. Little could be further from fact. There's a critical shortage of good day-care centers in this country—only about 1 million slots are available in day-care centers nationwide—and they serve a very small minority of children. This is especially true for infants—less than 15 percent of those in day-care centers are infants or toddlers under age three. Infant care is not offered in most day-care centers given the especially high adult-to-child ratio it requires, which makes infant day care especially expensive.

In most states, the law defines a day-care center as any facility where seven or more children are in care for more than three hours per day. In fact, centers are usually open from 8:00 A.M. to 6:00 P.M. to accommodate working parents. Day-care centers as most of us think of them are very much like nursery schools—child-centered "classrooms" or environments, with children usually grouped by age and headed by trained staff. These centers offer a wide range of enjoyable activities, appropriate equipment and toys, nutritious food and snacks and on-call medical care. This kind of center is called *developmental* day care and is day care at its best. However, developmental day care is expensive and hard to find. Many developmental centers have twice as many or more children on waiting lists as the number enrolled.

Publicly subsidized day care receives federal, state and/ or local funding and is supervised by a local government agency. Slots are generally made available to working parents with incomes below the state medium or to parents who pay fees on a sliding scale according to ability. The range is from free to $45 per week, and one does not need to be on welfare to qualify. Unfortunately, such subsidized childcare is woefully scarce. In New York City in 1983, for example, the subsidized childcare system was able to provide space for less than 5 percent of the infants and less than 20 percent of preschoolers overall whose parents qualified for the service!

Private day-care centers may be either profit-making— like the nationwide KinderCare or Child World chains— where parental fees are the centers' only support, or nonprofit organizations funded in part by sponsoring organizations such as churches, synagogues, hospitals, universities, etc., and in part by parental fees, which are sometimes set on a sliding scale. In nonprofit day care, the balance of the cost after sponsoring support plus parental fees is frequently made up from sources like the United Way or private contributions.

Good, privately run day-care centers generally range in cost from $35 to $85 per week, and more in large cities. In New York City in 1983, for example, such centers averaged $85 to $125 weekly for preschoolers, and when available, $110 to $180 per week for infants! In addition, many private day-care centers charge substantial *late fees*, if you're tardy in picking up your baby in the evening. For example, at San Francisco's highly regarded Magic Years infant-care center, where monthly fees exceed $450, I'm told you're charged $1 if 1 to 6 minutes late; $6 if 6 to 15 minutes; $8 if 16 to 25 minutes; and $16 if 26 to 35 minutes late!

Along with availability and expense, you have the problem with even the best day-care center of what to do when your baby is sick. Children in day-care centers tend to pass minor infections back and forth—one recent study showed preschoolers in day care have 30 percent more diarrheal illnesses than children who stay home. These illnesses cost parents an average of four days of work annually because they catch the disease themselves or must stay home with a sick child. Another day-care problem is that most centers have a number of different caregivers caring for your baby during the course of the day. That, coupled with high staff turnover, breaks the consistency and continuity of care.

If you plan to enroll your child in a family day-care home or day-care center:

• Start looking very early, particularly if you hope to enroll an infant. Day-care center places for infants are very scarce and you may be on a waiting list for a long while. Family day care for infants is easier to find—you could start with that and switch to a day-care center later on if you desire.

• Get basic information from the center or home over the phone: space availability, hours, fees, overtime charges, provisions (if any) for care of a sick child, whether payment is required over your vacation days or days when the child stays home, staff size and training. Turnover for day-care staff. Whether receipts

are given for the tax credit.
• Ask about number of children cared for, ages, and staff-to-child ratio. A 1979 investigation, the National Day Care Study, suggested that optimum group size for infant care is twelve; for toddlers, eight to twelve; for three- to five-year-olds, fourteen. State day-care center laws differ on number of staff required, but child development experts suggest one trained adult for every four infants under age two; one adult to seven older preschoolers. In family day care, the smaller the group the better. The average is 3.5 kids, although most state laws allow 6, *including* the caregiver's own. (More children and the home becomes a center, and subject to more regulations.) Hesitate to place your child in a family day care with only one adult in attendance and more than four children. With four children, it's best if only one is an infant.
• Ask if the day-care center is licensed. However, don't automatically exclude family day care that's unlicensed or you'll be eliminating more than 90 percent of the homes. Frequently, state licensing procedures for family day care are such that meeting them would drive the homes out of existence or make them as expensive as a day-care center. One problem with unlicensed family day care, however—the caregiver may insist on off-the-books payment.
• Of course you must visit any center or home you're considering. Plan to spend several hours. Be wary of any facility that discourages parental visits. Trust your instinctive reaction. You're looking for a clean, safe, well-ventilated space with easy access to enough toileting facilities. A good variety of toys. An opportunity for outdoor play. A warm, sensible, interested, healthy staff. (Ask if staff is required to have annual medical checkups—some parents ask to see the reports.) In a day-care center especially, expect staff to encourage creative developmental activities, but not a hard-nosed academic regimen.
• In family day care particularly, understand your re-

sponsibility for providing food, diapers, toys, etc. Many parents duplicate basic pieces of baby equipment and leave them at the home for convenience. This is expensive, however.

• Make sure of stable attendance of children, all of whom must show proof of immunization before enrollment. Don't leave your child in a home where new children get dropped off daily.

• Ask about accident insurance on the children.

• Child-rearing practices you feel strongly about—for example, no pacifiers, no junk food, no TV, no spanking, whatever—should be discussed thoroughly.

Childcare Tax Credit

Since 1980, there has been a shift away from direct federal support and subsidies to day-care centers, and toward the childcare tax credit—but unfortunately, it doesn't amount to much money. A tax credit is *not* the same thing as a tax deduction, which reduces gross income for the purpose of calculating your tax liability. A tax credit, instead, is a dollar amount subtracted directly from the taxes you owe.

You're eligible to claim a tax credit for childcare services if you have a child who requires care because both parents are working—either full-time or part-time—or actively looking for work; or if one parent is a full-time student and the other is employed and if, of course, you're paying for any of the kinds of childcare discussed above. (Also eligible are expenses for day or overnight camps, if your intention is childcare rather than just education or the camp experience.)

The amount of the tax credit is calculated considering your specific childcare expenses and your adjusted gross income. And here's the disappointment. First, the *maximum* amount of childcare expense against which the credit can be calculated is $2,400 for one child, $4,800 for two or more. Next, the credit is 30 percent of childcare expenses (subject to the maximum just mentioned) for taxpayers with adjusted gross incomes of $10,000 or less and is reduced 1 percent for each additional $2,000 of income. However, it does not drop below 20 percent, regardless of income. So, the maximum childcare tax credit for a taxpayer with an income above $28,000 is only $480 for one child, $960 for two or more. To repeat, those amounts would be directly subtracted from the tax owed. However, they won't seem like much if you're paying a day-care center $450 a month or a housekeeper $600.

To claim the credit, you must file IRS Form 1040 (the long form), plus attach Form 2441, on which you've calculated the credit you qualify for. Be sure to save for three years all receipts for childcare expenses, including relevant taxes you pay an in-home caregiver (Social Security, etc.) but excluding any transportation costs related to the care. Some *states* also have a childcare tax credit, so check that out, too.

Given how limited the childcare tax credit is, you'll have to resign yourself to paying childcare expenses with after-tax dollars—right out of take-home pay. Unless, that is, you're lucky enough to work for an employer that has restructured its benefit plan to take advantage of a recent change in tax laws.

Tax Incentives for Employer-Assisted Childcare

The government has made one other significant tax move regarding childcare in recent years. It has set up tax incentives for employers to help employees with childcare arrangements. Specifically, under the Economic Recovery Tax Act of 1981, employers can establish tax-favored programs to help pay for employee childcare expenses. Under this law, if childcare assistance is offered as part of a formal written benefits plan, and so long as it doesn't discriminate in favor of highly paid employees, those employees who use the benefit do *not* have to report its value as taxable income. In other words, you can pay for some or all (depending on the specifics of your employer's plan) of your childcare expenses with *before-tax* dollars! A very valuable benefit indeed—the higher your tax bracket, the more valuable. Moreover, any expenditures the employer

makes for childcare assistance can be deducted for its tax
purposes as a business expense. Everybody benefits! (One
unfortunate exception: this law does *not* apply if the care
is given by a relative.)

So far, the corporate response has been largely to do
new studies to assess employee interest. Some companies
have gone the next step and set up childcare information
and referral services for their employees. A small number
have purchased slots in existing day-care centers or family
day-care homes; others provide the employee with a coupon
in a dollar amount to go toward the expense of care in
such facilities. In a few instances, companies have joined
together to either back or establish day-care centers for
their employees. Fewer still—about four hundred employers
nationwide—have established *on-site* day care for the children of employees. More than half of these four hundred
employers are hospitals, another large block is universities,
and most of the remaining are high-tech companies concerned with competitive recruitment.

This all represents a significant departure from traditional employee benefits plans, so it's hardly surprising
that corporate response has thus far been slow and modest.
Some childcare researchers and human resources professionals, however, are quite optimistic. They expect the
popularity of flexible benefit plans to grow dramatically,
largely in response to the changing nature of family and
work in our society. When this happens, they think the
childcare benefit will become widely available. Maybe for
your next baby?!

❖ III ❖❖❖❖❖❖❖❖❖❖❖❖❖❖❖❖❖❖❖❖

Planning for the Future

❖ 13

WRITING A WILL

What Is a Will?

A valid will is a legal document that directs the distribution of your property after your death, according to your *expressed* wishes and intentions. In effect, a well-drawn will provides you with a degree of control over your assets and possessions even after death.

Who Needs a Will?

You do, definitely. With no exception, any adult reading these words should have a will. Whether man or woman, rich or poor, age twenty-five or forty, gainfully employed or not—you should have a will. Let me emphasize that both husband *and* wife should have wills. Becoming parents only makes this more pressing.

Why? Because a will allows the distribution of your assets (subject to some legal restrictions) in the manner you want and believe is in the best interest of your family. Without a will, the laws of the state in which you reside will determine how your assets are disposed of, according to an inflexible formula. Most people assume that a surviving spouse automatically inherits everything if the other spouse dies, and is free to use those assets as seen fit. Not true! Depending on the laws of your state, a surviving spouse may be entitled to only one-half or one-third your estate, or to a share equal to a child's share—so that what he or she gets depends on the number of children. Moreover, the surviving spouse could be restricted in the use of the inheritance of the children who are still minors—the remaining parent is not necessarily free to use the children's funds in the way he or she thinks best to provide for them. All of this can make for unnecessary hardship, especially if the estate is small. Say a young father dies without a will, leaving a dependent widow and a young child, and an estate worth $75,000. The wife would probably inherit $37,500 outright and so would the minor—but the wife would not have free use of the child's share. Instead, because the father dies without a will resulting in an outright inheritance by the minor, the court would be required to appoint a *guardian* for the minor's property. While the mother is the first in line for this appointment, she is not spared the trouble and expense of the legal formalities of guardianship. She must provide periodic accountings to the court, and in many instances must go to the court for authorization to spend some of the child's inheritance even if it's on the child's behalf.

Moreover, if you die without a will, you don't have the opportunity to choose your own *executor*. This is the person who safeguards the estate's assets while it's passing through the courts (called "probate") and makes sure the assets are distributed according to your wishes. If you die without a will—called "intestate"—the court instead will appoint an *administrator* to handle these tasks, and a *fee* will be charged against the estate for them. These fees are sometimes very stiff, and can take a disproportionate bite out of a small estate. Administrators must also be *bonded* in most states, and this results in additional expense. Instead, if you write a will and appoint your spouse or friend as executor, he or she will often waive an executor's fee.

And particularly if your estate is large, dying intestate may subject it to unnecessary large estate taxes. To minimize the taxes that larger estates are susceptible to requires expert planning embodied in a well-drawn will.

And finally, you need a will so you can name a legal *guardian* for your minor children in the event both parents die. If the parents don't name a guardian, the estate will have to pay a bond and fees for a court-appointed guardian. It can take many months before the court determines who the ultimate guardian will be, and sometimes court testimony is even required of the child! In the end, the children may go to someone other than whom you would have wished. It sometimes even happens that they are put under the care of the state, despite the fact that there are friends who would gladly have taken them and done a fine job of raising them. The issue of guardianship alone should send you scurrying to a lawyer to have a will properly drawn up.

In sum, a will can save your estate considerable expense in bonds and administrator and guardian fees. For larger estates, considerable money may be saved in taxes. With a will, you can choose your beneficiaries and leave property to your children in an intelligent way. You can also choose who will manage your estate, and can name a legal guardian for your children. With a will, your family will probably get their inheritance faster and with less legal fuss. Yet despite all these compelling reasons for writing a will, as many as seven in ten Americans die without one—and even more fail to name a legal guardian for their children!

Do You Need a Lawyer's Help?

Yes, you probably do. We've all heard stories about a hastily scrawled, "I, Jane Doe, being of sound mind and body ... ," but forget it. Some states will not allow a handwritten (called "holographic") will under any circumstances. Others may allow them, assuming they observe several formalities—formalities most of us don't know about. For example, did you know that most states require *three* witnesses to the signing of your will, and that none of them should be beneficiaries—lest they risk invalidating the will or disinheriting themselves? A will must be clear and unambiguous *in the eyes of the court.* Unfortunately, a will written in everyday language which is perfectly clear to a lay reader may in fact be full of legal loopholes and ambiguities.

What about "fill-in-the-blank" wills—standard forms that you can complete and get notarized and witnessed? These are available for a few dollars in some stationery stores or from some life insurance agents. However, these are not recommended for the same reasons cited for "do-it-yourself" wills. The only situation in which these become acceptable is if for some reason the alternative is no will at all. Wills and estate planning are a complicated business; they cry out for *personalized, professional* attention.

Many young people (and many young women who are full-time homemakers in particular) mistakenly assume that they don't have enough property to warrant a professionally drawn will. In fact, most people have more property than they think. You may not have a big savings account or stock portfolio, but what about your home, car, jewelry, family heirlooms, other personal effects? Or thrift, stock-option or profit-sharing plans at work? What about veteran or union benefits? Your IRAs? Or debts owed to you? Your interest in a small business? Even a smaller estate benefits from a professional will—assets are distributed in the manner intended, in a timely way, at the lowest cost.

By professional help, I mean an attorney specializing in estate planning. Particularly if you have a larger estate, not just any lawyer will do. Relevant law is too complex, there are too many formalities to be observed and traps to be avoided, and the potential cost of mistakes is too high. So go to a real expert. Moreover, the estate lawyer should be from the state in which you legally reside, pay taxes and would expect your will to be probated. This is because state laws have a lot to say about the final disposition of your property and they differ significantly.

How Much Will It Cost?

That depends on how complex your estate is. A simple, basic will might cost between $50 and $150—more in big cities, where the lawyer's cost of doing business is high. A more complicated will that sets up a trust and related provisions can cost $400 to $500; for a very large estate, the cost can be substantially more. However, if your estate is large, it's virtually certain that an estate lawyer will save you much more than you'll pay in fees by drawing up a "tax-sensitive" will. Be sure to discuss fees with the lawyer in advance. Comparison shopping is a good idea. If a lawyer draws up both a husband's and a wife's wills, you may get a lower fee for the second one.

If you cannot afford a private lawyer, there are legal clinics that can help. They will do an adequate job for you, and many charge fees of less than $50 for a simple will based on a standard form.

Will-Makers' Checklist

One way to save your attorney time and thus you money is for you to prepare in advance a comprehensive list of information needed to draw up the wills. This list should include information about your assets and liabilities, and about your personal affairs. Include the following:

PERSONAL INFORMATION

- Names, addresses, dates of birth of you, your spouse, children and other immediate family members.
- Location of birth certificates.
- Names and addresses of any others you want to make beneficiaries.
- Social Security numbers and location of cards.
- Date and place of marriage, and location of marriage certificate. Information on any prenuptial agreement.
- Military service branch, dates of service and discharge. Location of discharge papers.
- Names and addresses of guardian(s) for minors in the event of the death of both parents.
- If previously married, date and place, and name of former spouse. Location of his or her death certificate, or date, place and location of divorce papers. If divorced, note if contested and if so, who brought the action. Was there a divorce settlement/antenuptial agreement?

(This information will help the lawyer determine if the spouse retains any inheritance rights.)
• Note if you have any immediate relatives (especially children) who are handicapped or require special care.
• Name(s) and address(es) of the person or institution you want named as the trustee(s) and executor(s) of your estate.
• If you own a second residence, its address and the amount of time you spend there. Note where you vote and pay income taxes.
• Location of copies of income tax returns, and name and address of who prepared them.
• Names and addresses of accountant and stock broker. Name of any person to whom you have given power of attorney.
• Names and addresses of your employers and location of your employment contracts, if you have such.
• Funeral arrangements preferred.

ASSETS AND LIABILITIES

• Details of savings and checking accounts, including bank location, account number, location of passbook.
• Details of life insurance policies: insuring company, policy numbers, kind, face amount, location of contract, beneficiaries, name and address of your agent.
• Policies owned by others for which you are named a beneficiary.
• Details of any pension-annuity plan you are entitled to.
• Details of stock-option and/or stock-purchase plans in which you are enrolled, and any other employee benefits that may be payable at your death.
• Information on any trust for which you are a beneficiary.
• Details of stock and bond accounts.
• Details concerning annuity plans, IRAs, Keogh plans and/or deferred compensation plans.

- Details of any business interest you own. Any debts owed to you.
- Full itemization of any real estate you own: location, price paid, estimate of current marketable value, whether ownership is joint, location of deeds. Any other assets valued at over $200: cars, art, furniture, jewelry, furs, etc. Details of your mortgage debt: institution's name and address, amount owed, term, relevant documents and records. Note if you have mortgage insurance, which automatically pays off the mortgage in the event of your death.
- Location of safety-deposit box and key.
- Statement of your current income.
- Details of other debts you owe, to whom and under what terms. Car loans, significant credit card and bank loans, and lease obligations are common examples.

Make extra copies of this checklist and give them to your executor and beneficiaries, as well as to your estate attorney.

Some Assets Pass Outside the Will

Assets that are *jointly owned* (such as when husband and wife jointly own their home or a bank account) and assets for which a specific *beneficiary* has been named (like a life insurance policy) are assets that cannot be willed. These are said to "pass outside the will," because they go directly to the beneficiaries. (They are also protected from any creditor's claims.) Other common examples of beneficiary-designated assets that pass outside the will are pension and annuity benefits that continue in some form after your death and U.S. savings bonds. Despite the fact that such assets pass outside the estate, your attorney must be informed of them for estate-planning purposes. For example, planning can prevent these assets from being added to your gross estate for the purpose of calculating tax against it. This is an area in which literally tens of thousands of dollars can potentially be saved for the estate by virtue of professional planning!

Choosing an Executor, Guardian and Trustee

An *executor or executrix* is the person or institution you name in your will whose job it is to present the will to the court to have it probated. The executor takes title to the willed property, has it appraised for tax purposes where necessary, and files the necessary federal and state tax returns. He or she must also pay out of the estate any debts owed and collect any monies due. All this *may* take as long as a year or even more. Once these affairs are settled, the executor distributes the remaining assets in accord with the will's provisions.

The role clearly entails much responsibility and work. For this effort, an executor is paid a *commission*, which is fixed by state statute or determined by the court, based on the complexity and size of the estate. When the surviving spouse or a close friend is named as the executor, he or she frequently waives the fee. However, think carefully before naming your spouse or close friend as executor if he or she is financially inexperienced and if your estate is large or complex. It can end up costing the estate a lot more money than is saved by waiving executor commissions. A good executor is informed about appraisals, taxes, investments, accounting and filings, and he or she is organized, meets deadlines and keeps orderly records. If your spouse or friend doesn't measure up in this regard, consider naming your lawyer or bank as executor. If you wish, your spouse or friend can be co-executor. (Recognize, however, that two executors may mean double commissions.)

Before you name any individual or institution as an executor of your estate, discuss the situation fully with that person or an institutional representative. Private individuals may have reasons for not wanting to serve in this capacity, and a bank will sometimes not do so if the estate is too small. Never surprise someone after the fact with executorship of your estate!

Choosing a *guardian* for your children who are legally minors demands even more careful thought. Always put your children's welfare first—don't worry about insulting certain family members if you don't choose them. Don't even worry about insulting the entire family if you think that dear friends would do a better job of raising your children than any of your relatives. Things to consider in making your choice include the potential guardians' age and health; the stability of their marriage; whether you feel comfortable with their cultural and/or religious values; the compatibility of your children with theirs, if they have them; and their financial situation. (Although your children will have an inheritance, it may not be enough to cover their expenses over the years.) You should also decide if you want the guardian to be both guardian of the child *and* of the child's property. A bank or other institution can be named property guardian, and this may be a good idea if the child's guardian is financially inexperienced. Finally, you should decide and note in your will if you want the guardian to legally adopt the child.

Of course, you should thoroughly discuss all this with potential guardians before naming them in your will. This includes giving them at least an approximate idea of the inheritance you plan to pass to your children, as this is information they may need to help determine if guardianship is a responsibility they can handle.

A *trust* is an arrangement whereby you give assets to a *trustee*—an individual or an institution—to manage and invest for the benefit of the trust's beneficiary or beneficiaries. If your estate is a larger one, your attorney will probably suggest that you establish a trust of one kind or another. Not only are trusts especially useful in the instance when beneficiaries are young or financially inexperienced, but there are usually tax advantages, too. Trusts are subject to varying state laws, some of which are complex—you definitely need an estate lawyer to establish one for you.

In terms of a trustee, look for the same skills, knowledge and characteristics as in an executor. *The beneficiary of a trust should not be named its trustee, unless a co-trustee is named, too.* Chances are you'll choose an attorney or a bank representative. Trustees are paid commissions fixed by state law or decided by the courts, usually in accord with the size of the estate.

Periodic Review of Your Will

Once you have a will, you cannot, unfortunately, lock it in a safety-deposit box and forget about it. While a well-drawn will has some built-in flexibility—for example, wording allowing for the birth of a second child—it's essentially a precisely worded document reflecting a given situation. (That's as it should be. Ambiguous wording may result in a will that has to be interpreted by the court, and there's no guarantee that the court will interpret as you intended.) Of course, a person's situation can change significantly. When it does, the will should be reviewed.

It's appropriate to review your will at the birth of a child (even if you think it's written to cover that); at the death of a spouse; if you divorce; if your former spouse remarries; or if you have a significant change—for better or worse—in your property or income. (For example, if you suffered a significant financial reverse, you might want to eliminate a previously made special bequest to your alma mater to focus remaining assets on your family.) You might also want to review your will if your beneficiaries have a significant change in their financial situation. You should review your will if you move to another state in case formalities differ there. Review it if the tax laws change, or if your executor, trustee or guardian dies or is no longer able or appropriate to serve.

If a review of your will indicates a change is necessary, expect additional legal fees.

Another reason you shouldn't plunk your will into a safety-deposit box is that your safety-deposit box may be sealed by the court at the time of your death. A court order would then be required to open it, causing needless delay. Instead, leave it with your attorney or your institutional executor. Keep a copy in a safe place at home, and be sure your executor and beneficiaries know where it is.

❖ 14

LIFE INSURANCE AND DISABILITY INCOME INSURANCE

Like wills, life and disability insurance are subjects that many young couples find difficult to think about and tempting to put off. Even more so than wills, these are technical, complex subjects once you scratch the surface of them. And beyond the surface you must go, in order to figure out who in your family needs such insurance policies, of what type, in what amount and how to comparison-shop for them.

LIFE INSURANCE

What Does It Do?

The *main* purpose of life insurance is to protect dependents from the financial consequences of the death of a breadwinner. Life insurance creates an "instant estate" for your family at your death. This instant estate steps in to replace part of the income you would have generated over the years had you continued to live. It may be used for both immediate needs, such as burial and estate taxes; intermediate income for a period of adjustment so that a spouse can get back on his or her feet; and longer-term needs such as college education of children. While life insurance has purposes other than financial security for one's dependents—for example, as a tax shelter or as a forced savings plan—the primary focus of this chapter is family financial protection, which is the main reason that most people buy life insurance.

Who Needs Life Insurance?

First and foremost, a *primary breadwinner* with a dependent or dependents. It takes an income earner plus one or more people who *must* depend on that breadwinner for support to create a compelling need for life insurance. A spouse, who for whatever reason could not support herself or himself, creates a need for life insurance. Perhaps the most compelling need, however, is created by a child. With only rare exception, the birth of a baby—who will require support for twenty or more years—creates the need for life insurance on the primary breadwinner.

What if both members of a couple are breadwinners? In the absence of a child, perhaps neither would need life insurance. It depends largely on whether either one could support himself or herself in a satisfactory manner in the other's absence. However, with a baby, the situation changes, particularly if one of the adults (usually the mother) decides to stay home to raise the child. Suddenly, what was a two-income, no-dependent couple, becomes a threesome depending on one income into the foreseeable future—a situation crying out for life insurance on the remaining breadwinner.

When both adults continue as vital breadwinners after the birth of a child—increasingly common today—*then both should have life insurance,* if possible. Their life insurance policies should be in rough proportion to their contribution to overall family income. If one adult earns substantially more than the other, then that primary breadwinner should carry the more insurance. Let me emphasize this. The family priority should be to get the primary breadwinner adequate insurance—and "adequate" may be considerably more than you think, as we'll see below— before buying insurance on the secondary breadwinner.

Since more and more women are continuing to work outside the home even after the birth of a baby, and contributing vital economic support to their families, you'd expect statistics to show a big jump in the number of women life insurance policyholders. They do. In 1971, the ratio of men to women policy buyers was 2.5 to 1. In 1981, it was 1.5 to 1—and the average *size* policy purchased on women's lives has been increasing at a *faster* rate than that of men.

In fact, of course, a woman need not be a member of the paid work force to need or want a life insurance policy. These days, *an increasing number of full-time homemakers have life insurance policies, too.* After all, a full-time homemaker makes a vital contribution to the economic well-being of the family. If the homemaker should die, especially if there are still young children in the house, these services would have to be replaced, and that would create a new and considerable cash outflow for the household. So life insurance on a full-time homemaker *can* be a good idea. There are several "ifs," however. First, the breadwinner should be adequately insured before thought is given to homemaker insurance. Second, can the family afford a second insurance policy? If you're just starting out, and money is especially tight, you probably have higher priorities. And third, if a family has savings or other income to pay for housekeeping and childcare expenses in the event of the homemaker's death, it may not need homemaker insurance.

Should You Buy Life Insurance on Your Baby?

The answer is *no!* It rarely, if ever, makes economic sense to do so. Resist the blandishments of life insurance agents—who usually start to call as soon as the birth announcement appears in the newspaper—who want to sell insurance on your baby's life. Remember that the main purpose of life insurance is to protect dependents from the financial consequences of a breadwinner's death, and you'll agree it's not very sensible to take out a policy on a newborn.

Life insurance agents will argue that coverage for a child can be had at extremely low rates—so why not have it?

The reason that the rates are so low is that statistically there's an exceedingly small chance that the baby or growing child will die, requiring the insurance company to pay off. Agents will also argue that coverage bought for a baby guarantees later insurability as an adult, whatever the health condition. In fact, only about 3 percent of life insurance applicants are ever denied coverage for health reasons. An agent may further argue that life insurance bought now on the baby can provide funds for a later college education. In fact, there are more efficient and advantageous ways to save for a college education (see Chapter 14). And finally, if you've resisted all these blandishments, a life insurance agent may try to sell you a $1,000 or $2,000 policy to pay for the expenses of a final illness and burial. But don't be taken in by this. In the first place, it's health insurance, not life insurance, your baby needs. A $1,000 policy would probably not, in fact, be adequate to cover a final illness that was at all protracted. Second, if you're tempted to buy baby insurance out of worry over the cost of a funeral, you're living very close to the bone and surely have more vital things to spend your money on than insurance that covers against the exceedingly small chance of an untimely death of a child.

How Much Life Insurance Do You Need?

The basic question is, how much *income* would a surviving spouse with one or two young children need in the event of the death of the primary breadwinner? Begin by realizing that life insurance rarely has to shoulder the burden alone. Most of us have other income sources that come to the fore in the event of a breadwinner's death. *You must first figure how much income these other sources would provide*, before you can determine how much insurance the family needs.

First, there are *Social Security survivor benefits*. The families of most wage and salary earners working in jobs where Social Security taxes are paid are eligible. For those with substantial earnings, the benefits may be significant— up to about $1,050 a month—and they are *tax-free*. A good life insurance agent can help you figure out what your family's Social Security survivors benefits would be, or you can get instructions from your local Social Security office and figure it out yourself. Survivor's benefits are paid monthly, but they must be applied for—they don't start automatically. Social Security survivor's benefits are to a large degree *child-raising* benefits. They continue until the youngest child is eighteen, or twenty-two if the child is a full-time student. After that, the surviving parent generally will not receive further survivor's benefits until she or he turns sixty-five.

Next, does the breadwinner have a *group life insurance policy* through work? In what amount? Equivalent to a year's salary is common. Does the employer also offer a *family income-protection program?* Some companies provide that an employee's survivors receive a certain percentage of that employee's last monthly income for a period of years equal or double that of the employee's years on the job. And is the breadwinner eligible for any *pension* or *annuity* or is he or she a member of a *deferred compensation plan* (including a veteran's pension) that is available in whole or in part to survivors?

What cash and savings are available? Any stocks or other investment? Or equity in real estate or a business *that would be sold* in the event of the breadwinner's death? And finally, would the surviving spouse work outside the home for pay? What are the likely earnings?

Going through this exercise will give you at least a rough estimate of your monthly income needs against what would be available in the event of the main breadwinner's death. Now I'll give you the general rule the experts use. They maintain that *a surviving spouse with one or two young children usually needs 60 to 75 percent of the family's current after-tax income* to more or less maintain economic well-being. If you've calculated that your family *would* have that much income—which is perfectly possible if the surviving spouse has a high-paying job, if the deceased has lots of life insurance through work and/or if the family has substantial assets and few debts—then your (additional) life insurance needs may not be significant. You might want to buy just enough additional life insurance to pay off the mortgage on your home (assuming you don't already have mortgage insurance through the mortgage lender) plus enough to cover the cost of probating your estate (estimated at about 4 percent of the estate's value, exclusive of any life insurance). Or, if you've not made other provisions, you may want to buy a life insurance policy, the proceeds of which will pay for your children's college education. (And that *can* necessitate a fairly large policy!) If, however, the death of your family's main breadwinner would result in a monthly income much *less* than the 60 to 75 percent goal, that's where individually purchased life insurance steps in.

If you prefer a simpler approach to calculating your life insurance needs, there is another rule of thumb for doing so: *Have life insurance valued at five times your annual income.* While this formula is derided as simplistic by some expert observers, at least one such observer—NICO, the National Insurance Consumer Organization, a nonprofit public interest organization—thinks the rule is fairly sound. More specifically, *NICO thinks that the five times annual income rule is applicable to most families with two young children, who in addition have group life insurance at work equal to at least one year's salary and who are eligible for Social Security survivor benefits.* NICO maintains that those of you with only one child, with a spouse enjoying a high-paying job, with substantial net worth and/or with good pension or similar benefits available in the event of the main breadwinner's death can do with less insurance.

About 85 percent of American families have life insurance. Of these, the average amount owned is about $57,000. From this figure, the American Council of Life Insurance calculates average insurance protection for covered families equal to only *twenty-five months* of total disposable personal income—less than half of what the "rule of thumb" suggests. In other words, *most American families are underinsured.*

There are undoubtedly many and varied reasons for

this. Key ones include lack of understanding of the importance of life insurance and what it can do, an unwillingness to plan ahead, especially about one's own death, and differing ideas about security and the future. And, of course, *cost constraints* prevent many people from buying adequate insurance. Unfortunately, it can be one thing to calculate how much life insurance you need, and another to determine how much you can afford. However, there *are* ways you can cut the cost of life insurance. One is to buy the kind of insurance known as *annual renewable term* and the second is to *comparison-shop* for a policy.

What Kind of Life Insurance Is Right for You?

There are hundreds of policies on the market, with a bewildering array of names designed to sound persuasive. All these policies, however, basically boil down to two kinds of life insurance: *term* and *whole-life.*

Term insurance is the easier to understand. As the name implies, you buy this insurance for a specific period of time or term. Its *only* purpose is to provide survivors with a cash settlement *if* the insured dies within the designated term. There is no savings component or cash value to a term policy. You get nothing back out of it if you don't die within the specified term. For this reason, term is known as "pure" insurance protection.

Typical terms of coverage are one or five years. When the term is up, so is your protection—unless you've bought a *renewable* term policy. If you have, you've the right to renew your coverage regardless of any changes in your health or occupation, until you reach the age specified in the policy—usually sixty-five or seventy. Naturally, the premium you pay for this coverage increases each time you renew, to reflect the fact that you're older and so have an increased statistical probability of death.

Whole-life insurance, as its name implies, is designed to provide *lifetime* coverage. Whole-life is more complicated than term. Like term, it provides protection if the insured dies in the form of a cash settlement to beneficiaries of the face value of the policy. But *it also has a savings component,* a "cash value" that builds up over the years as one pays premiums. The insurance company also pays interest on this cash buildup. Understand that cash value is for the benefit of the *insured*, the *owner* of the policy, and *not* the policy's ultimate beneficiary. While the insured cannot withdraw money from the savings component of a whole-life policy (unless the policy is canceled or "surrendered" for cash value, which eliminates the insurance protection), he or she can *borrow* against it, usually at favorable interest rates. Because of its cash-value component, whole-life is pushed by insurance agents as both insurance and an investment.

There are many versions of whole-life or cash-value insurance. The most common is *straight-life*, in which you pay the same premium each year of your life for the same level of insurance coverage—that is, the premium doesn't go up as you get older, nor does the face value of the policy decline. This set premium is determined by your age at the time you take out the policy.

Does this permanent protection, at stable premiums, plus cash-value buildup sound too good to be true? Is there a catch? Of course there is! And it's just what you think— the *amount* of the premium.

Whole-life insurance works by charging a premium that is *far* higher in the earlier years than needed to pay death claims. This means that *for a younger person whole-life is dramatically more expensive than term insurance*—often five to ten times more! For example, a thirty-five-year-old, nonsmoking man might pay $130 for $100,000 of annual renewable term (ART) insurance. For $100,000 whole-life, he'd pay about *$1,300!* Of course, with ART, his premium would go up every year—but only slowly for many years. With the same policy at forty-five, he'd be paying $370; at fifty-five, $800. That's against $1,300, year in, year out for whole-life. While it's true that at some age, the premiums would cross and term would become more expensive on an annual basis, that would only happen when the person was considerably older. By that time, his life insurance needs might be much lower—or even nonexistent—because his children would have grown up and become financially independent, the mortgage have been paid off, etc.

The advantage of term insurance is that young families tend to need a lot of insurance at a time in their lives when it's most difficult to pay for. If you're one of these families, ART is the answer—it provides the most protection at the least current cost.

Arguments Life Insurance Agents Will Use to Get You to Buy Whole-Life

These are noted because it's practically guaranteed you'll hear them. Agents are trained by their companies to believe in whole-life, and they can be pretty persuasive. The first thing you should know is that whole-life is far more profitable than term for the companies *and* for the agents. It's not unusual for the agent's commission to be *50 percent* of your first-year premium (with some companies, it's more). Since (using the example cited above) 50 percent of $1,300 is ten times more than 50 percent of $130, which kind of policy do you think the agent will push? To convince you to buy whole-life, agents will argue that:

- *Term is temporary while whole-life is permanent.* In fact, term can and should be bought with a *conversion privilege* that allows you to convert to a whole-life policy within a certain period (usually up to age sixty), *if* you want to. However, it's by no means certain that one would want to. Many people don't need insurance in their later years. After retirement, there's no need to insure against earnings loss. Then, Social Security, pension, IRA and other retirement income takes over, and these income sources don't stop with one spouse's death. Another thing: after thirty or forty years of inflation, how much will a $100,000 "permanent" policy be *really* worth? You'll have paid years of high premiums in relatively expensive present dollars, for your beneficiaries to be paid off years hence in much less valuable future dollars.

- *Term premiums go up every year.* True, but gradually.

If you buy term young, you'll enjoy years of low premiums and far higher protection than you could afford with whole-life. And as you get older and your premiums get higher, chances are your income will have increased too, keeping you "even" in your ability to pay.

• *Whole-life is a way of forced savings; it's an investment.* True, but do you need to be forced to save? Even if you do, you probably have better vehicles—thrift plans or U.S. savings bonds at work, for example. And while there are tax advantages to interest earned on cash-value buildup of a whole-life policy, similar advantages are available elsewhere. In any case, you have to be in a fairly high tax bracket for this to be very meaningful. As an investment, whole-life insurance isn't very exciting. Most experts (including the Federal Trade Commission in a 1979 study) stress that the rate of return on most policies is inferior to what you could earn elsewhere. Note too that cash value usually builds up slowly—you have to stick with the policy for years before it's worth much in that regard. It's for this reason that consumer experts stress you should *never* buy whole-life unless you're reasonably certain of sticking with it for at least ten years. And yet studies show that one in five whole-life buyers drop their policies within two years—often because they're so expensive! But dropping these policies so early makes them *extraordinarily* expensive given the high premiums and little, if any, cash buildup. Why think of life insurance as an investment at all? Instead, buy term and invest your "left over" disposable dollars. That way you get both more insurance and almost certainly a better return on your investment dollar.

• *Term insurance is money down the drain, whereas you can always get something back out with whole-life.* A variation on this is that "you have to die to beat term," whereas you can make use during your life of a whole-life policy. In fact, of course, term premiums aren't wasted. They buy your family financial security. While it's true you can get something back out of whole-life, remember that cash values build up slowly, and surrendering such a policy early can result in the worst of all worlds—no more insurance, high expenses, little cash back out. Also remember that when you die the insurance company pays your survivors *only* the face value of the policy—*not* the face value plus your cash buildup. In other words, with most whole-life policies, the company uses your cash buildup or savings to pay part of the claim! In a sense, then, your survivors are getting less pure insurance protection, per se, with a cash-value policy.

• *You can do things with whole-life you can't do with term.* Yes, you can borrow against the *cash value* of a whole-life policy, once it builds up, and usually at good rates, too. However, if you do so, you're *reducing* your insurance protection until you pay the loan back. In the event of your death, your beneficiaries would get the face value of the policy *minus* the loan.

You'll hear these and more arguments for whole-life over term. And there *are* certainly some people for whom whole-life is a good idea. These might be people in high tax brackets who would benefit from the tax breaks of whole-life. People with large estates who will owe substantial estate taxes may want a major whole-life policy to pay off those taxes (especially if the estate is not very liquid). Whole-life is appropriate for the older, affluent couple with a new baby—and there are a rising number of such couples today—who need a lot of insurance protection for years ahead but for whom the cost of term is approaching whole-life because of their age.

If, however, you are young, of moderate to middle income, and have dependents who necessitate a lot of insurance protection, the better buy is annual renewable term with a conversion privilege. With ART, you get a larger bang for your insurance buck.

Comparison Shopping

Once you've decided on the kind of life insurance you need, start shopping for a policy. And make no mistake: comparable policies from various companies differ in price,

so comparison shopping can save thousands of dollars over
the years a policy is in effect. The bigger the policy, the
more important it is to comparison-shop. In fact, if you
comparison-shop for only one of the many services and
goods discussed in this book, it should be insurance.

Of course, *cost comparisons can only be made between
comparable life insurance plans.* Compare ART to ART,
whole-life to whole-life in the same face amounts. Other
features to compare: whether the policy pays dividends or
not, renewability and conversion privileges in term policies;
loan rights and rates in whole-life, and grace periods before
coverage lapses. The cost of a life insurance policy is not
the premium alone! Policies that pay *dividends* to you
obviously reduce the policy's net cost. If you buy a whole-
life policy, the rate of return on the cash-value buildup
will also obviously affect its real cost. The time value of
money must be considered too. And be sure to look at
what the policy will cost *over a period of years.* Don't be
fooled by a policy with an unusually low first-year premium.
Its rates may increase steeply after that initial "come-on"
premium.

To cover all these cost factors, and to provide a uniform
method of life insurance cost comparison, something called
an *interest-adjusted net cost index* has been developed by
the National Association of Insurance Commissioners,
whose members are state insurance regulators. It's beyond
the scope of this chapter to discuss how this index is
calculated. Nonetheless, the index is very useful for consumers, so *be sure* to ask for the interest-adjusted net cost
index for any policy you're considering. This index provides
the most accurate measure of relative prices of comparable
policies for given periods of time. *The lower the index
number, the less expensive the policy.* The cost index
definitely takes precedence over any premium differentials
based on such factors as sex or body build. Say company
number one offers a preferred rate to a lean, nonsmoking
woman, whereas company number two is indifferent in
terms of the premium to the sex or weight of the insured.
If the policy of company number two has a lower cost

index number, that's the cheaper policy, even if its first-year premium is higher than company number one's.

Another thing to ask about is *break points*—the levels of insurance coverage when rate discounts kick in. For example, you might be able to buy policies of $50,000 to $99,000 at one rate per $1,000 of insurance coverage versus policies of $100,000 to $249,000 for a lower rate per $1,000, and so on. Break points differ by company and kind of policy, so ask the insurer how much you have to buy to get a discounted rate.

And a final point about comparison shopping. The lowest cost indexes in town won't help you if you buy from a life insurance company that's not financially stable. To be on the safe side, most insurance and consumer experts suggest that you buy only from a company that has an A^+ or A rating, as awarded by *Best's Insurance Reports*. There are more than two hundred such companies, so you'll have plenty to choose from. Ask the agent what the Best ratings are for the company or companies that he or she represents.

Sources of Low-Cost Life Insurance

First, if you are covered by a *group life insurance program at work*, find out if you can extend your coverage. The rates are sometimes as much as 40 percent lower than what you can do on the "outside" as an individual—sometimes, but not always, so ask for the cost-index numbers. One plus about extending your group coverage through the office is that premiums are often paid by automatic payroll deductions, which many of us find less painful in terms of budget planning. However, one minus with group insurance through work is that if you leave the job, the insurance may get canceled, or if conversion to an individual policy is allowed, it's at a substantially higher rate. So know about the policy's conversion privilege if you elect to extend your regular employer-provided group insurance.

Group insurance is also sometimes available through a union, professional, alumni or trade organizations, or clubs or religious groups. These are not always a good deal, however. Sometimes dividends are payable not to you, the premium-payer, but rather to the sponsoring organization, so proceed carefully. All group life policies are term insurance.

If you're a veteran, you may be eligible for low-cost *veterans' insurance*. While the maximum amount isn't very high, and the kind is frequently five-year *non*renewable term, it may be worth having given its low cost.

In New York, Connecticut and Massachusetts, economical life insurance is available from mutual savings banks. The amounts of *Savings Bank Life Insurance* (SBLI) one can buy have been rising in recent years, and you may qualify even if you don't live in one of these states but a close relative does. Wisconsin also operates a state life insurance fund offering good prices. Both term and whole-life policies are available.

The National Insurance Consumer Organization, in its 1984 booklet *How to Save Money on Life Insurance,* mentions several commercial companies that offer across-the-board low rates. At the top of NICO's list is New York Life, whose policies are available through offices across the country. For younger people in particular, AMICA, in Providence, Rhode Island, is recommended. Connecticut Mutual, Bankers National, Transamerica Assurance (especially competitive for large policies) and Metropolitan also offer economical rates, according to NICO. If you do want whole-life, NICO recommends USAA Life Insurance Company of San Antonio, Texas, for your serious consideration.

And finally, a kind of whole-life that may be attractive for somewhat older people who are in higher tax brackets is a "Minimum Outlay Insurance Plan." With this kind of policy, after the first year the holder *borrows* from the insurance company money equal to the annual increase in the cash value of the policy. The holder uses this loan to pay part—in some years all—of the premium. The payments on the policy loan are tax deductible and the dividend the company pays to the holder is tax-free (because it's considered by the IRS as a partial refund of premium). While the first-year premium is high, in subsequent years when the above process takes over, the net cost is much lower. In fact, it may be lower than an ART policy—for the older insurance buyer, whose term premiums start out fairly high and increase fairly rapidly. Equitable Life is one company offering a Minimum Outlay Plan.

Other Ways to Keep Life Insurance Costs Down

If you do have an existing whole-life policy that pays dividends, but now need more coverage, be *very* cautious about dropping that policy and replacing it with a new one. While the replacement of older whole-life policies is common, it usually does not make financial sense. It's just too expensive to do so, for several reasons. First, as you've seen, if you drop a whole-life policy early on, chances are there will have been minimal cash buildup, so you'll have paid all those high premiums with little to show for them. Second, with the old policy, you've already paid those high front-end costs. You'll pay them again if you start a replacement policy. Third, you may have valuable loan rights built up with your existing policy. And fourth, a new policy is bound to carry higher premiums because you're now older. All this doesn't mean that you should never drop an existing whole-life policy, but rather that you should make a thorough investigation before doing so, using interest-adjusted cost indexes. Also talk with the insurance company that sold you the original policy, and let its representative analyze the new policy you're considering in its place. Instead of replacing your whole-life policy when you need more coverage, it's usually better to supplement it with ART.

Another way to watch costs: Be cautious about buying *riders.* They're usually expensive relative to the benefit provided. This includes the accidental-death benefit rider, which pays double or triple the face value of the policy if death is by accident. This rarely makes sense, when you consider that less than 6 percent of policyholders die by accident. Another way to look at it—are you suddenly worth more if you die in a car crash rather than of cancer? If you feel you *need* that extra coverage, what you're really saying is that you don't have enough life insurance, period. Another expensive rider is waiver of insurance premium in the event of disability. Instead of this, your priority should be adequate disability income insurance, as discussed in the next section.

Some Final Notes

As with your will, review your life insurance program periodically, especially when your financial condition and the needs of your family change. Remember that the proceeds of your policy will be distributed in accord with the policy's provisions. Life insurance "passes outside the will," so its distribution isn't governed by the terms of your will (unless the policy is payable to the estate, which for tax purposes isn't generally advisable). So a revision of your will doesn't result in a revision of your life insurance distribution—the latter has to be done separately.

Keep your policy in a safe place accessible to beneficiaries, other than a safety-deposit box, which may be sealed by the court at your death. Give photocopies to beneficiaries and to your lawyer. And if you move, be sure to keep your insurance company informed of your new address.

DISABILITY INCOME INSURANCE

What Is It?

This form of insurance provides you and your family with a monthly income if you become disabled and are unable to work for an extended period. Nearly every breadwinner—particularly those with dependents—should have adequate disability insurance, but in fact most of us do not. If you look at it pragmatically, disability income protection is at least as important as life insurance: For one thing, adults between the ages of thirty-five and sixty-five have a far greater statistical chance of being unable to work for ninety days or more because of a disabling injury or illness than they do of dying. Moreover, if you're disabled, not only are your earnings lost—you're actually a financial *burden* to your family. To become disabled without adequate income protection is, then, the worst of all possible worlds, financially speaking.

Sources of Disability Income Insurance

There are several, and the majority of us are covered by at least one—*Social Security disability benefits.* Social Security pays more than $15 billion annually in disability benefits to covered workers. An individual's benefits are determined by salary and number of years covered under Social Security. However, the fact that most breadwinners qualify for these disability benefits shouldn't make them complacent, because Social Security alone is rarely enough for a family to maintain an adequate standard of living.

To be eligible for Social Security disability benefits, you must have earned five years of Social Security coverage within ten years before you were disabled, if you're thirty-one or older, less if you're younger. In other words, you don't have to be fully employed at the time of disability to potentially qualify. Nor do you have to be the primary breadwinner. For Social Security purposes, you qualify as disabled if the injury or illness is severe enough to keep you from substantially gainful activity and if this disability is expected to last at least twelve months. However, you cannot start collecting Social Security payments until the sixth month of your disability. The dollar amount of your benefits can be calculated for you by a local Social Security office or an insurance agent. In addition, each of your dependents may get 50 percent of the benefit due you, subject to certain maximum levels. Once you've collected these benefits for two years, you also become eligible for Medicare benefits. Also important: *Social Security benefits are tax free.* The top monthly benefit for a family is, however, only $1,047—probably not enough to meet your needs.

Other disability protection programs many of us enjoy are provided by our employers. Your employer may provide short-term disability income protection, a long-term protection program, or both. The short-term program is by far the more common. Benefits under short-term employer programs can run up to two years, although twenty-six weeks is the most common duration of a benefits period. Benefits usually start immediately, especially if the disability is due to an accident. Some policies may delay benefits one week if the disability is due to an illness. Not only are benefits started promptly—they're usually substantial, too. Nearly all short-term employer-provided disability plans pay benefits of at least half of predisability income; many pay two-thirds. Some plans will pay full salary for a stipulated number of weeks (sometimes determined by the employee's years of service), followed by a number of weeks at half salary. In most cases, employers offering this kind of insurance coverage pay *all* of its cost. In other instances, the employee is asked to share the cost. Less often, the employer doesn't pay for the coverage but arranges with an insurer for a relatively economical group plan for employees, who then pay for their own coverage through payroll deduction. Who pays the premium determines whether the benefits are taxable. Generally, if your employer does, the benefits *are* taxable to you, but you may be eligible for an annual exception of $5,200. If *you* pay the premiums, the benefits are not taxable. This kind of disability benefit program is sometimes called *sick-leave benefits* or *paid sick leave.*

Working mothers-to-be take note! If your employer provides this kind of disability benefit program, then by law you must be granted a comparably paid pregnancy disability leave. While you probably don't like thinking of pregnancy and childbirth as a disability, since the passage of the Pregnancy Disability Act in late 1978, that's what it is in the eyes of the law—and this law can really work to your financial benefit and protection and your job security. The Pregnancy Disability Act states that an employer's practices of hiring, promoting and calculating seniority cannot be influenced by the fact of an employee's pregnancy. Nor can a maternity leave of absence affect the computing of sick leave, vacation, service or salary. This is *not* to say that a maternity leave *must* be a paid leave. If the company's benefit plan makes no provision for paid disability leave, it isn't required by law to make a special provision for paid maternity leave. On the other hand, if your employer grants paid sick leave in most situations, then that policy must be applied to maternity disability, for the period of time a woman is unable to perform her normal job functions. So, if you're a working mother-to-be trying to inform yourself of your overall employer-provided disability coverage, be aware that if you have such coverage for most situations, you have it for maternity-related disabilities. Ask your employer specifically how many weeks of disability pay you'll get following a "normal" delivery, and how many if birth is by Cesarean, or if there are complications. Employers differ significantly in how much paid pregnancy disability leave they grant—some give as little as two weeks, others give as many as twelve. Your physician may be called on to "certify" the period of disability, and I know of many doctors who have successfully "negotiated" longer disability coverage for their patients with those patients' employers.

If you're lucky, your employer may provide long-term disability income protection through an Employee Group Disability Plan. Such coverage usually lasts at least five years, but often goes up to age sixty-five or seventy-two, or even for life. Most long-term policies provide at least 60 percent of predisability income. As with the short-term plans, your employer may pay all or part of the premiums, or simply make group coverage available to you as an employee, with you paying the premium through payroll deduction. In some instances, disability income payments are included in profit-sharing plans or pension plans (the latter if the disability is "total and permanent"). Similar benefits to all of these may be available to members through their *unions*.

To further understand what disability coverage you have through your employer, ask if a stipulated number of years of service is required for eligibility. Ask also how disability is defined; how benefits are calculated; the waiting period before benefits begin and their duration; and whether disability caused by illness as well as accident is covered.

There are other sources of disability protection that you may be eligible for, too. If you're disabled as a result of work-related injury or illness, there's a good chance of eligibility for *workers' compensation,* which also usually starts promptly. Coverage is paid for by the employer for the employee's benefit, but under the auspices of state laws and rules that vary widely. So you must find out the rules for eligibility, proportion of lost wages or salary covered, and duration of benefits in your state. Some states give an extra allowance when the disabled worker has dependents. Moreover, in many states, workers' "comp" continues for the entire duration of disability. All together, your state law may provide for benefits up to 65 percent of previous take-home pay, subject to certain ceilings that would affect those of you with high salaries. Workers' comp benefits are free from tax. You can also receive Social Security benefits along with workers' comp, up to a maximum of 80 percent of your predisability monthly earnings. (Disability benefits are usually coordinated, so that one program's payments are reduced in recognition of benefits from another program.)

If you're a veteran and your disability is service-related, you're entitled to compensation, no matter how high your income may be. If it's determined you're 50 percent or more disabled, there's an additional allowance for dependents. These *veterans' disability benefits* are free of tax.

And finally, some states (New York, California, New Jersey, Hawaii, Rhode Island) have cash sickness programs providing coverage for disabilities that are *non*occupational in origin. *State disability coverage* is short-term—less than a year—and the maximum weekly amount is usually less than $100.

As you can see, the disability income programs that many of us already have can offer substantial protection, but they are still frequently not enough for a family to live on comfortably. Don't forget that a person's disability brings with it many new expenses, frequently including household and/or nursing help. Or one spouse's disability may require the other to stay at home to provide care, thereby eliminating the possibility of an outside income. This is where *private or individual disability income insurance comes in.*

Who Needs Disability Insurance?

The family priority should be to get adequate disability income insurance on the *main breadwinner.* Experts say that *"adequate" disability insurance is an amount that will replace at least 70 percent—preferably 80 percent—of pre-disability income.* Your preference is naturally to get as much of the coverage from Social Security and employer programs as possible, because these are no cost or low cost to you. So, with the help of an insurance agent, calculate the benefits you would get from these programs, and set that figure against your goal of 70 to 80 percent of regular net income. Before buying an individual policy, however, investigate eligibility for coverage or extension of coverage through a group plan. As noted earlier, while your employer might not pay for long-term disability for you, he might offer a group plan that employees are eligible for if they elect to pay the fee. Or you may be able to extend or expand coverage you already have under an employee group plan. As with all insurance, group disability plans are generally much cheaper than individually purchased ones.

Still, even people eligible for Social Security and workers' comp and having good employer plans usually find they must supplement these programs with private insurance to arrive at the goal of 70 to 80 percent of regular income. And for those of you who are *self-employed* main breadwinners, private insurance is a virtual must.

(Once the main breadwinner has adequate coverage, you can consider if a policy is needed by a secondary breadwinner or a homemaker. Yes, for a homemaker. Although there are no earnings to be replaced if a full-time homemaker becomes disabled, there is the cost of replacing the household services, and today, some insurance companies are writing disability insurance for these individuals. It may be relevant in this regard to note that statistically, women are disabled *more* frequently than men.)

To help illustrate the importance of disability insurance, and the need to approach it in a specific, practical way, let's look at the situation of one young couple. Sara and John L. live in Pennsylvania, with their six-month-old son. John, age twenty-eight, is two years out of graduate school and earns $24,000 as a computer technician. His monthly take-home pay is $1,334. Sara has quit her job as a computer programmer to take care of the baby. Unhappily, while waterskiing one summer afternoon, John takes a horrible fall that leaves him partially paralyzed. While there is some hope of eventual recovery, it will be, at best, a long process. John is certified as totally disabled and unable to do gainful work.

Unfortunately, John and his family will suffer in another way, too—financially. John has not worked long enough to be eligible for Social Security benefits. His disability was not occupational in origin, so he isn't eligible for workers' compensation. John does have a long-term disability plan through his employer, but it has a duration-of-service stipulation. John has not worked for the company long enough for coverage, so his disability benefits are drastically reduced. He even has to pay tax on some of the benefits, because the employer paid the disability insurance premium! All in all, John receives $580 a month from his employer in disability benefits—about 44 percent of his predisability take-home pay. And out of that, the family now has to pay $100 a month for continuation of John's group life insurance and the family's health insurance—premiums that were paid by his employer when John was working. That leaves $480 for rent, food, clothing, car and all the other household expenses. Sara could go back to work, but because John can't get around, someone would have to come in to take care of the baby and provide some nursing assistance to John. After those expenses, Sara wouldn't do much better than break even.

If John had examined his disability coverage carefully, he would have recognized its inadequacies. He easily could have made provisions to double coverage through his existing group plan at work for about $16 a month! That way, his family would have been adequately covered until he was eligible for Social Security and for the fuller benefits of his employer plan. The insurance coverage John needed to protect his family against financial disaster was only a little analysis, planning and money away.

How to Shop for Private Disability Income Insurance

The cost of private disability income insurance is determined by the dollar *amount of income* you seek to receive; *the length of the waiting time* before benefits start; and the *duration of benefits*. The latter two are really the key determinants, because the insured income amount is largely determined by your existing monthly income and calculation of Social Security and other benefits in the event of disability. In other words, an insurance company will not encourage you to "overbuy" disability insurance to insure yourself for an income when disabled that's larger than your normal income. (One reason is that they're afraid of encouraging claims.) In fact, private insurers will usually allow you to insure for two-thirds of your salary at most. For example, if you're earning $750 per week, you'll be eligible to buy private insurance of about $450 to $500 per week. Any Social Security or other benefits would be in addition.

Obviously, the shorter the waiting period for benefits and the longer their duration, the more expensive the policy. You can choose a policy that starts from day one of disability, from a week, a month, or six months. If you're covered by an income protection-disability insurance program through work that starts promptly, and/or if you have significant assets you can draw down, you can better afford a longer waiting period to get lower premiums. Remember, too, that Social Security benefits will kick in at six months. If you don't have disability benefits at work, nor substantial assets, you need a shorter waiting period. Because you pay the premiums, private disability benefits are tax free.

As to duration of benefits, experts advise, in effect, to assume the worst—that once disabled, you'll be permanently disabled and so will need long-term payment of benefits. How much good, for example, would it do a young father, permanently disabled in a car accident (not work-related, so no workers' comp), to receive private benefits for twenty-four or even sixty months, when faced with a lifetime disability preventing him from providing for his family? It's for this reason that NICO, among others, recommends buying a policy that covers you for life or at least until age sixty-five. To keep costs down, choose a policy that doesn't begin paying benefits for at least 90 to 180 days, if you can manage.

Comparison-shop among several insurers for the best price for the given amount, waiting period and duration of benefits you've decided on. According to NICO, disability income policies are usually offered by quality companies at fairly competitive prices. To give you an idea of cost, a thirty-five-year-old man seeking $1,000 of long-term monthly benefits beginning one month after becoming disabled will pay about $600 a year. If he extends his waiting period to three months, his premium will drop to about $450. If a waiting period of six months is selected, the premium drops substantially again.

Be sure you understand the *definition* of disability covered by a policy. Some policies pay out only when you're completely disabled and precluded from *any* gainful employment. Other policies pay out if your disability keeps you from your *customary* occupation—and this is usually the smarter buy. Some policies will cover for partial disability (although usually only after a period of total disability), while most will not. And some policies will pay only for disability resulting from an *accident,* and not from an illness, or will pay for a longer period for an accident versus an illness. You definitely want a policy that covers disability caused by both accident and illness, preferably for the same duration. Do *not* buy a policy that defines disability in part by saying it requires you to be completely confined to your home. Confinement is not a valid element of the medical definition of disability.

Do be sure your contract is noncancelable or *guaranteed renewable*, so long as you continue to pay the premiums. Otherwise, a company can choose to renew or not at the end of each year, if your health should deteriorate.

Disability income insurance is an important (although often neglected) part of a family's overall insurance program. A family's need for disability insurance protection, like their need for life insurance, nearly always increases with the birth of a child, so if you're parents-to-be or new parents, now is the time to think about this kind of family protection.

❖ 15

SAVING FOR A COLLEGE EDUCATION

What will college cost in 2003, about the time your new baby is ready to attend? No one really knows, because there are so many variables that will be in play over the next eighteen to twenty years to affect the price—not the least of which is inflation. But with the cost today of some state universities approaching $5,000, and top private schools $10,000 or more, it's easy to conclude that most of us will not be able to pay for twenty-first-century college costs out of even then current income. That means that an intelligent savings and investments plan is in order to finance your baby's future education.

When to Start

Too soon to think about your newborn's college education? Not at all—any more than it's too soon to think about a will or life insurance. *The sooner you start an educational savings plan, the more years you have to accumulate the needed funds, and the less money you have to put in annually to achieve your goal.* It's a lot more likely that you'll reach your goal if you have eighteen or twenty years to do it, rather than ten or five.

To show you what a difference a few years can make, consider this. Say you want your child to have $75,000 for college costs by age eighteen. If you start saving the year the child is born, you'd have to put away $1,854 annually to achieve that goal, assuming an 8 percent interest rate. However, if you wait until your child is ten years old to start, you'll have to contribute $6,529 a year to reach the same $75,000 goal. These figures take into account *compound interest*—the annual interest computed on both the principal (the money you deposit in the account) and the accrued interest (interest that builds up each year). If you have a dollar goal in mind, a bank officer can help you compute how much money you should try to contribute annually. The point is not to procrastinate. Start early, even if you have to start small.

Select Secure Investments

There are many ways you can invest the money you put into your child's education fund. However, given the fund's purpose, select steady, secure investments, not risky ones. If money and time are in short supply for you, as they are for many new parents, choose investments that don't require a large initial outlay or a lot of time to administer and manage.

Tax-Advantaged Funds

It's also smart to set up the education fund in a way that's tax-advantaged. There are many ways to do this— some simple, others more complex. The point is that using tax-advantaged techniques, you can, in effect, pay for your child's education with *pretax* instead of after-tax income— a very big advantage, particularly for those in higher tax brackets. However, setting up and administering the more elaborate tax-advantaged arrangements require expert professional help, so let's start with the simpler—but still smart—ways to save for your baby's future education.

U.S. Savings Bonds

U.S. savings bonds are back in style. That's because they're a secure, steady investment, available in a wide range of denominations, so you can "start small." They're easy to buy and easy to administer. And, if you make certain simple arrangements, U.S. savings bonds can be a

254 **THE AFFORDABLE BABY**

tax-advantaged way to save for your child's education.

Before late 1982, U.S. savings bonds were decidedly out of favor with sophisticated investors, because they offered low, fixed yields, at a time when interest rates were at record highs. Since money-market funds were offering much better rates, market-wise savers who could afford the minimum deposit put their money in them. Now the situation is changed. In late 1982, the government established the *new series EE U.S. savings bonds, with interest rates geared to those of current money markets.* If held for at least five years, series EE bonds yield a guaranteed return of 85 percent of the average interest paid on five-year marketable Treasury securities—no matter how high the latter may go. And on the downside, series EE bonds offer a unique guarantee: no matter how *low* the other interest rates may drop, series EE bonds will pay a minimum return of 7.5 percent—again, provided the bonds are held at least five years. As an additional security measure, if U.S. savings bonds are ever lost, stolen or destroyed, they're replaced without charge upon application, bearing the original issue dates.

The series EE bond is an appreciation-type or discounted security. This means *its purchase price is 50 percent of its face value*—for example, a $100 bond costs you $50. EE bonds are available in face values or denominations of $50, $75, $100, $200, $500, $1,000, $5,000 and $10,000—to repeat, you'd pay "half price" to buy one. The maturity of the EE bond is ten years—pay $50 for $100 face-value bond in 1985, and in 1995 you redeem it for the full $100 face value. If you hold the bond for less than ten but at least five years, you'll get 85 percent of the average market yield on five-year Treasury securities, compounded semiannually. If you redeem the bond less than five years from issue, you earn fixed, guaranteed interest starting at 5.5 percent at one year and rising gradually thereafter. Should the need arise, an EE bond is eligible for redemption six months after issue, making these highly liquid assets. Series EE bonds are guaranteed as to both principal and interest by the U.S. government. You'd be hard pressed to find a more steady, secure investment.

Series EE bonds are also tax-advantaged. They are exempt from state, local and property taxes. More important, *if you buy them in your child's name, you don't have to pay federal income tax on the interest.* Here's how it works:

When you buy a bond you have a choice of registering it in one name, in two names as co-owners, or with one owner and one beneficiary (who would get the bond if the owner died). *To create a tax-free education fund with series EE bonds, you must put them in the child's name as owner.* You can sign on as beneficiary, but *not* as co-owner. Then file a federal income tax return for your child indicating an intention to report the interest income from the bonds annually. In fact, however, in any subsequent year, you're only required to report the interest income *if* your child's investment income in that year exceeds her personal exemption, which is $1,000 in 1984. (To do so would require a $10,000 asset paying more than 10 percent. The excess will be taxable, but at least at the child's lower rate.)

Using this approach, your child can cash the bonds when they mature and get tax-free, full value. How important is this tax advantage? Very. If you're in the 30 percent tax bracket and have savings bonds with a face value of $20,000 in your name, you'll pay about $3,000 in taxes when you redeem the bond at maturity. You'll net $7,000 over the $10,000 you originally paid for the bonds. If, however, the bonds are in your child's name, there's an excellent chance no taxes will be owed at maturity.

Another advantage of series EE bonds for an education fund is that they're *easy to buy*, because many employers offer special savings bond payroll deduction programs. You decide how much you want to set aside each week or month, and it's automatically deducted from your pay and credited to your savings bond account. When the deductions add up to the (discounted) price of a series EE bond in the denomination selected, a bond is issued. This is a convenient, systematic and automatic way to save that over the years can build a sizable education fund for your child. Particularly if you find it difficult to discipline yourself to save, this kind of "forced savings" program can be a godsend. If your employer doesn't offer a savings bond payroll deduction plan, check with your local bank—there's a good chance they do.

Not only are savings bonds easy to buy—once bought, you don't have to spend any time administering them. They "tick over" by themselves. And the fact that they're available in small denominations makes them especially appropriate for those of moderate means. All in all, series EE savings bonds are an excellent vehicle for secure, convenient, systematic, tax-advantaged saving for the college education fund of a moderate-income family.

However, for those of you in higher tax brackets—30 percent or more—educational savings vehicles involving more sophisticated family tax planning may be in order. Let's look first at the approach for those of you who have significant income-producing assets. With these, you can use established tax-saving devices, including outright gifts, short-term trusts and interest-free loans to shift income to your child, reduce overall family taxation and thereby maximize after-tax benefits.

Custodian Accounts

Making an *outright gift* to your child by establishing a custodian account at a bank is one way of taking advantage of the minor's low tax bracket to build an education fund more rapidly. Income-producing assets—cash, quality stocks or bonds, bank certificates of deposit, rental properties, etc.—are shifted to the child under the auspices of your state's Uniform Gift to Minors' Act and put in a custodian account. The interest or dividend income earned on the assets is taxed at the child's low tax rate—usually, there's no tax obligation at all. In contrast, if you had kept that asset in your name, any income earned from it would be taxed at your tax rate—making the asset less valuable in net income terms. With the custodian account, not only is the tax bite from the asset eased, but in that way more after tax dollars are accumulated to build the education fund.

Let's look at a specific example. Say you're in the 30 percent tax bracket and have a $5,000 asset returning 10 percent a year—or $500. If kept in your name, you'd pay a tax of $150 (30 percent) on that $500 interest earned, and so net only $350. In contrast, if you give the asset to your child through a custodian account, it's likely that no tax will be owed—the full $500 interest will accumulate in the education fund for your child's ultimate benefit. This kind of advantage can really build up over the years. Each parent or grandparent (or for that matter, aunt, uncle, godparent or friend) can give the child up to $10,000 a year without having to pay federal gift tax on it. And no matter how much income the assets in the custodian account return, you can still claim your child as a dependent for deduction on your income tax returns.

You should understand that a gift like this is *irrevocable*—you as the giver cannot get it back, and it belongs outright to the child at the age of majority. Your child can do with it whatever he or she sees fit, and there's no way of guaranteeing it will be used for college as you intended. However, you *can* name yourself as custodian of the account, which means you have control of the property until the minor attains majority (between eighteen and twenty-one depending on the laws of your state). As custodian, you can sell the asset, collect income from it, reinvest the proceeds, whatever—as long as it's kept in holding for the child's benefit or actually used for the child's benefit. The child's *benefit*—not the child's *support*.

This is an important distinction, if an unfortunately ambiguous one because there is no federal standard. It comes down to state law. The distinction between benefit versus support is important, because benefit income isn't taxed while support income is. That is, income used to pay for the "support" of the beneficiary is taxable to the person who is obligated under state law to provide that support. That's you, the parent. So it all boils down to what your state defines as "support" or parental obligations. In most states, it's only the necessities: food, clothing and shelter. In those states, a college education is *not* considered a necessity or a parental obligation, so income generated by a custodian account to provide the *benefit* of a college education would enjoy the tax advantage. If, however, you live in a state that recognizes a college education as one of your parental obligations or duties of *support*, using that income to pay for the child's college would make that income taxable to *you*. The basic point of the exercise would be lost; you'd clearly want to find another vehicle for your child's education fund. So find out what the law is in your state in this regard, before taking any action.

A custodian account is relatively easy to set up through a local bank—at little or no cost. An exception is if you transfer income-producing real estate into the account. That's more complex and requires a lawyer's help.

Clifford Trusts

Another option for those in a high tax bracket who can afford to shift assets to the child for tax purposes and the building of an education nest egg is the short-term or *Clifford trust*. This differs from an outright gift administered through a custodian account because with the Clifford trust, *you eventually get the principal back*. This is called having a "reversionary" interest—the principal *reverts* to you at the end of the trust period, which is a *minimum* of ten years. During the trust period, all of the income generated by the assets you've contributed is accumulated for the benefit of the child, and so is taxable at the child's lower rate (if at all). It's the investment income, then, and not the original principal, that is the education nest egg. In more detail, here's how it works.

As with a custodian account, you transfer income-producing assets to your child, but this time through a specially established trust fund, with specific provisions made for the earned or investment income. The income can either be paid into a savings account in your child's name, where it's perhaps used to buy tax-free government bonds, or simply be allowed to accumulate in the trust for payment to the child at the end of the trust period. The latter may be simpler, especially if the trust is timed to end when your child is ready to start college. Remember that the trust by law must last at least ten years (most are set up to last ten years and a day) *from your last "deposit" in the trust.* So if you contemplate making more than one contribution to the trust, then the trust period provided should be longer than ten years. If you *don't* respect the ten-year minimum term and have the assets revert to you before it's over, the tax advantage is lost—the trust investment income would be included in your taxable income.

How important is this tax advantage? Once again, very. If, for example, you're in the 30 percent tax bracket and own a $10,000 asset returning 10 percent a year, you'd earn a $9,672 net return after a decade. The same asset placed in a Clifford trust, in contrast, would return nearly $15,000. The higher your tax bracket, the bigger the advantage provided by the Clifford trust.

With the short-term trust, then, you substantially ease the tax bite on an income-producing asset, thereby maximizing after-tax benefits and building a larger education fund for your child (or building one faster, if you prefer)—and at the end of the trust your asset is returned to you, along with any capital appreciation.

A final advantage of the Clifford trust is that the legal principles, statutory rules and Treasury regulations relevant to it are established and supportive. If the trust is set up and used correctly, the Clifford trust will succeed in income shifting with scant risk of a challenge by the IRS. You'll need expert help from a tax attorney to ensure that everything is done properly. Prices for these services vary considerably, depending on the complexity of the trust and what part of the country you live in. A ballpark range for these lawyer fees is $200 to $500, more in the biggest cities. So in calculating your actual after-tax benefits from the trust, you should subtract the lawyer's fee for its establishment, plus expenses for a trustee, tax-return filings and periodic, further professional advice. This is another reason why Clifford trusts are appropriate only for higher tax bracket individuals with a significant income-producing asset whose use they can afford to give up for a decade.

A final note: At the end of the trust, you'll be responsible for paying taxes on any *capital gains* its original asset realizes.

Spousal Remainder Trust

The spousal remainder trust is rapidly gaining favor among tax advisers and the financially astute as another tax-advantaged way to provide college education funds. It is similar to a Clifford trust, in that interest accrues to the child's account and low tax bracket. However, the spousal remainder trust is funded by one parent, with legal title to the principal passing to the spouse at the end. Because the ownership changes in this way, there is no requirement for a ten-year minimum term as there is with a Clifford trust. You can also put more money into a spousal remainder trust in a single year than you can into a Clifford trust without incurring a gift tax. This results from recent changes in the tax laws regarding calculation of the value of a gift in the form of income generated by the trust's assets. However, this difference will affect only the very largest givers. A spousal remainder trust is generally more appropriate for the very affluent who can afford to put large assets into a trust and would prefer to confine the trust to the time period of the child's college years.

Custodian accounts, Clifford and spousal remainder trusts—these income-shifting techniques are good ways for those of you with liquid, income-producing assets to build an education fund for your child. If you *don't* have such assets but do enjoy a high income—and suffer a high tax bracket!—you may want to consider using *borrowed* funds to build a tax-advantaged education nest egg. You also shift income with this technique, but the special advantage is the *tax deduction* created for you. The basic idea is to borrow money and make an interest-free loan or a gift to your child's trust. The child receives income from the invested funds, and you get tax deductions of the interest payments on the loan. The family's after-tax benefits are increased, and the money resulting from reduced overall family taxation is used to build the education fund.

Before getting to the details, let me emphasize that these borrowed funds and tax-deduction techniques are not for the faint of heart. They all run a risk of IRS challenge. Moreover, they are complicated, and you usually need the help not only of a tax attorney but of an accountant and a bank official, too. To be worth the effort and expense of establishing and administering the arrangements, you'll probably have to be willing and able to borrow a significant amount of money. Nonetheless, there are a fair number of highly paid professionals for whom this approach would be appropriate for consideration. Moreover, even if this approach isn't right for you now, it may be in the future, when your income increases.

Interest-Free Loan with Borrowed Funds

With this arrangement, you borrow funds from a bank in order to make an interest-free demand *loan* to a short-term trust established for your child's benefit. The trust invests the funds in Certificates of Deposit (CDs) with the bank that made the original loan. Interest paid on the CD is paid through the trust to your child, and so is taxable at the child's low rate. Although the CD rate will be lower than the rate you'll be paying back to the bank on your original loan, the tax deduction makes this arrangement attractive. You get a major tax deduction on your interest payments to the bank, at the same time your child (through the trust) has the use of an asset that's generating income taxable at a low rate. The family's overall taxes are thus reduced, after-tax benefits increased, and an education fund starts building up.

Let's look at a specific example that assumes you're in the 50 percent tax bracket. You borrow $50,000 from a bank at a rate of 15 percent, resulting in interest payments by you to the bank of $7,500. That $7,500, in turn, is a deduction that will result in a tax savings of $3,750. As a result, the net after-tax cost to you of the loan is $3,750.

The loan is placed in the trust, which invests it for your child's benefit in bank CDs paying 13 percent. That will return $6,500 through the trust to the child. Assuming the child has no other investment income, the $6,500 return will result in about $420 in tax payments, and so a net after-tax income of $6,080. Subtract the net after-tax cost from the net after-tax income ($6,080 − $3,750 = $2,330) to calculate the total after-tax benefit to the family.

Bear in mind that this is a simplified explanation and that the "real thing" requires professional help. Setting up the trust may cost a few hundred dollars in legal fees (some of which may be tax-deductible because tax advice is involved). However, by looking at the example above, it's easy to see how significant the family tax advantage can be and how that advantage could contribute to the rapid buildup of a substantial education fund.

Gift and Borrow Back with Borrowed Funds

This arrangement is even more complicated, but it can generate even larger tax savings. It involves borrowing money and then making a *gift* of those funds to a short-term trust established for the benefit of your child. Next, you borrow the money *back* from the trust and repay your original loan. You then owe interest payments to the *trust.* Those payments are the trust's investment income, which are payable to its beneficiary—your child—and taxable at his or her low rate. For you these payments are an interest expense, and so a tax deduction.

This all must be done formally and be fully documented. There are any number of possible pitfalls that can render the whole arrangement very vulnerable to IRS challenge, and so professional help in setting up and administering the arrangement is essential. But for certain people, this complex method can be well worth the effort and expense involved, because it in effect converts (otherwise non-deductible) education payments into interest-expense deductions.

The main point of this chapter is to get you thinking creatively about financing your child's future education. While there's a fortune in scholarships and financial aid out there (millions of dollars of which actually go unused each year!), it would be imprudent to assume you won't have to provide a significant share of your child's college costs. In financial matters, it's always best to keep your assumptions conservative.

So assess your family's future needs and present capabilities, and start an education savings program. Definitely make family tax planning part of your strategy in this regard. It's just not smart to create an education fund by simply putting after-tax dollars into a savings account or money-market fund. Even moderate-income families can save considerable money over time using tax-advantaged ways to build an education nest. If you have a thrift or profit-sharing plan at work—especially if it contains untaxed employer contributions—that may be an excellent education savings vehicle. But if you don't have such a plan (or do, but have its funds earmarked for something else), then you need to make other arrangements. Whether your choice is a simple payroll deduction plan for U.S. savings bonds registered in your child's name or an elaborate Clifford trust, what's important is that you *start.*

WHAT THREE COUPLES SPENT

Of course you can afford a baby. It's more a question of how well you anticipate and manage the many expenses associated with new parenthood. Knowing what expenses lie ahead, understanding your options, avoiding financial surprises and pitfalls, planning ahead—all will smooth your financial transition to parenthood.

Let's see what we can draw from the experience of three couples living in different parts of the country, at different income levels, having different preferences, but all giving birth to their first babies in 1984.

ANDREA AND ANTHONY DELGADO

. . . live in a small community about fifty miles from Houston. Andrea, twenty-three, works in the area hospital, where she earns $13,200 a year as a licensed practical nurse. Anthony, twenty-six, is a social studies teacher at the local high school. He earns $14,800 there, and an additional $1,700 over the summer months as the swim coach at a nearby country club. The couple have lived in a one-bedroom rental apartment since they were married three years ago, and are carefully saving money for a house.

Andrea's pregnancy was planned. Although they felt it would have been nice to have a house of their own to bring their baby home to, it was a matter of priorities—a baby, *now*. Although the DelGados did not have a clear picture of how much a baby might cost in the first few years, they weren't too worried about being caught short, since they were willing to take money out of their $7,500 house saving fund, if necessary. They *did* make a pact to try to save an additional $75 per month during Andrea's pregnancy. However, they weren't able to do so, finding that pregnancy involved many new (and unexpected) expenditures that made savings—never easy—all that much harder.

The DelGados were covered by a health insurance policy that they'd never really called on before Andrea's pregnancy. Anthony contributed $31 per month to it for the two of them ($54 per month for family coverage). They knew little about the policy's details, but were lucky—it included good maternity coverage. Moreover, Andrea knew a young doctor at the hospital who offered to deliver the baby for whatever the insurance would pay—$750, it turned out. That helped, but the DelGados still had to contend with a $250 deductible and 25 percent co-insurance on the lab work, two sonograms and three nonstress tests that Andrea needed. She had a normal, uncomplicated delivery and required only a "local" anesthetic for the episiotomy, which the insurance didn't cover ($65). All her other in-hospital bills were covered—after another $200 deductible, which had been recently added to hospitalization coverage by Anthony's employer, to help slow the growth in premium increases. Hospital bills for newborn Andrew were covered, except for a $35 fee for circumcision. All together, medical expenses associated with pregnancy and delivery left the DelGados with about $620 out-of-pocket expenses.

Andrea's maternity clothing needs had been satisfied simply. She bought three maternity nursing uniforms at $32 each and three bras for under $20, sewed two jumpers for about the same, bought three T-shirts for $33 and a nightgown for $14 and borrowed everything else from a sister, friends and Anthony. As for the "nursery"—the couple just moved furniture around in their bedroom, buying only heavier drapes ($39) to block out the light better. Andrea also borrowed a good crib, for which they purchased a $50 foam mattress. Crib linens came to about $65. The changing table, which included a chest of drawers, cost $179, which Andrea worried was too expensive. Maybe for this reason, they bought a cheap, sling-back stroller for $32. (This backfired. "It fell apart in three months and we had to replace it with a Maxi Taxi we paid $69 for at J. C. Penney.") They decided to do without a swing and a jumper, because they would have taken up too much space in their small apartment.

They received a soft carrier and an infant seat as gifts, along with a lot of cute baby clothes. ("Too many," Andrea said. "Andrew hardly wore half of them before they got too small!") Anthony's parents also bought them a playpen. Although it was a good wooden one, Andrea wished they'd asked her before buying it. She's opposed to putting Andrew in a pen, but didn't feel comfortable returning the grandparents' gift.

Another significant purchase for the DelGados was a camera. They bought the kind that develops pictures instantly. "The film is expensive, though—about eighty cents a picture. I guess we think twice before taking them." The camera cost $129, and the DelGados estimate they've spent $100 or so on film so far, judging from the number of pictures in their album.

Andrea took a three-month maternity leave from work, during which she received six weeks' pay from accumulated sick leave plus vacation. She breastfed the baby during her leave, but when it was time to return to the hospital ("I would have liked more time off, but we needed my salary if we're ever going to buy that house!" she said), she quickly weaned him to the bottle. Andrew consumes a lot of formula; Andrea buys the liquid concentrated kind by the case to save money.

When she was home, Andrea used a diaper service, which she thought was good value for $9.50 weekly. Now that Andrew is in family day care, he gets disposables for the convenience of the caregiver, and Andrea found she couldn't resist the convenience for herself and Anthony, too. She buys the Toys-R-Us disposables by the case, and spends about $9 a week on them.

About their childcare situation, the DelGados feel pretty lucky. The caregiver watches only one other child—a three-year-old girl, who loves the baby—and is affectionate and responsible. In terms of cost, the caregiver is a bargain—$35 a week for forty to forty-five hours of care. However, the pay is "off-the-books," so the DelGados can't claim a childcare tax credit, which they had not in fact heard of before we discussed it. They did, of course, know about the federal tax exemption of $1,000 for their new dependent.

The unpleasant surprise for the DelGados—as it is for many new parents—was learning that health insurance would not cover Andrew's well-baby visits and immunizations. Lucky for them, Andrea's hospital has a baby clinic, which provides well-baby checkups at a nominal cost—$3 a visit, immunizations for $5. Andrea feels comfortable about using the clinic (although she acknowledges that many of its clients are welfare recipients), because she knows the doctors and nurses who staff it and enjoys bringing Andrew in to "show him off" to her colleagues. She estimates that using the clinic will save them at least $500 in Andrew's first two years.

In terms of preparing for the future, the DelGados still have some work to do. They have no will, although a life insurance agent did mention he could get a fill-in-the-blank one for them—at the time he sold them a $5,000 policy on the baby. (A mistake.) Anthony has only his employer-provided life insurance, equal to two times his annual salary—about $30,000. This is way too little. Supplementing it to a total of $100,000 would cost only about $60 the first year, but all the DelGados financial attention now seems focused on getting the house they want so badly. An important exception is that Anthony has $20 a paycheck (twice a month) automatically deducted and put toward savings bond purchases for Andrew's education. Andrea commits $20 a month to the same goal. A banker told them how putting the bonds in the baby's name would save tax dollars.

Andrea and Anthony describe themselves as "very budget-conscious, particularly once we decided to have Andrew. A few of our friends asked us why we didn't wait until we were more ahead to have a baby. But there's a danger in waiting until you can really afford a baby to have one—you may be too old by then!"

NEIL AND DANA ZIMMERMAN

. . . thirty-one and twenty-eight years old, respectively, live in Oakland, California, in a home they've owned for four years. In 1983, Neil bought a record store, and the new business made life hectic as he expanded into video-cassette sales and rentals. Because he was trying to build the business fast, Neil took only $26,000 out of it in salary—not much considering the seventy-hour weeks he routinely put in. Also in 1983, Dana earned almost $11,000 as a realtor.

The surprise of 1983 for the Zimmermans, however, had nothing to do with real estate or records—it was Dana's pregnancy. Their lives had been going so fast, she was nearly three months pregnant before she even realized it. Their first reaction of "Oh, no! Not now!" quickly changed to excitement and happiness—they'd certainly intended to have a family anyway. But there was anxiety, too—the Zimmermans had no health insurance. It was one of those things Neil "had been meaning to do" but hadn't gotten around to because of the store. Dana was especially worried because a good friend had recently had a difficult Cesarean delivery that resulted in a week-long hospital stay for mother and newborn and medical bills in expensive California of nearly $8,000.

"Because of buying the store, we had practically nothing in savings when Dana realized she was pregnant. Plus we had—and still have—some big fixed monthly bills, like an $842 house mortgage. These ate up just about everything we were bringing in," said Neil. "It was really unclear where we were going to find the money to pay the doctor and hospital," Dana continued. "I knew a couple of women

who'd had their babies at home, and I'd heard of a birth
center nearby, where costs were a lot lower. But I was too
nervous about being outside a hospital, after my friend's
experience."

So, after a lot of thought, Dana settled on a community
hospital that offered an in-hospital birthing suite staffed by
nurse-midwives. There, if all went well, Dana would get
most of her prenatal care from the midwives; delivery, too,
with hospital discharge within twenty-four hours. Preset
cost for these services: $1,950 fully payable sixty days in
advance of due date. Prenatal labwork was extra ($65), as
were vitamins ($35). Lamaze training was included in the
set fee.

Everything went well for Dana and newborn Joanna.
Dana particularly enjoyed going home so quickly after the
birth (her mother came to help for two weeks). The Zimmermans estimated they saved at least $3,000 over the
traditional hospital delivery by an obstetrician. The Zimmermans then joined an area HMO, for which Neil pays
(through the store) $188 per month for comprehensive
family coverage. So there are no pediatrician bills to contend
with.

During her pregnancy, Dana made an effort to cut back
overall household expenses but wasn't really successful.
Rather, it was more a financial reshuffling—decreasing
expenses in some areas like entertainment (although at the
end of the pregnancy she was quite tired, so they found
themselves eating out or ordering take-out food a lot)—in
order to make baby-related purchases. For example, although
Dana tried to exercise restraint, as a self-described "clothes
horse" she spent more than $400 on maternity clothes. She
"justified" this because she was selling real estate right up
to the last two weeks. "It's a people business. You have to
look nice." And she did close a sale at 8½ months!

The Zimmermans redid a small bedroom as a nursery.
New carpet, Marimekko wallpaper and Levelor blinds came
to $520. They also made a conscious decision to buy quality
baby equipment and furniture, in part with baby number
two in mind. They bought a Simmons crib for $199, a $75

extra-firm spring crib mattress, and designer crib linens for about $70. They also bought a $250 coordinated Simmons dresser ("which doesn't look like baby furniture, so Joanna can use it for years"). A crib mobile cost $11, and a Strolee birth-through-toddler car seat, just under $60. They also bought an infant seat for $19 and a mesh playpen with a safety seal for $150. All these purchases were made at J. C. Penney. Joanna proved to be a very active baby, so to have a little time with hands free ("self-preservation!") the Zimmermans later bought a swing for $35, a walker for $31 and three spring-loaded safety gates for $16 each.

Neil's mother gave them a frilly bassinet ("A waste of money, whatever she paid for it," groused Neil) and Dana's parents gave them an Aprica stroller. Dana got a Snugli baby pack at a shower, a diaper bag, plus "a ton" of both new and "gently used" baby clothes.

The Zimmermans used Pampers on Joanna from day one, and spent between $9 and $11 a week on them, depending on finding coupons and in-store promotions. Highly committed to breastfeeding, Dana joined the La Leche League (dues: $15) and breast-fed Joanna until she was eight months old. She used her food processor to make baby food from whatever she and Neil were eating. Dana had time for all this because she decided not to go back to real estate for a while. "I just couldn't tear myself away from the baby. Besides, after paying someone to take care of her, there wouldn't be much left from my up-and-down kind of work." However, Dana is an active participant in a parents' babysitting co-op, which works on a "chit" system. Each of the five mothers in the group starts the month with ten chits, each worth an hour of sitting time. When she wants some "time off," Dana calls around until she finds a mother willing to watch Joanna, and gives her a chit for each hour she does so. No money changes hands. "There are certain rules. You're not allowed to go into 'debt'—once you've used your chits, that's it. You can only carry up to five unused chits over into the next month. This promotes an even use of the co-op."

The Zimmermans learned from their mistake with health

insurance and have no intention of being unprepared in other ways. Right after Joanna was born, Neil increased his life insurance to $150,000 annual renewable term. The policy costs him $237 a year—again, bought through the store. They've even finagled a $50,000 policy on Dana (cost: $169) through the store. Neil is also now one of the minority of Americans with disability income insurance. It guarantees an income of $1,500 per month in the event of disability after a three-month waiting period. It costs $770 annually.

A lawyer charged the Zimmermans $125 for a will, in which they named Neil's brother and sister-in-law as Joanna's guardian. About education savings, the Zimmerman's say they recognize the need to start early, but need a year or two to get a little ahead after all the baby expenses.

All in all, the Zimmermans feel that getting caught without health insurance as they did was a valuable lesson. It focused their attention on financial preparation and planning "as an attitude, as much as a practice."

CHRISTINE AND JONATHAN WOODS

. . . both thirty-three, live in Stamford, Connecticut. Stamford is the site of corporate headquarters of several Fortune 500 companies, and Christine, who has an MBA, works in the accounting group of one of them. Jonathan commutes daily into New York City, where he works in the creative department of an advertising firm. Christine earns $36,000 and Jonathan, $33,000. Both their employers offer a generous benefits package—comprehensive health insurance, life insurance equal to annual salary in Christine's case and twice his annual salary in Jonathan's, disability insurance and a savings incentive plan.

Christine's pregnancy was planned—very planned. She had been trying to get pregnant for two years before she finally did so in late 1983. Her pregnancy came only after extensive fertility treatment: an operation called a laparoscopy, which lets the doctor inspect the fallopian tubes and ovaries for damage; and drug therapy to induce ovulation.

The laparoscopy cost $800, and the drug therapy, just under $400 per month, including doctor's visits for ten months. Luckily—unusually—this treatment *was* covered under Jonathan's health insurance policy (but not Christine's own). So after an annual $250 deductible, and 20 percent co-insurance, the policy reimbursed about $3,700 of Christine's nearly $5,000 in fertility treatment.

After all they'd gone through, Christine and Jonathan were ecstatic about her pregnancy. Their emotion, plus the belief that "this will probably be the only baby we'll ever have," led them to a "best-of-everything" approach. Christine chose a prominent obstetrician (she heard of him because he authored an excellent pregnancy book) whose fees were at the top of the scale in the Stamford area— $1,800 for usual delivery, $2,200 for Cesarean. She spent nearly $100 on pregnancy and baby books, and then (as she put it) "practically badgered the doctor into every test that exists. I was terrified something would go wrong." Prenatal lab work cost $125, vitamins $35 and iron $27. She had two sonograms at $90 each when she began light spotting in the third month. Two years short of the "threshold" age of thirty-five, Christine agonized over whether to have an amnio. Finally, her doctor suggested she do so. ("Probably because he thought I'd worry myself really sick if I didn't.") The amnio cost $850 and turned up nothing to suggest any problems. Only then did Christine begin to relax. "My behavior only sounds crazy to the twenty-four-year-old who gets pregnant the first month she tries—or even without trying."

In any case, nearly all these bills were 100 percent covered by insurance, because the Woods enjoyed double coverage and coordination of benefits. One exception was $400 of the OB fee, which both insurers refused because it was deemed to be in excess of "reasonable and customary."

So just when she was really beginning to "show," Christine was also calming down and able to focus again on her work. Jonathan told me that Christine had, in fact, worked very hard during the previous two years, in part to distract herself from her pregnancy problems. Her efforts had been repaid with two good promotions and raises, and Christine clearly prides herself on being every inch a professional. Her maternity wardrobe illustrated that. She bought maternity "suits" (jumpers and jackets) in conservative colors, button-down shirts with bow ties, and some patterned blouses—most of which were ordered from Mothers' Work. These, along with stockings, slips, etc., cost exactly $589. Christine bought her casual maternity clothes—jeans, two pair of trousers, T-shirts, a sweater, two nightgowns—at an off-price maternity store, spending $244 more.

The Woods' best-of-everything attitude was apparent in other ways, too. They didn't just convert a bedroom into a nursery—they sold their in-town condo and bought a $189,000 house outside of town in anticipation of the baby. Housing was clearly their biggest baby-related expense—moving expenses alone were several thousand dollars. The Woods moved into their new home six weeks before Lara was born.

Lara's birth had its tricky moments. Twenty hours into a painful labor, the fetal heart monitor showed signs of fetal distress. The obstetrician quickly decided on a Cesarean. By then, Christine had already had a lot of anesthesia, but was naturally given more. Jonathan stayed with her. Lara was born with a one-minute Apgar score of 6, which improved to 8 a few minutes later as the staff worked on her. Christine was in the recovery room for several hours and Lara was put in intensive care for her first day, just to be extra careful. Mother and baby stayed in the hospital seven days, and their bill totaled $5,892. The Woods paid $495 of the bill, mostly because Christine had a private room. In-hospital pediatrician bills amounted to $320. Christine had earlier decided not to breastfeed, because the plan had been to return to the office in four weeks (although that didn't work out because of the Cesarean).

Christine and Jonathan brought Lara home to a brightly decorated nursery. When I asked the two of them if they could remember what they'd paid for all the furniture and equipment filling the nursery, Christine laughed and said,

"I can do better than that. I'm an accountant, remember?" and proceeded to produce a complete list, receipts attached, of every significant baby purchase (a researcher's dream!). Here's what she showed me:

Cradle (antique)	$225
Cradle mattress & bumpers (specially made)	90
Childcraft crib	249
Crib mattress	79
Calliope bumpers and sheets	111
Crib quilt	56
Three crib blankets	42
Crib dustruffle	34
Musical crib mobile	17
Childcraft dresser	279
Childcraft changing table	259
Nursery lamp	39
Cosco car seat (birth to toddler)	79
Gerry cradle bath	12
Nursery scale	19
Saks layette	119
Dior christening gown	69
Century baby swing	39
Padded playpen	95
Aprica walker	37
Brevi high chair	115
TOTAL	$2064

Christine and Jonathan bought most of these items at a nice Stamford baby boutique (they could have found many of them for about 20 percent less at Sears or J. C. Penney). Christine acknowledged that some of the purchases were luxuries—like the christening gown and the cradle; and some—like the scale and the full layette—a waste.

In addition, the Woods received as gifts an infant carrier, a Sassy seat, a Snugli, lots of baby clothes (these seem to be about the most common baby gifts) and "as a joke" (a good one, I think) a month's supply of Luvs disposables. Christine's parents gave them a MacLaren stroller (which probably cost more than $200) and a beautiful French reed bassinet-carrier. They also paid a professional photographer $65 for an hour's worth of photography of the newborn, and bought $110 worth of prints. Jonathan's parents gave the baby $1,000 to start her education fund (and Jonathan thinks they plan it as an annual gift).

Christine's company routinely grants eight weeks full disability pay for childbirth, plus a maternity leave without pay of up to six months—with a guarantee of the same or an equivalent job upon return. In Christine's case, because of her difficult delivery plus a lingering, if minor, complication, her physician successfully made a case with her employer for twelve weeks' full disability pay, after which she returned to work.

As to childcare, the Woods were set on a progressive developmental day-care center, in part because they continue to think it's unlikely Lara will ever have a brother or sister—they wanted her to know and be with other youngsters from babyhood. There's an excellent center in Stamford, but there's also a waiting list. Christine signed Lara up but was told it might be a year before she gets in. The cost is just under $400 per month. Until then, the Woods have an English au pair they pay $70 a week. They located her through other couples who'd made similar arrangements, and they paid her airfare to the States. She's "off-the-books," so no childcare tax credit.

For the longer term, Lara is equally well provided for. Both parents supplemented their employer-provided term life insurance with $100,000 of whole-life. These are expensive ($1,105 for Christine, and $1,225 for Jonathan), but the couple (who are in the 50 percent tax bracket) like the idea of tax-advantaged cash-value buildup. The Woods also have mortgage insurance and both their parents are in a position to help if anything disastrous happens.

When I asked the Woods if they'd written wills after Lara's birth, they seemed taken aback. "Of course!" was their response. They had an estate specialist do the wills for them, which cost $575.

Lara's education fund is off to a great start with the grandparents' gift and the tax-protected savings plans that both Christine and Jonathan's employers offer. In Christine's case, she puts 6 percent of her before-tax pay into her fund and her company matches it. Jonathan puts 10 percent and his company matches 4 percent—so the Woods savings are mounting fast and earnings are free of tax until withdrawal.

Christine and Jonathan are clearly an affluent young couple, and the family has a bright financial future. I closed our interview by saying, "I don't suppose you consider yourself very budget-conscious." Their reply: "Budget-conscious—no, not exactly. But financially minded—yes, *very*."

And is there really much of a difference? Whatever our incomes, we can all benefit from money "awareness"— money management and consumer sophistication can make our own lives, and those of our children, easier and more pleasant and secure.

INDEX